Fire
IN THE HOLE

Fire
IN THE HOLE
The Untold Story of Hardrock Mine

J E R R Y   D O L   H

Washington State University Press
Pullman, Washington

Washington State University Press, Pullman, Washington 99164-5910

Printed and bound in the United States of America on pH neutral, acid-free high quality recycled paper. ✸

Library of Congress Cataloging-in-Publication Data

Dolph, Jerry, 1943-
    Fire in the hole : the untold story of hardrock miners / by Jerry Dolph.
       p.   cm.
    ISBN 0-87422-112-9. — ISBN 0-87422-108-0 (pbk.)
    1. Silver mines and mining—Idaho—History.   2. Silver mines and mining—Idaho—
Anecdotes.   I. Title.
TN433.I2D65 1994
622'.3423'09796—dc20
                                             94-25176
                                               CIP

There would not have been a book if it was not
for the support and encouragement of my wife,
Jo Ann. I am afraid that just saying "thanks" is
not going to be enough.

Acknowledgments

In the mineral-rich regions of the American West, the history of hardrock mining usually began with a lone prospector, armed with a pick, shovel, and pan, and accompanied by a donkey or mule. From these prospectors' surface discoveries in the 1880s and 1890s, large mining companies quickly took the search for valuable minerals deep into the bowels of the earth itself.

Extracting valuable ore from the ground was an extremely complicated, competitive, lucrative, and hazardous business, requiring extraordinary cooperation between miners and the mining companies they worked for. After a century, however, hardrock mining in the United States now has run its course with the closures (at least temporarily) of most deep underground mines.

In the 1970s and 1980s, I "tramped" through many mines, particularly in North Idaho's fabulous Silver Valley. This book is meant as a tribute to the men and women who I knew in the mining industry, both past and present. I think it is only fitting that this story be told by the miners themselves. In many cases, these individuals are descendants of the early prospectors and miners of a hundred years ago.

I have done my best to try to avoid errors, and I apologize for any unintentional mistakes in the text that I might have made, or if I have misspelled anyone's name. I did my best. In some of the less flattering stories, I have changed the names of certain individuals.

I wish to thank the following people from the mining companies, government agencies, businesses, libraries, and museums who provided me with photographs, documents, printed materials, and other information. Their assistance was most welcome, and critically important, in the preparation of this book—

Chris Pfahl, Fred Owsley (ASARCO Inc., Wallace ID)
Bill Booth, Sonya Westfall, Linda Capp, April Robertson, Art Brown (Hecla Mining Co., Coeur d'Alene ID)
Harry Cougher, Susan Shiplett, John Ackerman, Tim Burns, Daryl Jerome, Gordon Burdick (Sunshine Precious Metals Inc., Kellogg ID)
Allen Young (Sunshine Precious Metals Inc., Boise ID)
Bill Vanderwall (Sunshine Precious Metals Inc., Silver Peak NV)
Art Johnson, John Howard, Isabell Scott (Coeur d'Alene Mines, Coeur d'Alene ID)
Lin Car (Homestake Mining Co., Lead SD)
Roger Smith (Energy Fuels Nuclear Inc., Fredonia AZ)

Earl Bennett (University of Idaho, Moscow ID)
Collin Galloway, Earl Frizzell (Mine Safety and Health Administration, Coeur d'Alene ID)
Ted Williams, Frances Baker (Bureau of Mines, Spokane Research Center, WA)
Clay Martin, Ed Hollop (Bureau of Mines, Denver Field Office, CO)
Jim Robbins (BLM Mining Engineering, Coeur d'Alene ID)
Dan Drewry, Charles Fernandes, Don Sauer (*Shoshone County News-Press/Wallace Miner,* Kellogg ID)
Larry Reisnouer (*Spokesman-Review,* Spokane WA)
Steve Morris (Alaska-Pacific Powder Co., Rathdrum ID)
Mary McCulloch, Harriet McConnel, Arlene Kastelle (Kellogg Public Library [Bunker Hill photos], Kellogg ID)
John Amonson (Wallace District Mining Museum, Wallace ID)
Bill Rautio (Silver Bow Chamber of Commerce, Butte MT)
Gerry Walter, Allen Hooper (World Mining Museum, Butte MT)
Don Toms (Black Hills Mining Museum, Lead SD)

I also wish to express my gratitude to the following individuals who likewise provided essential photographs and assistance in the preparation of this work—

Richard Caron (Wallace ID)
Steve Thomas (Coeur d'Alene ID)
Steve Voynick (Leadville CO)
Bruce Baraby (Wallace ID)
Phillip Lindstrom (Silverton ID)
Gene Hyde (Post Falls ID)
Bob Yost (Osburn ID)
Tom Wobker (Post Falls ID)
Bill Lytle (Coeur d'Alene ID)
John Fahey (Spokane WA)
George Lander (Pinehurst ID)
Marvin Chase (Spokane WA)
Jim Arnoldi (Hayden Lake ID)
Pete Deitz (Coeur d'Alene ID)
Larry Dolph (Post Falls ID)
LaRene "Billie" Stone (Post Falls ID)
Ruth and Bob Hanna (Coos Bay OR)

Finally, I would like to thank the staff of Washington State University Press for their very fine efforts to preserve this important part of our American experience—

Thomas H. Sanders, Director
Mary Read, Assistant Director
Glen Lindeman, Editor
Keith Petersen, Editor
Doug Garcia, Designer

Contents

CHAPTER I

Miner Entree Training

Kelley Mine
Butte, Montana

I'd spent nearly six years in the U.S. Air Force and, after finally being discharged in 1966, joined the ranks of the unemployed... again.

For a few years I tried working in lumber mills and such on the Oregon coast, but that kind of work just didn't seem to suit me at all. I didn't mind, though. "Tramping" around from job to job and trying out new things just seemed to come naturally. I suppose it must have been something in my genes. I had itchy britches.

Then in 1968 I moved to Kellogg, Idaho, and went to work as a laborer for a construction company that was building a new junior high school. After about six months of intermittently pulling nails, carrying boards around, and drinking oceans of watered-down beer, I met my special lady, Jo Ann. It seemed like we were meant for each other too; a perfect match. I was so smitten that I completely forgot my vow to be especially careful about choosing a mate and proposed that first night. She said, "Yes," and we were married one week later.

Actually, the B & M Restaurant where she worked was closing in a few days, so she said, "I need a place to go, and you sure need someone to take care of you [that was the God awful truth too] so, yes, I will marry you."

I figured there was no way I was going to continue in my dad's footsteps of moving all the time, following the construction trade with my own family. I quit my job, loaded up our few belongings and my new wife, and left

Idaho, headed back down to the Oregon coast. I enrolled in Coos Bay's Southwestern Oregon Community College and majored in law enforcement. I figured that was a career that wouldn't involve much tramping around.

Everything went well for about a year. Jo Ann and I had our share of problems, like most newlywed couples I suspect, but we stayed together out of spite if nothing else. Then something happened that was to change both of our lives forever. We became the proud parents of a beautiful baby boy we named Jason.

Money—or should I say, the lack of it—became an instant problem, so I went to work for the Coos Bay police department as a patrolman while I continued attending college classes. I was trying to earn enough money to take care of my wonderful new son and finish up my education at the same time. I had only about three more months of school to complete before I'd earn my two-year Associate degree in law enforcement.

I'd been on the department as a probationary "let's see how he works out" patrolman for only about a month when I received a frantic call one day from the dispatcher: "High speed chase in progress... center of town... several officers involved... request assistance."

That was what I was waiting for: a chance to prove myself. I'd been assigned to an officer who turned in daily progress reports and was there to keep an eye on me. His nickname was "Spud," and he was sitting beside me on the passenger's side of the patrol car. I wanted to make a good impression on him.

Spud normally was an easygoing, subdued kind of fella whose composure was seldom ruffled. In fact I visualized him as the kind of a guy who'd be able to do

Deep in a Butte mine, circa 1950, holes have been drilled in the face of a stope and loaded with dynamite and primers.
World Museum of Mining, Butte MT

the unenviable job of taking high school kids out on the driving part of their driver's license examinations: something that I'd decided I could never do.

After I heard the dispatcher's excited announcement, I quickly glanced over at Spud, who only nodded. I knew the chase was on. The big, green, Ford patrol car leaped forward when I stomped down on the gas pedal. The 440 cubic-inch police interceptor engine fairly screamed with all of its gas-guzzling power. I reached down and flipped on the siren and lights. Instantly the squawk of loud insistent warbling blended with the bright blue-colored, side-to-side, flashing lights. I glanced over at Spud. He still didn't say anything, only nodding in approval.

Rain had sprinkled all day and the patrol car was sending off sprays of water as it roared through an occasional street-wide puddle. I felt good and wondered if that wasn't the way Dirty Harry felt on one of his high speed car chases.

Ocean Boulevard is a long, winding stretch of two-lane road, lined on each side by houses. Every once in a while I caught a glimpse of someone standing and watching as we roared by. Then I remembered that the Boulevard, just before it entered the main part of town, made a tight, left-hand, 90-degree turn. About then I glanced down at the speedometer… 87 miles an hour! I quickly looked up and saw that a church, located on the outside of the sharp corner, was only about a city block away. About then the patrol car hit a low spot and all four wheels left the road.

Before the car returned to the pavement, I planted both feet firmly on the brake pedal, all the way to the floor. I looked at Spud; he didn't say anything, but I noticed that his face was ashen colored and his eyes stared ahead. He was instinctively trying to apply the brakes, I guessed, since he was pushed back hard in his seat.

As the car touched down I heard a loud "thud" and saw a spray of sparks shoot out the sides from underneath. The car had bounced on a washboard section of the road, but for that instant its brakes grabbed at the wet pavement. One bounce, then two and they grabbed even more. The church loomed about half-a-block ahead as we began skidding sideways.

The car went into a full sideways skid in front of the church (which must have been built on that corner to watch over fools like me). Finally the brakes overcame our forward momentum, and the interesting thing about it was that we came out pointed in the right di-

rection. In all the confusion, I looked ahead and somehow saw our quarry. I yelled to Spud, "There he is," and fought the steering wheel for control. After a few violent side-to-side swerves, we were again in hot pursuit.

Being new to the force, I didn't know the city's streets very well. When Spud replied "Turn here"—the only thing he uttered the whole time—I took his word for it. I pulled hard on the steering wheel and the car careened onto a side street. Then I saw my mistake; I'd turned one street too soon. As we sped by a Dead End sign, I knew some serious trouble was coming up. I stomped on the brakes and wrenched back on the other side of the steering wheel. The car began a full broadside skid again, toward a curb. It slid right up and stopped at the curb, as if I'd parked it there on purpose.

The chase was over for us. I sat there white-knuckled, gripping the steering wheel. Both of us stared silently ahead, with the car's engine idling quietly. Its steaming hood and a faint odor of oil were the only evidence of our recent chase.

Spud didn't turn in a favorable report on me that day. In regard to the perpetrator, the police in neighboring North Bend pulled him over and gave him a warning ticket for driving too fast in a residential area. A few weeks later I was out looking for another way to make a living. The report Spud turned in on me probably made our police chief decide that instead of speeding by that church in a patrol car, I should have been down on my knees inside of it.

Ashamed, and feeling like a complete failure, I withdrew from college and returned to Kellogg, Idaho, looking for work. I still had to support my wife and baby son. In Idaho, construction work seemed to be at a low point and other jobs were scarce. Through the Idaho State Department of Employment, the only prospect I could find was a miner entree training program at Butte, Montana.

Butte was about 250 miles from Kellogg, but I signed up for the training, because I needed work. I left my young wife and little baby in Pinehurst, which was only five or six miles from Kellogg; that way they'd be near her relatives.

The drive to Butte was great… and a step into the future. After I arrived and checked in with the Butte Vocational Technical School, I went out in search of a room. I found one on the second floor of the Leggett Hotel on Broadway Street. My room was clean and simple, almost Spartan really, with its nearly bleach-white walls and sparse furniture.

Officer trainee Jerry Dolph with wife Jo Ann and son Jason, in Coos Bay, Oregon, early 1972.
Jerry Dolph

I threw my stuff on the bed, walked over to the window, and pulled it up. Placing my hands on the sill, I leaned out and looked to the right down a row of aged buildings, butted tightly together. I then looked left… a fella was sitting on the window sill of the room next to me, his legs dangling against the building's brick wall. Surprised, I almost fell out the window! He didn't notice me, however, because just then he stood up on the sill, grabbed the window frame with his left hand, and then gingerly swung onto the next window sill and, crouching down, went into that room.

I stood back contemplating what I'd seen and thought, "What a novel idea. I think I'd rather use the hallway, but to each his own, I guess."

When I'd arrived in Butte, I had $49 in my pocket. Six days later it was "all" gone. I knew that sooner or later I'd run out of money, and I wasn't wrong. On the first day of being completely broke, I got up and went off to training like usual, but worried about where I was going to spend the night. After class I began looking for a new home, and it soon began to get dark. Then I remembered my days as a police officer in Oregon and how the police department sometimes gave lodging and meal vouchers to persons down on their luck. I looked down the hard, cold sidewalk, thinking about the pros-

pect of sleeping on it and eating out of garbage cans. I certainly qualified as a man down on his luck!

I walked straight over to the Butte police department. I told the big cop behind the desk that I was going to miner school and that I was broke and needed a room. He was busy with his paperwork, but after I'd finished my tale of woe he looked up, sort of half smiled, and said, "Get use to it kid." Then he handed me vouchers for meals and for two nights' lodging in the same hotel where I'd been staying.

I went back to the hotel and gave the vouchers to the desk clerk: the same shifty-eyed little fella who'd already taken most of my money. All he said was, "Oh… you're back," then he handed me the key to the same room I'd been occupying, and I went back up to "my" room. I called Jo Ann that night on the phone and she sent me some money that she'd borrowed, bless her heart.

Before long, I was settled into a steady routine. Leaving Butte right after class each Friday, I drove the 250 miles to Pinehurst to spend the weekend with my family. On returning to Butte, I drove through the early morning darkness arriving in time to start training at 7:30 AM. I had to drive through the night, but it was worth it. The arrangement worked well until my car was stolen. Then I hitchhiked back and forth for about a month before I was finally able to get another car.

There were two different classes going on at the same time in the center—our miners' class and one for mining truck drivers. The trucks that the other class's students were learning to drive were huge 100 and 200-ton monsters that hauled copper ore up from the bottom of Butte's Berkeley Pit. The Berkeley Pit is a giant open-pit copper mine more than a mile wide. Over the years, it had steadily been growing and eating away at Butte's scenery.

One day during a break, some of the guys in my class were standing out in the hallway grabbing a smoke and started talking with one of the fellas in the truck driving class. Their classroom was just down the hall from ours. I was sitting inside and suddenly heard a muffled roar of laughter from the hallway. Then the door burst open and the laughter trebled in strength.

It was in response to a story that the driving trainee told. The day before, one of the "big shot" bosses at the pit was racing around in a brand new pickup truck chasing after some errant employee. The boss spotted the fella up on a bulldozer, slammed on his brakes, and skidded to a stop in a cloud of dust. He jumped out of his company pickup and was walking briskly toward the dozer with a mean look in his eye. About that time the boss must have heard "the big crunch," because he turned around to see the new pickup disappear beneath the huge, rear tires of a two-hundred ton'er.

The tires on these monsters are at least 10 or 12 feet high and, I heard, are powered by their own diesel engines. It smashed the boss's little pickup flat like a beer can. I never did find out what happened to the employee on the bulldozer, but I'll bet you a dime to a doughnut he got a really great laugh out of watching the boss's pickup truck getting recycled.

My class of hopeful miners was 23 strong and we all seemed to get along pretty well from the beginning. Four weeks went by, and the classroom part of our training, where we learned mine safety procedures, ended. We now were ready to go into the Anaconda Mining Company's Kelley Mine.

The big day, our first trip down into the mine, had arrived. None of us had ever been underground before and, up till then, we had only read about it in books. I'll have to admit, it was a little spooky. There was an aura of excitement in the air, almost like static electricity, as we checked out our web belts, mine lamps, batteries, and the rest of our gear. Then, as we dressed in our funky clothes and put on all the stuff they gave us, there wasn't much to say. Even as we walked over to the shaft and got into the skip, or cage, there wasn't much conversation. We all just stood there waiting for what was to happen next.

Everybody was sort of within themselves. Personally, I was thinking about the 91 miners who'd died in North Idaho's terrible Sunshine Mine fire a few months earlier. That mine was still closed down, too. Then there were all the stories I'd heard about guys who had died in the mines back East. But that was in the coal mines, so I didn't really know what to expect. I thought of our classroom studies over the past four weeks. The messages we'd learned to prepare us for the day when we finally did go down into the mines were "Watch out for this," and "Be sure of doing that."

There wasn't much conversation as we walked toward the shaft and got into the skip. The skip resembled a large elevator cage. I'll say it was large… the sign on the wall declared flatly, "Capacity 50 men." We all stood there checking things out in silence. I got to looking down at the see-through grating of the metal floor. It was about 2 inches or so thick, sort of like the hundreds of little hollow squares on the floor of a bridge that

you could look down through into the water. Deep in thought, I shined the beam of light from my cap lamp down through the grillwork and into what looked like nothingness beyond. By then we were all looking down.

We were startled by the sudden appearance of a stranger as he noisily got into the skip with us. He closed the two swinging doors on the front and "clanged" the metal locking bar down into place between them. He then jerked down on a cord a couple of times to signal the hoistman that we were ready to go down. (In all of the hardrock mines, the standard signal was three pulls for up, two for down, and one for stop. If people in the skip wanted things done faster, they just belled faster.) He turned around to face us and said, "My name is Jim Arnoldi and I am your instructor when you're underground. I noticed that you were all looking down at the floor when I got on. This shaft is over 4,000 feet deep and…"

I looked down again into the blackness beneath the floor and tried to fathom how far 4,000 feet really was. Finally he finished talking and I heard someone else say, "I hope this floor is pretty solid."

That did it. You could sure tell that we were all a bunch of greenhorns because we started stomping our feet at the same time on the "see through" floor trying to scare each other. Then Jim's deep voice barked out, "Knock it off." At about the same time the skip began to move downward and we all fell into silence again. We'd begun our long descent into the mine. We felt warm exhaust air rush up to us as we dropped lower and lower in the shaft. Everyone remained quiet as we experienced this new, sinking feeling.

After about five minutes or so at what seemed to me a dizzying speed (man speed for the shaft was 800 feet a minute), we finally slowed down to a mere crawl, creeping downward. Then Jim reached out and pulled the "bell" cord (every stop had one beside it), signaling the hoistman to stop the skip at this level. The hoistman in the hoist room on the surface knew when to slow the skip down by looking at his gauges and instruments.

Jim hadn't said much on the trip down. He reached out and pushed open the shaft gate (a large, screened, swinging gate), and opened up the doors of the skip. We got off.

In a commanding voice he said, "I want you all to pay close attention to what I'm doing now." He secured the doors of the skip back in its doorway, commenting, "So they won't swing out and be torn off by digging into the timber when the skip is moving in the shaft."

Looking west toward Butte, Montana, and the Berkeley Pit in 1972. Started in 1955, the Berkeley Pit was the largest truck-operated open pit copper mine in the nation. It obliterated the working-class communities of McQueen and Meaderville, as well as deep shaft mines. After mining ceased here in 1982, ground water began filling the pit at the rate of 20 or more feet a year. By 1994, the lake was 800 feet deep and still rising; it is the deepest body of water in Montana.
G. DeBruyne

Jim shut the large shaft gate and, reaching through an opening in it, grabbed the signal cord again and belled the skip away. "This signal tells the hoistman we are done with the skip," he said.

Then Jim declared loudly, "Never forget to close the shaft gates when you're through... it's a long way down."

The image he so vividly painted—of someone falling down the shaft because some fool forgot to close a gate—gave me real respect for the safety those gates provided.

He continued, "You're now on the 3,900 foot level and the mine's different levels are 200 feet above one another. This is where the transfer of men, materials, blasting powder, muck [broken rock], and equipment takes place."

I looked around as he talked and saw that the station seemed a lot like a subway tunnel and a cave at the same time. Jim started walking from the shaft. We fell in be-

hind, following him. The guys finally started to talk among themselves a little bit.

We walked to about the middle of the station, where Jim stopped, pointing down to the floor, "This is the ore pocket and that iron grillwork on top of it is called the grizzly."

I looked down and saw a big hole that looked about 10 feet square and at least a hundred feet deep. The grizzly over the top of the hole looked like a hollow chessboard for want of a better explanation. Its iron framework was about an inch and a half thick and 4 inches deep, with 10 inch square holes in it.

Jim yelled out, "The idea is, when the muck train comes out of the drift [tunnel] with its cars loaded full of broken rock"... he pointed down to the small railroad tracks that went by the pocket... "the guy working the grizzly waits till the motorman [the person driving the ore train] unloads the cars into the pocket and leaves. Then he gets down and stands on top of the bars of the grizzly and cleans out the holes so all the muck

Kelley Mine at Butte, Montana.
World Museum of Mining, Butte MT

falls through, down into the pocket. After he's finished, he gets out and waits for the train to come back again. Now that doesn't seem too hard—does it?"

As he talked I noticed three broken sledgehammers and a pick head laying on the floor near the grizzly. When he said, "Now that doesn't seem too hard—does it," I heard some of the guys sort of chuckle.

Jim walked on along the narrow, 18-inch-wide railroad tracks that ran through the station and we followed. We passed by lunch tables, tool bins, piles of boxes, and junk that looked like it should have been thrown away, it was so rusty. I found out later that metal begins rusting in just a few days in the humid, warm environment of a deep mine.

The station was lighted with bulbs hanging from electric lines running overhead. We left the station and entered into the darkness of the drift. The drift looked like a railroad tunnel only not as big. It was only about 12 feet high and 15 feet wide. Four pipelines and several power cords hung on the wall to our left and seemed to go on as far as I could see in both directions.

Jim yelled back to us, "These pipes you see are for air, water, sand fill, and pump water. That big green one is the fan line [32-inch plastic looking pipe] for ventilation back in the work places. The power cords are for the electric equipment."

Then Jim pointed out a nearby chamber, which we went into. We saw a row of enormous electric motors. Their constant roar was deafening—so loud, in fact, that I shouted as loudly as I could and wasn't able to hear my own voice.

After leaving the pump room, Jim said, "The Kelley Mine acts as a pumping station for pumping groundwater out of all of the mines hereabouts. Those motors pump 7,000,000 gallons of water a day from down here on 3,900 level straight up to the surface."

He continued, "We are now on our way back to your training stope [work place]. It's about 1,500 feet from the station."

We walked along talking about the different things that we saw when I noticed other drifts that branched off in different directions from the one we were in.

I couldn't help thinking, "Damn, this is a big place. I'll bet that it wouldn't be hard to get lost down here at all." I found out later that there were direction signs at intersections.

Jim talked about the mine as we walked, and his loud voice made it easy for us to hear him: "When the earth was in a molten state, during its volcanic period, veins of ore squirted up through fissures in the rock where they remained even after the ground cooled. Then some hard-working geologist or a lucky prospector came along and discovered them. These veins can be thousands of feet long, miles high, and anywhere from a fraction of an inch to many feet wide."

He continued, "This main drift was mined through hard country rock that parallels the vein so it will last as long as possible without a lot of costly maintenance. The ground near the vein structure itself is crumbly and caves in. It's hard to hold in place. Then a crosscut [side tunnel] is mined [driven] out toward the vein which is usually about a hundred feet or so away. After the crosscut finally goes on through the vein, it stops, and there you are, the stope."

Old Jim must have given that same talk to a lot of other classes because as soon as he said, "the stope" he suddenly stopped, turned toward us, and gesturing with an outstretched arm and bow, said, "This way gentlemen."

I thought, "Well, at least this guy has a sense of humor."

We turned into the crosscut he was pointing to and walked on for a few more minutes. Then Jim suddenly stopped dead in his tracks again, threw up his arms, and shouted, "This is it."

To tell you the truth, I wasn't expecting that at all and he just scared the hell right out of me. I noticed some of the other guys sorta jumped when he did that too. We'd finally reached the bottom of our stope.

"The term 'stope,'" he said, "describes a section of the vein which is several hundred feet long, or just long enough for a crew to mine. If the stope gets longer than that, then removal of the blasted rock gets to be a problem."

Jim went on, "The stopes are aligned end-to-end along their respective veins of ore and numbered for identification purposes."

I looked up and saw my first timbered raise. Jim pointed out the man-way part of it and the bottom of a ladder. Stepping back, he said, "Start climbing."

We climbed up nearly 90 feet of ladders before finally reaching the working floor. As we topped the last ladder and stepped out onto the floor we had to spread out to make room for everybody. Jim brought up the rear. After Jim straightened himself up and stepped out of the man-way, he dropped the hinged gate down over the hole behind him.

He said, "Make sure you keep the man-way gate closed unless you are going through it." He then continued, "This is the first time that this place has been used as a student stope, so we'll have to try to stay out of each other's way."

Our stope was only about 10 feet high, 8 feet wide, and disappeared into the darkness on both ends. I almost had to laugh, because we were a regular mob and the darting beams of our cap lamps lit up that small area so brightly it seemed almost like daylight.

Jim then described the different types of equipment in the stope and how they were used. Then he noticed some of us weren't paying attention. There was a small group of fellas huddled together and talking in low tones over in a corner. They were looking at the wall. He stopped talking, walked over to where they were, and looked over their backs to see what they were so interested in.

That was the first time I heard the term "vug hole." The ground in the Butte mining camp, especially in the Kelley Mine, was just full of vug holes. They were pockets in the rock caused by water and chemicals. The holes, some football-sized, were full of crystals, many as large as a man's fist. As soon as the rest of us found out that the damned place was full of "diamonds," we hammered and chipped at the walls with whatever we could find. Jim had lost us, and even though he yelled menacingly, he couldn't regain control. Finally he just threw his hands up in disgust and declared an early lunch.

The student stope we trained in was narrow and long, so only a few of us were able to get close enough to Jim at any one time to get personalized instruction. That left much to be desired in regard to learning, but it gave us a chance to talk and get to know each other. In the days that followed, I often talked with Frank. He was just a young fella, but he seemed to have a lot to say. We talked about the story in the daily newspaper that described how two kids were shooting their 22 caliber long rifle at an old powder magazine from about 50 yards away. The high-explosives exploded, blowing up the storage building. All that was found of the two young men was one tennis shoe and part of a shirt.

A HISTORICAL VIGNETTE OF HARDROCK MINING, BUTTE, MONTANA—

Above left—Trucking out equipment after drilling a round of holes for explosives. The holes are visible in the stope's face behind the miners.
World Museum of Mining, Butte MT

Left—Checking caps and fuses while loading explosives into holes.
World Museum of Mining, Butte MT

Above—After blasting a round, a miner uses a slusher to drop copper ore down an open chute. The ore then is loaded into ore cars at the bottom of the chute. A century ago, miners drilled rounds and shoveled ore by hand.
World Museum of Mining, Butte MT

Then Frank said, "Did you hear Jim say that when electric primers [electrically ignited blasting caps] were first being tested here a few of the miners were killed by them? Yeah… no one could figure out why the primers were going off by themselves without being charged. Then someone happened to notice, up on the surface, that along the electric trolley line a few of the copper connectors that were supposed to be in between the rails were missing. Hell, they found out that some kids were stealing them and selling the copper for scrap. The juice was going through the rails all right, but instead of continuing on through the copper connectors to the next rail, it went straight down into the ground and charged the rock where the miners were trying out their brand new electric primers."

We learned a lot from Jim in the next 10 weeks; he was a good instructor. The Kelley, and the whole Butte camp in fact, was mostly one big copper mine. The copper water draining through the rock was highly acidic. Jim told us that a lot of people couldn't even work in it because their skin was too sensitive and the water burned them. None of us had any problems with it, but I could sure see what he meant. Sometimes I felt my own skin getting warm too.

Just to give you an idea of how acidic the copper water was, picture this: we had to cut our pant cuffs off with pinking shears, otherwise the "seams" around the bottoms of the pant legs would rot, drop down on one side, and trip us up. The acidic copper water really did a job on denim. I noticed too that one of the metal rails leading to the bottom of the student stope had a drip of copper water hitting it dead center. The rail had to be repaired in only a few days because the copper water cut it in two. Incidentally, the water was the most beautiful green color you'd ever see. It dripped down from little seams in the rock and actually formed stalactites that hung down on the walls like giant green icicles.

There was a "poor box" in the Kelley Mine's dry, or locker room. Guys threw articles of clothing into the box that they no longer wanted. Poorer miners sorted through the box to try and find something usable. In essence they traded clothes. Diggers, or miners' clothes, are tough on washing machines. If you don't believe me just ask laundromat owners. Machines wear out fast because of grease, rocks, 60 penny nails, etc. that go into them with the diggers. Sometimes, unfortunate persons put their nice dresses, or whatever, into digger machines by mistake. Their clothes don't get clean; they just get punctured, stained, and ripped.

Each morning, before starting down the shaft for our day's training, we could look out over the opening above the skip's door and see Butte's impressive landscape. I remember thinking, "Man look at all of that stuff. It must have taken thousands of men a hundred years to build all of this."

I also was discovering that miners were a hard lot who pushed life to its fullest in their search for the almighty dollar. They spent most of their days deep in the earth, struggling with materials and equipment in oppressive heat. They installed vast quantities of timbers and wood into their work places to shore up the ground and keep it from caving in on them. Then, they drilled holes, which were filled with high explosives to blast the rock apart. Then they hauled out the valuable ore. Except for the introduction of modern power equipment, mining has been done in pretty much the same way for many, many years.

I once heard a story about a hard-core miner, known as Uncle Fudd, who lived in a turn-of-the-century Montana mining town. He was as rough, tough, and nasty as they come, and at one time or another he'd beaten up practically every man in town. Finally, the townspeople couldn't stand it anymore and held a town meeting. After a heated discussion, they decided to hire John Boggs, a notorious roughneck, to fight Uncle Fudd for them. Boggs was well-known throughout the region for his vicious thrashings of opponents, sometimes leaving them crippled for life.

After several weeks of hopeful anticipation, the big day came—Boggs arrived by train at the station, which was overflowing with Uncle Fudd's past victims. Townsmen were ecstatic when they saw Boggs's hulking form standing in the passenger car doorway. He was big! Surely, all the tales they'd heard about his fighting reputation were true. With an enthusiastic cheer, they rushed forward and crowded around as the town council members kept them from pushing right up to the passenger car. Enjoying the warm reception, John stepped proudly down from the train onto a red carpet that the townsmen called "the carpet of revenge."

After lengthy greetings and backslapping from the hysterical crowd, big mean-looking Boggs impatiently demanded, "Now, where's this Uncle Fudd?"

The town's mayor stepped forward and, pointing with a finger, said, "He lives up there on the hill in that white house with the picket fence. Here take my horse."

John took the horse's reins and swung his big frame up into the saddle. Sensing revenge, the crowd cheered wildly and followed behind on foot as he rode off toward Uncle Fudd's house. After a brief ride, Boggs arrived at the house in front of the shouting, laughing mob, which contained nearly all of the town's population. They then stood expectantly, at a distance, waiting to see what was going to happen next.

John urged the horse on with his knees. The horse's big hooves sank into the freshly planted flower bed gracing the white picket fence, and the horse's shoulder pushed against a corner post, collapsing a section of the fence. Out of the corner of his eye, John noted the crowd's obvious pleasure and he smiled. He swung a leg over the saddle horn and dropped to the ground. The crowd stood motionless, watching him climbing the stairs up onto the porch. None of them had ever been up those steps before, for fear of their lives.

John purposefully stepped up to the door, and with a big fist pounded on it, rattling the window frame. A few moments passed and the door swung open. The crowd gave out an audible sigh of anticipation. A giant, dark complexioned man appeared in the doorway. Townspeople claimed that Uncle Fudd's dark demeanor had come up with him from deep within the earth where he worked. John suddenly paled, stepping back in uncertainty at this first sight of the enormous dark figure in front of him.

Uncle Fudd said, "Yeah?"

Girded up by the crowd behind him, John drew up his courage again and replied, "Are you this Uncle Fudd that everyone says is so tough?"

Uncle Fudd patiently said, "Yeah, I guess I am."

John then reached down, picked up a piece of wood from a rotting plank on the porch, and placed it on his own shoulder. He said, "Knock that off of there."

Quickly, Uncle Fudd reached out with one of his huge hairy hands, crushed the material to fragments all over John's shirt, and, with a one-handed bear-like grip, lifted John's thrashing, twisting body easily from the floor and hurled him 30 feet through the air, and over the broken white fence and the flowers.

Then Uncle Fudd said calmly, but with a raised voice, "Is there anything else I can do for you?"

John, lying there in a heap, looked up through the picket fence at the huge dark figure on the porch. He answered, "Yeah, throw me my horse, will ya?"

I don't know how much of the story is true, but it illustrates the aura of "strength" and "hardness" that I was talking about regarding the traditional hardrock miner.

There were two weeks left in our training program when my friend Frank went into one of the local bars and began drinking heavily. Butte was just plum full of bars, located practically in every other building, and these bars were filled with old-time miners.

Now Frank was the kind of guy who'd done everything, gone everywhere, and had twice as much fun as it was really possible to have had doing it. You know the type. He was sitting there at the bar, bragging and swaying, trying to get the fella he was talking with to believe his claims about mining experiences he'd had. Frustrated in his conversation with the stranger, the young "miner" reached into his jacket, pulled out a stick of dynamite, and promptly slammed it down onto the bar saying, "See there?"

I spoke with Frank a couple of days later down at the city jail. Recounting the incident, he said, "Things are a little confusing for me after that, all I can remember are sounds. The wailing of sirens, jingling of keys, and the clanging of iron doors."

You'd think that after seeing what the evils of drink had done to my young classmate, I would have been more cautious, but no. You've no doubt heard the expression, "Put your brain in gear before you start moving your mouth," or however it goes.

Same scene, Butte bar, and too much to drink. The only difference… I was the one who was staggering around making a fool of himself. I must have gotten someone mad too because I was severely beaten about the head and shoulders out behind the bar. The fella I met up with was intent on remodeling my alcohol induced attitude, and my face, with a brick, and succeeded on both counts. I finally came out of a coma two or three days later in a hospital in Missoula, Montana. I found out later that the ambulance drivers who took me on that 100+ mile flat-out ride fully expected me to die en route.

After several weeks of recuperation, plastic surgery to reconstruct my cheek bones, and having a broken jaw wired together in three places, I was released from the hospital. I didn't get to drive back to Kellogg. Jo Ann wouldn't let me. She drove. I'm proud of my little lady. She stuck by me in my time of stupidness. ❀

*"There were a hell of a lot of things they
didn't tell me when I hired on at this mine."*

CHAPTER 2

First Meeting with Mr. Air Blast

Lucky Friday Mine
Mullan, Idaho

There I sat in Kellogg, Idaho, unemployed, and watching the weather turning colder day by day. It was nearing the end of September 1972, and I knew that a brutal Pacific Northwest winter, with its unforgiving freezing temperatures, was coming up fast.

The "Butte experience" was behind me... almost. I'd finally healed up enough to go out looking for work. Even though I still had my jaw wired together, I hired out at Hecla Mining Company's Lucky Friday Mine, located beneath Mullan, Idaho, and the eastern-most active mine of North Idaho's Silver Valley.

The Silver Valley is one of the richest mining districts on earth. Its deep hardrock mines (once nearly a hundred strong, but eventually numbering only six, and, in 1994, only two) produced millions of ounces of silver, much gold, and many tons of lead, zinc, copper, and other metals each year. For years the Valley was responsible for over half of the nation's silver output (many of the mines are on stand-by and can be re-opened should an increase in metal prices make them profitable to operate again). In a hundred years of production, over a billion ounces of silver have come from the Valley's mines. At the time of my hire out, it was "rumored" among the men of the Lucky Friday that the mine was producing enough in gold alone to pay for its employees' wages, as well as all of its other expenses.

The Friday was one of the Valley's biggest, and a deep hardrock mine just like all the others. The mine's main

"My powerful cap lamp could just barely penetrate the thick choking dust... I could see that the dust was shaking from the concussions of repeated blasts hammering the stope over and over again"—Jerry Dolph.
ASARCO Inc.

shaft reaching a depth of well over 4,000 feet, was much the same as the Kelley Mine that I'd just left in Butte. I'd heard that originally silver bearing ore was discovered on the surface of the Lucky Friday and, as its shaft was sunk deeper, levels were laid out every 200 feet, one above another. But, presumably because of mining methods, the top level was 850 feet below the surface. The rest of the mine's levels were 1,050, 1,250, and so on, all the way to the bottom.

I could never really tell about the actual depth of the top level itself, though, because of all the hustle and bustle, and excitement, of loading onto the skip. We always "swooshed" on down past that first level in our little iron cage at a speed of about 800 feet a minute, the same man-speed as in all of the other shafts of the Silver Valley mines too.

My first job at the Friday was beating rocks up with a sledgehammer so they would be small enough to fit down through a grizzly on the mine's 3,450 foot level. This grizzly was a 10-feet-long, 5-feet-wide iron grill made up of 10-inch square holes through which the ore was dumped from a train of mine cars down into an enormous 125-feet-deep storage pocket. At least I knew what a grizzly was, because of my "extensive" three-month-long training in Butte.

It was really hard to get air at first, as I tried to work with my jaws wired together. I had to suck in what little air I could around the bands. Of course, I could still breathe through my nose, but most of the time that just wasn't enough. And that left me with the feeling that I was suffocating. Something else that I had to filter between my teeth at work was lunch. Now I hadn't eaten Gerber's baby food for a considerable amount of time.

But you know, it wasn't half bad. Another "dish" that I took in through a straw and liked was blended steak.

I really missed being able to use my tongue, though, and had a devil of a time trying to mail letters. Picture this: you go into the post office with a letter to mail and buy a stamp. So then what do you do with the stamp—ask someone else to lick it for you? The lady behind the postal counter had the answer. She brought out a damp sponge and said, "A lot of people have to use this." The only reason I could think of for them to need the sponge, too, was that they must've met up with the same fella over in Butte that I did.

When Doc Chambers, my new shifter, or boss, first put me on a grizzly, I felt a little degraded somehow. But then I figured, "Hey, a guy's gotta pay his dues right? After all, most miners start their mining careers on the grizzly." Or, at least, that's what everybody told me at the time.

Somehow that still didn't seem to satisfy the feeling I had of, "Damn it... I just got out of school and here I am pounding rocks. Something must be wrong."

I had the cleanest grizzly in the mine, though. One day a crusty-looking old gent walked through the drift by my grizzly. He stopped and visited for a while.

As he spoke I thought, "This old fella must be a mechanic."

He turned out to be Bill Anderson, the mine's superintendent. I liked Bill a lot. He always wore railroad type coveralls and acted like he was just one of the workers. I'd seen mine superintendents before and was wary of them. In Butte, with their foremen in tow, they acted like, "Boy you'd better watch what you say around me, because if it's the wrong thing I'm either going to laugh in your face because you're stupid or I'll fire your dumb ass."

I was doing just a cracker-jack job on my grizzly. Then one day Doc came up to me and said, "Fred [one of the miners] didn't show up for work and I want you to take his place. So go on up into the stope with his partner, Bill, today."

I thought "All right... I've made it."

Actually, all Doc needed was a body to baby-sit his miner in case the miner got hurt, but I didn't know that. (In addition to being just plain stupid and dangerous, it is illegal under federal safety laws for a miner to work in a stope by himself.) As it turned out it was the first time I was to be introduced to "Mr. Air Blast."

I fell in behind Bill and we walked on back through the drift toward his stope, which was about 1,000 feet from the shaft's station where I'd been working. As we walked along, I looked over my surroundings and thought, "This is almost like the Kelley Mine. The rails are bigger because of the different sized ore cars down here, but there are the same strings of air, water, and sand pipes hanging on the wall, and the big 32-inch vent line for ventilating air back into the stopes."

I looked down and saw the piss ditch (a drainage ditch at the base of the wall beneath the pipes) running alongside the tracks too. I think mining engineers must have all gone to the same school because all of the mines I ever worked in were pretty much the same.

It didn't seem like very long at all before we reached the bottom of Bill's raise (a vertical timbered shaft). We started the long climb up from the track level through the man-way to the stope itself. My doctor had just removed the bands that had wired my jaws together for the past month, and I guess I was feeling pretty good over just about everything that day.

As we climbed along I began to notice that the man-way was sort of "octagonal" in shape and made of 3-feet-long, 8 x 8 inch timbers that joined together at their ends. I figured that the man-way must have been put together like that to give it the ability to give way as the ground pressed against it. But then, I also noticed as we climbed that much of Bill's man-way was crushed in or had been pushed out of shape, and that many of the wooden ladders we were climbing on were twisted and broken too.

I yelled up at Bill, who was just a couple of ladders above me. "What caused your man-way to get so screwed up?" He only grunted and said, "You'll find out."

His voice sounded deep and vibrated as he spoke, because of the acoustics of the man-way. I thought his answer a little strange, but let it go at that. Eventually, we'd climbed 140 feet before finally reaching the top of Bill's raise and entered the stope itself.

Later on that morning I did find out what had messed up his man-way. I was moving tools up into a different section of the raise just before lunchtime when "Mr. Air Blast" came a-callin'. There was suddenly a horrific blasting roar which just shook the hell right out of me, right down to my bones. I was in shock. It seemed to last for hours—actually, only a couple of seconds, I guess. During those seconds, though, I was frantic. It happened so fast… I searched desperately for some kind of cover from all of the rocks that were dropping around me from out of the back, or ceiling, of the stope.

A deep grinding noise blended in with the roar. I glanced over in its direction and saw a solid rock wall collapse right there in front of me. I couldn't believe it—a solid granite wall just fell apart. It not only fell apart, it sort of heaved out toward the center of the stope as it collapsed, looking almost like there was a giant pushing it over from behind. I just had a brief

glimpse of the wall as it dropped when an almost instant cloud of dust belched out from everywhere. My powerful cap lamp could just barely penetrate the thick choking dust hanging like a heavy cloud in the air, but I could see that the dust was shaking from the concussions of repeated blasts hammering the stope over and over again.

I searched desperately for Bill through the wall of dust and the fear that clouded my mind as I dodged falling rocks. And then I saw something that really looked weird—a head with a big toothy grin, seeming to be body-less and floating in the air. The dust was so thick that all I could see of Bill was his big, stupid grin.

Finally it was all over and, after I was able to talk again, I shouted angrily, "What the hell was that?"

Bill had looked almost insane to me during the blasts, shrouded in dust. Rocks were falling everywhere, and there sat Bill roaring with laughter. He didn't answer my question, either.

Finally suppressing his laughter, all he said was, "You know you climbed up and down that ladder three times."

We walked over and sat down for lunch, and he explained what had caused my initiation ceremony. "These mountains are moving and building up stresses. When the stresses get to be more than the rock can stand… the rock breaks. Sort of like little earthquakes. I don't know, guess it's got somethin' to do with the movement of the earth's plates."

As he talked I heard the rumble of a sudden rush of rocks breaking loose and falling. Simultaneously, we looked over at the top of our man-way and saw the wall

Lael Pohto breaking up pieces of ore on a grizzly.
Bruce Baraby, Wallace ID

above it come down, burying its gate, or hinged trap-door. The top of the man-way was gone. It had suddenly been buried under more than three feet of muck. It then took us well over an hour and a half to dig out the man-way trapdoor—our only escape route. I'll have to admit, I was having some serious doubts about my decision to become a hardrock miner right about then.

(Experts say rock bursts are caused when, in the pro-cess of mining, ground is blasted loose in one area of a mine, causing stresses to build up in the surrounding rock. When the ground can no longer withstand the tremendous strains and pressures, it suddenly bursts in a shower of rock, relieving the stress in the area. The more extensive the initial mining activity, the larger the burst.)

We spent the rest of the day fixing up his stope. It was a lot like crawling into a garbage can and trying to straighten it up from the inside out.

There was something else Bill told me that day: "The parts of a drift were named after the body parts of a snake. The ceiling is called the back. The sides are the ribs. The old mined out end of the drift is called the tail drift. And the other end, that's being blasted, is the face."

I worked with Bill a few more times afterward. Gradually I became almost numb to the efforts of Mr. Air Blast to shake my confidence in man's ability to

A man-way in good shape.
Bruce Baraby, Wallace ID

control the ground he works in, although there were moments when I wished I was home hiding under my bed. I was still a greenhorn—green as pitch—in the Lucky Friday and what really impressed me was the strength of the miners who worked there. I'm not talk-ing about their muscular strength especially, but their strength of will. Here was a group of fellas who had fire in them.

They never ceased to amaze me with their feats. In the short span of an eight-hour shift, they'd go down in the "hole" and literally cause the earth to shake—"drill-ing" with heavy jack-leg drilling machines, "timbering" with tree sized logs to shore up the ground so it wouldn't cave in around them, and "blasting" with high explo-sives to break up the rock. It was amazing to me.

One of those who impressed me most was a big man named Joe Hunter. His job was to replace support tim-bers worn-out from use and time, or when they had rot-ted from exposure to the constant drizzle of water com-ing down the shafts.

I was impressed and thought, "Now this guy must be the ultimate miner—big, tall, and deep-voiced. A man to be reckoned with."

Joe liked to "kid" around with Hugh Campbell, his pardner. In one way or another, the two of them always seemed to have something going on. One day, as six of us were jammed together in the shaft's skip, dropping like a rock through the blackness into the mine's depths, Joe and Hugh started playing one of their little games. They liked to show each other, and the rest of the crew too I think, how much hand strength they each had. They interlocked fingers and began grap-pling, each trying to force the other to "give" while putting their whole bodies into it. Space was tight, with

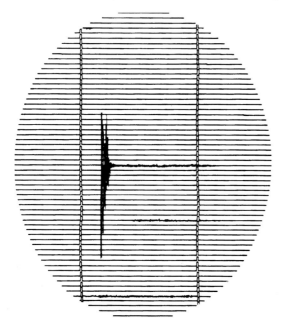
Rock burst at the Lucky Friday Mine on September 20, 1987, registering 73 mm.
Bureau of Mines Research Center, Spokane WA

the six of us all crowded in the skip together. Like it or not, we were all participants in their little game. First they would wrench one way and someone would howl from an accidental elbow in the ribs. Then they jerked in another direction, and an unlucky crew member had his face mashed into the skip's wall as his hard hat went a-flyin' (that was me). In the furor of their battle, they were oblivious to our pleas. This went on for a seeming eternity, even though the ride lasted only five minutes.

Finally Hugh howled in pain, and said, "Damn it, you broke my finger."

Their intense, heated battle was over, and my blood pressure suddenly returned to its normal simmer. I thought "Whew, what a relief, I'm glad that's over."

The two eyed each other fiercely for a moment and what happened next was probably the biggest surprise of all. They started laughing. I couldn't believe it. There Hugh stood laughing, while wincing in pain with a broken finger. Joe's thunderous laughter was almost deafening—I could actually feel the metal wall of the skip that I was leaning up against vibrating under my shoulder from his deep base voice.

Then he thundered out, "I got you back for the broke finger you gave me last year."

Like I said before, "These guys were powerful." Joe and Hugh had been partners for many years and actually were very good friends, although it sure didn't seem like it at the time of their "pitched battle."

(In 1981, Joe, who was working as a shaft repairman, slipped and fell several thousand feet to his death. I was deeply saddened by it; he was a great guy. It gave me a rude reawakening too, saying to me, "For God's sakes be careful, this is dangerous stuff." I eventually talked with Hugh about Joe's terrible accident. Hugh explained how it happened: Joe was in the process of changing positions on the shaft's timber. After unhooking his safety rope and trying to get resituated, he grabbed hold of a rotten post. He tried to gain another handhold, but the old timber that he had ahold of gave way, leaving Joe with a handful of "rot." He plunged down into the darkness of the shaft, to his death.)

Hugh was involved in some near fatal accidents himself. Betty, who drove a muck train and was one of the fine lady workers at the Lucky Friday, later told me the following tale about one of them: "One day Hugh's partner didn't show up for work so his shifter told me to go up and baby-sit Hugh in his stope. I did so, and just before lunch as I was putting away some timber in the

raise, a bad air blast hit. I was stooped over at the time and just happened to look up at the very second it hit.

"Hugh was back in the stope about 50 feet from me drilling with his jack-leg. I heard a horrible roar when the blast hit. Then I saw him look to his left and put his left arm up trying to protect himself. The hanging wall just sort of leaned over and collapsed down on top of him. Then everything disappeared in a cloud of dust.

"I knew that Hugh was badly hurt and maybe even dying so I hurried down the hundred feet of man-way ladders to the level below and ran out to the station. Then I told the guys I found out there about what had happened to Hugh. Before I knew it, there were all kinds of fellas rushing back toward Hugh's stope with me.

"It didn't take long either before we were all up in there. The dust was gone then and one giant slab of rock was laying right where Hugh should have been.

"The ground was still snapping and popping, and I heard a bigger 'thump' once in a while as we hand dug, pried, and jacked the slab up trying to get Hugh out from under it. We finally found him. Just as we pulled him out from under the mess and dragged him back under the raise timber, another big one hit. Then the whole back caved in right down on top of where we'd all been working."

Hugh was off work for over a year with a broken hip, broken ribs, and legs, but eventually came back and went to work in the same stope where he had nearly been killed. ✿

A man's feeble attempt to thwart the forces of nature. A miner jokingly tries to push back "Mr. Air Blast."
ASARCO Inc.

CHAPTER 3

Hung Up in Ten Shaft

Sunshine Mine
Kellogg, Idaho

The combination of the Lucky Friday's air blasts and the word given to me by a friend that the Sunshine Mine was paying a dollar more per hour was enough to make me quit the Lucky Friday after a couple of months of working there. I went to work for the 'Shine, located just above Big Creek, near Kellogg, Idaho.

It was December 1972 and all of the Silver Valley mines were hiring. They all seemed to have three different crews at the same time too: one hiring out, one working, and one quitting. It was the heyday of the tramp miner.

I am reminded of a story my friend Pete Rule told me about tramp miners. He said, "This miner was killed and immediately found himself standing at the end of a long line of other miners in front of the pearly gates of heaven.

"Well…" Pete continued, "the miner stepped out of line and walked up to the front. Saint Peter was there and the new guy asked him, 'What's this really long line of miners here for?'

"Saint Peter replied, 'They're all trying to get into heaven so you'll have to go back to the end of the line and wait your turn.'

"With that the miner thought for a moment about what Saint Peter had said and asked, 'If I can get these fellas to leave their places in line, can I be next?'

"Saint Peter, after some deliberation, said, 'Yes, I suppose that would be all right.'

Miners entering the Sunshine Mine's Jewell Shaft.
Sunshine Precious Metals Inc.

"The miner quickly returned to the line again and began speaking with the others. Saint Peter was astonished to see the line quickly dissolve leaving only the new miner in front of him.

" 'That's amazing,' Saint Peter said. 'What did you say to them?'

"The miner replied, 'Oh, that was easy, I just told them that there was a new mine down the road that was paying $200 a day and they all left.' "

As Pete was telling his story, I listened to the tone of his voice. It was harsh and raspy. Some would have called it a whiskey baritone.

I thought, "This is a hard-drinking, hard-working, rough and tumble miner who's had a really tough life."

A year later, Pete was my partner for a while. He eventually died of cancer, courtesy of the tobacco company that produced his smokes, I suspect. He was a hard man right to the end. The doctors had to open up his wind pipe and insert a tube so he could breathe. Pete, not wanting to miss an opportunity like that and no longer able to smoke cigarettes in his mouth, used the tube. I've often wondered if he didn't wind up being the new miner at the end of the line.

I'd heard that the Sunshine miners were considered to be real pros, having a reputation in the Silver Valley of collectively being some of the best hardrock miners anywhere. My first day there in the 'Shine, left me in awe of all the new mining stuff and people I saw around me. There was the new dry, lamp storage area, shifters office, and so on. I felt like a real rookie as I put on my diggers and prepared for my first trip down the shaft into the mine. In such strange surroundings, the sight of my funky old clothes somehow seemed comforting. They

A man-train on the Sunshine Mine's 3,700 foot level. On this level, the distance from the bottom of the Jewel shaft over to the top of Ten Shaft is about a mile, requiring miners to be be transported by rail.

Sunshine Precious Metals Inc./Photo by Harry Cougher

were almost like old friends who showed up to go down with me on my first day underground.

Memories of the Sunshine Mine's disastrous fire which claimed 91 lives earlier in the year were firmly embedded in my mind as I silently went on with the business at hand. I noticed that silence was the order of the day for the other guys, too, as they "suited up." My full gear consisted of old rotten clothes and hard-toed boots complete with the wear holes that had been accidentally ripped into their sides in various places, which helped with their drainage. Then, of course, there was my hard hat that had been gashed up many times by low clearance objects and falling rock.

I got up from the bench and walked toward the door on my way out of the room. That's when I happened to see my reflection in a mirror above a wash basin as I passed by. I tentatively approached the mirror and turned on the water in the sink, like I was washing my hands, so no one would notice that I was looking at myself.

I saw the new Sunshine miner and thought, "Damn I look bad… this is great, I'll fit right in."

I always figured that the worse a miner looks, the better a miner he is, and I knew some awfully good ones. No one seemed to notice as I picked up my lamp and headed down the long flight of stairs toward street level and the shifters office. I was really afraid that someone was going to say, "Hey, look at the new guy… bet he don't know much."

As I pushed open the door and walked into the 40-foot-long shifters office building, I saw that I was in a hallway with time cards and a clock hanging on the wall to my left. To the right was a countertop running the full width of the place and behind it, a room full of men busily milling about talking loudly about God only knew what. I pulled my new time card from its holder, trying to act like I'd done it a thousand times before. I noticed that someone had already filled in my name and employee number. Undaunted, I pressed on and was just about to punch in when I heard someone yell out from behind the counter deep within the room. "You Dolph?"

I replied, "Yeah." I thought, "The jig's up, someone's spotted me. Guess my disguise wasn't as good as I thought it was."

Several of the bosses in the room looked up for a second from their duties and saw me in all my infant glory… I felt bad. A stocky-looking guy got up from his desk and walked toward me through the thick cigarette smoke that filled the room and said, "I'm Larry Hawkins, your shifter. You're going to be working on the 4,800 level and I'm sending Jeff down with you to show you around. I've already told him about it and he'll meet up with you at the top of the Jewell Shaft."

I said, "Okay," finished punching in my time card, and walked on through the short hallway.

I opened the door and was outside again. I stood there for a couple of minutes looking up at the mountainside and the tunnel's portal with the words "Jewell Shaft" etched into the concrete above it.

I thought, "I've seen this drift before. It was on television when I was with the police department down in Oregon. When the bodies of the 91 fellas who died in the fire were taken out of this mine, the rescue crews brought them all out right through here." The Sunshine had been closed down for a long time after the terrible fire and had only been back in operation for a few months.

I fell into line with the rest of the crew and walked several hundred feet through the drift into the mountain before reaching the shaft. That's where I met Jeff, as the shifter had told me to do. Jeff was an old-timer who'd been there at the 'Shine for many years and was just a fountain of information about the mine. We stood there for what seemed like ages waiting for the hoistman to lower the first skip of the day. I was trying to see what the place looked like, but Jeff stayed right in front of me—every time I moved, so did he.

After about 15 minutes of listening to the impatient urgency in his voice as he blurted out nonstop facts and trivia about the mine, I thought, "I'll bet I know why Larry put me with this guy. He probably got tired of listening to him and pawned him off on me."

We finally loaded up onto the skip and were soon down on 3,700, the main haulage level. That's when I first saw the man-train. According to federal regulations, only electric motors and diesel engines are used underground because exhaust fumes from gas driven engines can be deadly if there is poor ventilation. The motor, or electric locomotive, that pulled the man-train looked a lot like the ones at the Lucky Friday and the Kelley, but it was enormous—I'd never seen one that big before. It looked to be about 6 feet wide, 7 feet high, and somewhere between 15 feet and a mile long… a real mean-looking machine. Jeff saw that I was admiring "his" motor and predictably charged in with a barrage of information that ended only with the report that the motorman's kids were all down with the flu.

The train behind the motor was nine cars long. Three small doors were "holed" into the side of each car, providing access to the three compartments in each car. Jeff and I climbed into one of them and sat beside each other on a narrow bench. Our bench was just two butts wide. Two other guys got into our compartment, too, and sat across from us. As they did we all interlocked legs so we could "fit in" together. I kept thinking of the television commercial, "Aren't you glad you use dial, don't you wish everybody did?" Three of the guys in my compartment didn't—at least I thought it was them.

We were riding on the first skip down. As I sat on the man-train, I could see the entourage that was following us out of the shaft onto the level. Looking out through the car door, I watched the train steadily filling with men. The hoistman raised and lowered the skips in the shaft over and over again, letting off more men each time. I couldn't believe the number of guys who kept getting off the skips and walking over towards us. I thought, "Hell, there must be hundreds of them."

Suddenly our little car jerked forward and began moving. I thought, "This isn't right, there are still fellas coming out of the shaft."

As we pulled out, I guess I screwed up by asking Jeff, "Why are we leaving those guys here?"

He half choked on the coffee he was drinking and quickly replied, "There's another train." Then he talked on… and on.

I thought, "That damned Larry, I'll bet he's having a hell of a laugh about giving me to old Jeff here."

The train picked up speed and soon we were rolling merrily along. A sign stenciled on the wall just inside the door of the car read, "Keep hands and feet inside the car." I thought of how terrible it would be to suddenly lose a hand or foot outside the door, as we clickety-clacked down the tracks. Gazing out through the open doorway as we bumped along, I saw that we were passing many crosscuts taking off into the darkness as we rolled on by them.

I thought of the Lucky Friday Mine: "This is sort of funny, the Friday boasts that it can get its whole crew out from underground in a matter of minutes because it only has one main shaft. I'll bet it'd take a week for these guys to get out of here."

As our train took the curves, its wheels shrieked, scouring against the twisting, turning iron rails. The cars groaned and shook. The drift we were traveling through looked like most every drift I'd been in so far, but I decided right there that riding in a man-train just beat the living hell out of walking. It was sort of neat. Then I saw something I wouldn't have believed. The two miners sitting across from Jeff and I were already asleep. I sat there studying their faces for a while and thought, "Their heads flop back and forth together at the same time, sort of like the little dolls' heads that my dad used to have stuck to the back window of his pickup truck."

We rolled along about a mile. Finally, making one last screaming curve, we slowly came to a stop. I was thinking of how the ear-piercing screech of the train's wheels compared with dragging fingernails across a blackboard, when Jeff blurted out, "Well here we are… this is Ten Shaft station, we'll go on down to the 4,800 level from here."

Everyone got out of the train and soon the station was full of fellas who were standing around in small groups waiting to get on the skip. They chattered together about everything from the amount of powder, or dynamite, they were going to need, to how the fishing was over the weekend.

Then I heard the familiar "clang" of a skip gate's locking bar being thrown open and the clear voice of a cager. Cagers worked in conjunction with the hoistman in loading and moving men, equipment, and muck in the shaft. In a loud demanding voice, the cager called out levels, starting from the bottom of the mine and going up: "Five thousand, forty eight hundred…" Then the guys who worked on those levels stepped into the 3-level skip and stood there settling themselves in for the trip down.

Ten Shaft, although bigger, was a lot like the Lucky Friday's shaft in that it too was relatively small and crowded. Fully loaded, a single deck in the skip held about 11 guys. I don't think that rating was meant for full-grown, lunch-box-carrying miners, though. Once a deck of the skip was full, the cager closed the swinging gates and dropped the locking bar down securely in place. Then he belled the hoistman to slowly raise the skip up the shaft a few feet. That brought the next empty deck up into the loading position where it was stopped and filled with men. Jeff and I got on then, too.

The rule was to load the men who worked in the mine's lower levels on upper decks of a skip first, finally ending with the men working at higher levels on the lower deck. On the way down, the upper-level workers (who would be standing on the lower part of the skip) unloaded first. If there happened to be a power failure, the hoistman could utilize gravity to lower the upper

Sunshine Mining and Refining Company on Big Creek, Idaho, circa 1970s.

part of the skip down to the station floor and off-load the crew. At the end of the shift the order was reversed. Thus, first on, last off (on the way down)… last on, first off (on the way back up). This allowed all of the miners to have equal time working in the stopes.

Our "ride" was finally full—all three decks worth—and after the cager signaled the hoistman which level to stop at first by pulling on the bell cord (which looks like a length of plastic-covered clothesline), we began our second trip down a shaft that morning. We quickly picked up speed. Soon we were at the 800-feet-a-minute speed, dropping like a stone down the shaft. As I stood there watching the timber whizz by the front of the skip, I began thinking about the poor souls who died in the fire.

"Hell, they didn't have a chance. Here we are, thousands of feet underground and going down the second shaft that I've been in today." I tried to imagine how it must have been for them in their last moments of life as we hurled certainly and steadily deeper down into the earth.

Finally the skip began to slow down. We were approaching 4,800. I thought, "How in hell can this mine make any money? Everybody here is making pretty good bucks and none of us have done a thing productive at all since we started work today. And here it is 30 minutes into the shift already."

As I stood there in the skip looking at the backs of the hard hats in front of me, I thought of how many guys I'd seen walking toward the man-train at the bottom of the Jewell Shaft. I was brought back to reality again by the sound of the shaft gate being swung open. We'd stopped. Jeff got off the skip first and I quickly followed out onto the 4,800 station. After getting off the skip, and as I walked away from it, I could hear the sounds of its doors being swung closed, the familiar "clunk" of the iron locking bar dropping in place, and the tugging noises as the cager jerked on the "spring resisting" bell cord, signaling the hoistman to lower the skip further on down the shaft to the mine's 5,000 foot level.

About then I turned and just caught a glimpse of the top of the skip as it disappeared beneath the floor into

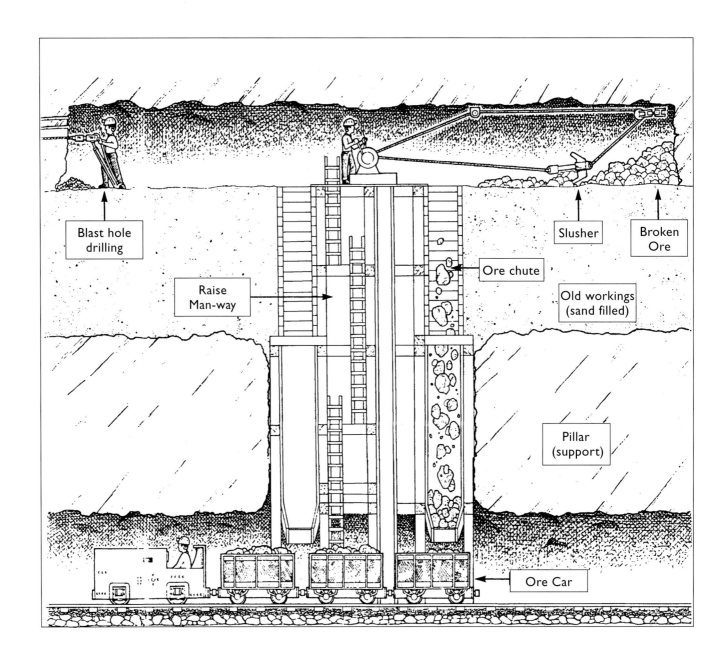

Blast hole drilling

Raise Man-way

Slusher

Broken Ore

Ore chute

Old workings (sand filled)

Pillar (support)

Ore Car

STOPING

The cut-and-fill method essentially involves the extraction of horizontal slices of ore, usually from a steeply dipping vein deposit, followed by filling of the resulting void with waste material, commonly "tailings" sand from milling. The method is generally applied to orebodies which are relatively high in grade but require a greater degree of support of the working place or "stope." It has been in use at the Sunshine Mine for many years and is presently the most common method employed there. It is cyclical in nature, with "stoping" and "sandfill" being its two main components. Ore is produced during the stoping portion of the cycle, while there is no production while the stope is in sandfill.

At the Sunshine Mine, mining proceeds from the bottom of one ore block to the top. Stoping involves drilling and blasting slices or "cuts" of ore which are usually about eight feet high and at least as wide as the vein. Horizontal holes are drilled in the "face" and, after being loaded with explosives and blasted, the broken ore is transferred to a chute using a device similar to a dragline called a "slusher." The ore is then pulled from the bottom of the chute and loaded into rail cars, which are used to convey the ore to the main production shafts. During stoping, geologists regularly inspect and sample the face to insure that ore extraction is optimized. Cuts are usually about 100 feet in length and, once completed, any broken ore remaining is carefully cleaned out before proceeding to the sandfill portion of the cycle.

Sunshine Precious Metals Inc.

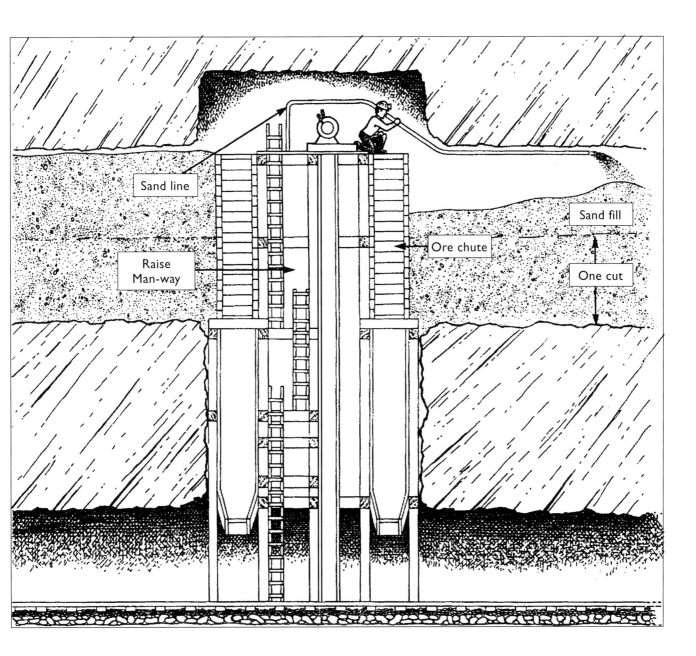

Sand line

Raise Man-way

Sand fill

Ore chute

One cut

SANDFILL

The sandfill portion of the mining cycle begins with "raising up," which creates the room necessary to extend the raise timbering up to the elevation of the next cut, where a new slusher platform is established. Once this is completed, "sand walls" are built using plastic sheeting and similar materials to seal off the raise from the areas to be filled with sand. Sand lines are then extended from the raise into the stope. Finally, a sand slurry mixture is delivered from the surface in a continuous "pour" until one side is completely filled. Each side of the stope is filled separately. Once the sandfill material has been allowed to drain, the mining cycle begins all over again, with the sand in the newly filled areas providing the necessary support for the next cut.

Sunshine Precious Metals Inc.

the darkness of the shaft. The cager yelled out, "Remember the Alamo."

I saw the thick, black, dope-covered hoist cable working itself back and forth in the shaft. It reminded me of a fishing line being fed out of a fishing reel. Everything was really quiet then and I could hear the cable humming as it sped by, and occasionally a "thunk" as it smacked against the timbers somewhere in the shaft.

Jeff and I were left standing alone on the station. There were other crews working on this level too, but I guessed they must have held back so they could take a later "flight." He sat down on a pile of burlap that looked like a big, well used nest and said, "Have a seat, it'll be a while before Larry gets here. You want a cup of coffee?"

I thought, "Oh… that's right," and I proudly held out my brand-new stainless steel coffee jug, the first one I'd ever owned, showing him that I already had coffee. I said, "No thanks."

He looked back down at his own cup.

I couldn't find anything that looked nearly as comfortable as Jeff's nest to sit on, so I drew up a pile of boards and sat down. Then I listened as he began to talk. He told me about the mine, his life, my life, and God I can't remember what all. I looked around the station as he talked. We were in an area about 20 feet wide, 15 feet high, and 40 feet deep. The main drift took off from where we were and disappeared into the darkness toward who knew where. He talked about his kids. I got to noticing that the station's timbers, instead of being wood, consisted of enormously thick metal I-beams. I wanted to ask Jeff about them, but he looked like he was really involved in a part of his conversation that was vital to his very existence. I let him continue.

We sat there for at least another 10 or 15 minutes drinking coffee and talking about stuff, or should I say in my case "listening," when I heard voices coming from the shaft. The rest of the crew was coming down.

I thought, "Thank God… I only hope that Larry is with them, then maybe I can get busy and do something. If I don't, I can see right now that this is going to be one hell of a long day." Jeff slowly screwed the lid back on his little coffee thermos and gently placed it in his smallish, black-metal lunch box.

I really love lunch boxes. I know that probably sounds dumb but I grew up in the desert country of Wyoming in the 1940s and times were hard. All my brother and I had for lunch boxes in those days were the ones with ducks and cowboys painted on them. I was the youngest so I got the "duckie" one.

Suddenly, I was brought back from my deep reverie by the arrival of the skip as it dropped into view. Looking over at Jeff, I saw that he'd gotten to his feet. I did too. We stood there like a couple of dummies, waiting for the boss to get off the skip. Anybody in his right mind would have known that we'd been sitting there drinking coffee… I felt used.

Larry and three other guys got off the skip and it continued on down the shaft. He walked over to us, while the others continued on down the drift into the darkness. Larry looked at me, nodding his head toward Jeff, and said, "He showing ya around is he?"

Now I want you to know, I sort of have a strange way of looking at life. I put real stock in realistic life experiences, like the ones I saw once in a movie about prisoners in an Alabama chain gang. One of the prisoners had to relieve himself. As was the routine, he yelled out loudly to the guards, "Use the bush, boss?" Granted permission to go, he made his way out into the bushes and was busily fulfilling his promise to the guards. A guard grew suspicious because he'd been gone so long and yelled out at him, "You in the bush boy?" Whereupon the prisoner shook the bushes together and replied loudly, "Rattlin' the bush boss."

Well, when Larry asked "He showing ya around is he?", without thinking I automatically replied, "Rattlin' the bush boss." He gave me a look that I still think was a real classic. It had elements of surprise, curiosity, misunderstanding, anger, impatience, and so on in it.

Larry sat down, held out his coffee thermos toward me and said, "Want a cup of coffee?" I declined his generous offer and sat back down on the pile of boards. Then I gave Jeff my best "Why the hell did we get up a second ago?" look.

We sat there for about five more minutes, talking about the 4,800 level mostly, when Larry suddenly said, "Well I gotta get going." With that he screwed the lid back on his coffee jug, got to his feet, and grabbing his aluminum clipboard, headed off down the tracks following the three miners who'd gone on before him. As he walked away, he looked back over his shoulder toward me and yelled, "You work with Jeff here today, he's the motorman and he'll show you what to do."

As soon as Larry had disappeared around the corner, Jeff sat back down and unscrewed the lid from his coffee jug again. I thought, "Now I know this damned place is going to go broke."

After more time passed by, we got up and he finally began showing me around. As we walked down the tracks back into the level, he talked about the fire they'd had there and the miners who'd died in it.

He said, "I was lucky, because I was on the opposite shift on the day the fire broke out. I did get in on the rescue attempt though."

I was comparing the drift and its crosscuts to both the Lucky Friday and Kelley mines as we walked.

"When we finally got in here," he continued, "we found two guys there by that post, and another one over there by that screen," gesturing with his hand. He went on, "The heat was so intense during the fire that they were baked and we had a hell of a time bagging 'em up."

I couldn't help but think, "This guy should have been one of them."

My first day was sort of a "hello how ya doing" kind of a day. I pitched in and helped Jeff load up the timber and stuff that the cagers brought down the shaft. We stacked it and all the other junk in storage areas—lagging, or boards, timber, and so on. Storage areas were strung out up and down the sides of the drift.

Paul was one of the fellas who'd gotten off the skip with Larry. He was the grizzly man, and I talked with him during breaks. It didn't take me long to decide that I liked Paul; he was a real character. He told me he'd worked in the Sunshine about six years ago, but had been gone from the area and just came back about two weeks ago. I asked him where he had been for those six years. He calmly replied, "Prison."

That sort of took me back for a bit; I didn't know how to react at all. Here we were, an ex-con and an ex-cop, hashing over the good old days.

Paul went on, "I was working here and doing good. Then I met these two guys uptown in a bar. We got to talking and hit it off real good too. I saw them 'bout every night from then on and found out that they were going to go over to Montana and rob this little bank. They invited me to go with them and I agreed. We got caught and that's how I wound up in prison."

Paul had been there about two weeks longer than I so he got to work with Jeff on the motor after that, thank God. I was reintroduced to a sledgehammer and the iron bars of the grizzly—seniority, you know. So as it turned out my first job there at the Sunshine was working on a grizzly… again.

Hauling out muck was the same in all of the mines. When a motorman pulled a string of ore cars back into the level beneath a stope, he would stop the first car under one of the stope's two ore chutes (most stopes usually had two chutes—one for each of the two miners working in the stope). The motorman then pulled up the chute's handle, opening its gate and dumping in as much muck as needed to fill the car. Then he'd close the gate and pull the train ahead to the next car, and so on. After all of the cars were full, he'd return to the station to unload at the grizzly.

I liked that part… that's where I came in. When Jeff and Paul made their return trip to the grizzly pocket and dumped their muck cars, there I stood with my trusty sledgehammer waiting for them. The way I figured it, I really had the most important job of all. After all if I wasn't there to break up the rocks too large to fit through the 10-inch-square holes of the grizzly, then the muck couldn't fall down into the 150-feet-deep, or whatever it was, pocket. The motorman wouldn't be able to pull the chutes anymore because there wouldn't be any place to put the muck. With him out of the picture, the stope's chutes would get full to overflowing, or "muck bound," and the miners would have to quit slushing (scraping the muck out from the ends of their stopes into their chutes). If they couldn't get rid of their muck, then they wouldn't be able to blast anymore; they wouldn't have room to work.

So you see, if I wasn't there with my little hammer, then hundreds—nay thousands—of miners and support people would probably be put out of work and have to line up for soup somewhere.

Much of the rock that the muck train dumped onto my grizzly was extremely hard—so hard in fact that when I smacked it with my hammer it was sort of like hitting a chunk of rubber. Sometimes I'd hit the rocks with all the strength I could muster and the hammer just bounced back. In one instance when I hit a flat chunk as hard as I possibly could the hammer bounced back so fast that I wasn't expecting it. The hammer flew out of my sweaty hands, up over the side of the hole that the grizzly sat in, which was about 7 feet deep, and clear across the tracks. I found it laying up against the wall, about 20 feet from where I was working.

Things went smoothly during most of the three months I worked on the grizzly. But one day the train came out of the drift onto the station and dumped "The slab from hell." Or at least that's what I called it at the time. It was nearly 2 feet thick, 4 feet long, and just as hard as it could be. After cleaning off the grizzly, I beat on it for a while. The train came back and dumped another load and headed off down the tracks again into the darkness, its warning bell "clanging" for all it was worth. The bell looked a lot like a cowbell. It was supposed to alert anyone who happened to be close enough to care that the train and its muck cars were moving… so get the hell out of the way.

I went back to pounding on the slab in my spare time. Now I was young, feisty, and figured that there wasn't any dumb old rock that was going to get the best of me. My blows with the hammer got harder and harder. I'm sad to say I killed my hammer and several of its grandchildren that day. With sparks flying, I beat that rock down to about half its original size and rounded off its corners and edges. I decided to roll it over so I'd have a flatter, better place to beat on.

It took awhile because it was still very heavy. When I finally turned it over, I found out that it had a secret. Inside was a stick and a half of dynamite that hadn't gone off with its round, and, yes, there was still a live primer, or blasting cap, in the stick of powder. Using a water hose, I flushed the dynamite out of the hole and very gently pulled out the primer and dropped it into the pocket. The good Lord must have been watching over me because when I reared back and smacked it again, what was left of the slab from hell broke in half. If it had broken one swing before that I'm sure the concussion of the hammer's blow would have set off the primer and then the dynamite.

When I'd worked in the Sunshine for about a month, something happened that scared the socks right off me. It was the first shift of the week and a Monday, when 11 of us were in the skip on our way down Ten Shaft. Ours was the first skip to be lowered down that day.

We'd "swooshed" past the 4,000 feet level when Mr. Air Blast made one of his frequent visits. We'd been talking on the way down, but when the air blast hit everybody froze into deathly silence. I looked up at the ceiling knowing that falling rock always followed air blasts. I only heard a few of them crash on top of the skip and thought, "Maybe we're going to be lucky this time."

About this time the skip suddenly slowed, and then came to an abrupt stop with a shuddering groan. We were wedged in between the shaft's guides, or timbers. I didn't think it possible for a skip full of men to fall to their knees all at the same time because of a sudden stop; it seemed like it would be too crowded, but it wasn't. Without a word we all rose back to our feet, then

someone started laughing. Before long we were all laughing; it must have been a reaction to the stress.

At first only a few rocks fell. They rattled off the sides of our skip and into the thousands-of-feet-deep shaft below us. Then the trickle turned into a torrent. We were really being bombarded… and we laughed even harder.

The doors on the front of the skip were only about five feet high, with an opening above. Everyone dropped their chins and hid their faces under the bills of their hard hats, pushing their hats up against the guy's back in front for protection from the rocks and constant spray of thick dust and gravel flying in over the door. We must have looked like a bunch of turtles.

"Thank God for the tall guy standing in front," someone shouted over the roar of flying debris. That would have been all right but the tall guy was me. Talk about ringing your bell! I must have been hit dozens of times and took little comfort in the sounds the rocks made as they rattled off my hat and onto the hats of all the little turtles behind me. A few were even big enough that they drove my hat right down over my ears.

Some of the rock pounding the outside of the skip must have been much bigger because, as our little fortress was hit, the skip sagged and groaned like it was alive. The pounding suddenly died down and stopped. It became ominously quiet. We wondered what was going to happen next. Our answer was… nothing. Nothing happened, not for a good hour at least. Surely the bosses hadn't forgotten that we were hanging in the shaft, suspended between daylight above and God only knew what below. We could only guess what was happening above us.

We finally heard a voice shouting down from somewhere up above, "Don't worry, we're working on getting you out. The hoistman is going to lower another skip down the other side for you."

Then came two words that we thought were absolutely hilarious. He said "Hang tight"—as if we had any choice. We laughed for a good five minutes. Whoever called down to us probably thought we were hysterical.

Ten Shaft had three compartments in which skips were raised and lowered. We were in an outside compartment, but our rescuers planned to lower another skip down to us in the compartment on the other side of the shaft, and not the middle compartment. I guess they figured that whatever hung us up could easily "catch" another skip too if it came close to us.

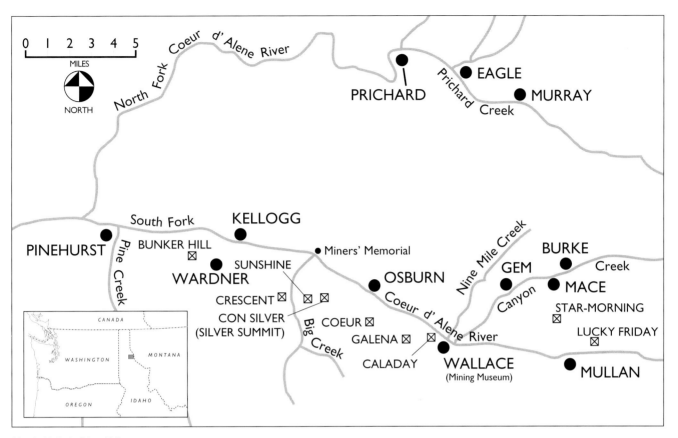

North Idaho's Silver Valley.
Dave Hoyt

Needless to say, we did "hang tight." Sure enough, about 45 minutes later we heard the welcome rumble of a skip making its way down the shaft. Listening intently, we heard voices coming from it too when it came closer to us. Then came what sounded like planks falling on timbers. Suddenly, someone was pounding on the top of our skip. Skips have escape hatches on top for just such emergencies. Our escape hatch hadn't been opened in some time, though, and the rock that had fallen down the shaft on top of it didn't help much either. It took a while for the fella on top of our skip to break through, but he finally pried the hatch open. We all cheered and shoved a little guy up through the hole to see if everything was all right. After not hearing any screaming or anything we decided to give it a try too.

Wouldn't you know it? I had to be next. After I'd climbed up onto the roof of the skip, I found out what had sounded like planks dropping on timber. Our rescuers had laid a double thickness of lagging over the empty shaft compartment between the two skips. A rescuer knelt on top of the other skip leaning out to me with hands outstretched, saying "Don't look down."

Naturally I looked down... and down, and down, into empty space. Beneath the pair of 3-inch-thick and 8- or 10-inch-wide planks, one laying atop the other, there was blackness, only interrupted by dim lights on the level stations. At 200 feet apart, the level station lights grew ever dimmer deeper down into the shaft. I was staring into a 2,000-feet-deep barrel of death.

The empty shaft was wide and the planks only had a few inches of "footing" on the timbers at each end. I figured this was the only way I was going to get back to the surface, so I took a deep breath and began crawling on my hands and knees across the sagging planks toward the outstretched hands of my rescuer. I made it!

Actually, the rescue operation went well. We all made the "crawl" without any problems and were soon on our way back up the shaft. We got the rest of the day off, with pay too. The shaft repair crews worked, though. They went back down and spent the rest of the day replacing timbers and guides that were blown out of place or broken up by the air blast.

Things were going fine for me at the Sunshine. I was getting along pretty good with everything and everybody. Then I got to thinking, "This is sort of like when I was with the police department down in Oregon. I just hope it doesn't turn out the same way."

Then one day, seemingly right-out-of-the-blue, Larry told me to go to the doctor's office and have another chest X-ray taken, which I did. I'd completely forgotten about the stupid lung X-ray in all the excitement of hiring out at the 'Shine. A few days later I was called into the office to see the foreman. A fella was usually never called into the boss's office unless he was really in trouble for something.

He said, "When you took your pre-employment physical, a spot showed up on your lung X-ray. You were told then that if the spot was still there in a month, you would have to be terminated before your probationary period ran out." Then the foreman said something sorta like I'd heard before, "I'm sorry but we're going to have to let you go. The chest X-ray that you took a few days ago still showed the spot on your lung."

Of course I was worried, and I called the doctor up. I asked, "What does that spot mean Doc? Do I have cancer or something?"

I was a heavy smoker and fully expected his answer to be, "Yes," but he just laughed and said, "No, it's true there is a spot on your lung but we've decided that it's just scar tissue from a scratch that was caused by a broken rib. I'll send a letter of explanation to the Sunshine so you won't lose your job." I'd already told him, when the new X-ray was taken, that I was about to be fired.

For the rest of that day, I thought about what he'd said but I couldn't remember ever breaking a rib… unless it was that time when I was working on a pulp mill's fuel pile in Oregon. It was one of the jobs I took just after getting out of the Air Force. I can truthfully say, "That was about the worst job I've ever had." I had to use a short-handled pitchfork to work wood chips and sawdust loose so they'd fall onto a conveyer belt that took them into a boiler. When the boiler operator decided that he needed more sawdust and wood chips to fuel the boilers he signaled with a whistle. Then I had to take that damn pitchfork outside and bust loose the wood chips.

The thing I hated most was the fact that the overhead conveyer belt dribbled wood shavings and slivers down my neck all of the time. I didn't mind that I had to work all night, or even that I often was out in the rain, fog, or cold. The thing I hated was those "itchy" slivers of wood. I just couldn't see how sawdust and

wood chips could pack together so tight either, just from gently falling through the air and landing in a pile. In fact, the chips were packed so tightly together that when I'd go to drive the pitchfork deep into the pile to break them loose, the pitchfork would only bounce back.

I wondered what the guy I replaced meant when he said to me, "You have to stay mad on this job to do it well." It was the only thing he said as he left. He was right. To do the job well or any other way, I practically had to work myself into a frenzy so I had enough strength from anger to consistently dig the pitchfork into the fuel pile.

One day I was especially hyped up and plunged the pitchfork really hard into the chips. I immediately felt a stabbing pain in my leg and the side of my chest. I quickly looked down, seeing that I'd ripped my pant leg with the pitchfork. I thought, "Man that was close, I almost punctured my leg good with this damned thing."

That didn't explain the searing pain in my chest, however. Every time I took a breath, I felt like throwing up. It just so happened that my shift was ending, so I went straight home and to bed. Looking back on the incident, the only thing that I can figure is that the pitchfork's handle must have cracked a rib.

At the Sunshine Mine, I talked with Larry and told him what the doctor had said to me about the scratched lung and all. Larry replied, "I'll talk to the foreman today, call back tomorrow."

All told, I lost three days' work because the mine didn't want me on the payroll without written proof from the doctor of what he had told me. I couldn't blame them, because once a guy had gone through his probationary period and become a bona fide employee, the mine was responsible for medical costs in a big way. Finally, the Sunshine agreed to put me back to work after someone in the hierarchy of the mine, probably the foreman, called the doctor for confirmation.

Larry did say though, "We're putting you back on again but if we still don't have the paperwork back from the doctor within 30 days so we have this in writing, we'll have to let you go again."

I thought, "Hell, I'm in, surely it won't take another month for the doctor's report to reach the mine."

How wrong I was. Twenty-nine days later, right out of the blue, Larry said, "Guess what?" For some reason I just knew what he was going to say next. Larry was about to let me have it again. It seemed like his lips were in slow motion as he talked. Then I heard the familiar phrase, "I'm sorry we are going to have to let you go."

Again I had no job, or for that matter no future in mining. If I couldn't work in the Sunshine because of some spot on one of my air bags, then who'd hire me? Surely other mines would check with the Sunshine people, who then would pass along my medical information. I just couldn't understand how I'd been able to hire out at the Lucky Friday; maybe the doctor there missed seeing the spot. Usually there was much cooperation between the mines as far as passing along information about tramp miners like myself.

I have heard that years ago—in the 1930s or thereabouts—some mines used "broken wing" letters to secretly inform each other about tramps. When a miner quit a job, the bosses would write a glowing referral for him, including their feelings of remorse at the loss of his services with something like, "Whoever is able to hire this fine miner, should do so by all means."

The tramp invariably would show up at a new mine clutching his referral letter tightly in his greasy little hand. The hiring guy at the new mine would make some kind of excuse to leave the room with the referral, and step into a back room out of the miner's sight. He'd hold the letter up to the light and look at the eagle bonding seal in the paper. If the eagle was intact then the letter was telling the truth about the miner. If, on the other hand, the eagle had a broken wing, then everything in the letter was false. From what I understand, companies used the broken wing letter because one of their hiring guys was murdered by an angry miner who was given a bad written recommendation.

Shortly, I again missed a couple of days of work, though for a different reason: the miner's United Steel Workers Union went out on strike. Two days after the strike started, the mine sent me a letter saying, "We have received your doctor's report and decided that the time you missed because of this misunderstanding shouldn't be counted against you. We are reinstating you as having completed your probation. You are a full-time employee as of your original date of hire."

The Sunshine's decision to reinstate me was somewhat untimely, though. It dashed any hopes I had of drawing state unemployment compensation during the strike. Unemployment checks were considerably higher than picket line pay from the union. I had to consider my beautiful wife and little baby son, who was steadily getting bigger along with the bills. I knew we couldn't survive on picket line pay.

I came to the decision, "Ah, the hell with it." ❀

CHAPTER 4

Motorman Gets Even

Bunker Hill Mine
Kellogg, Idaho

I had friends who were working for the Bunker Hill Mine and they encouraged me to go to the hiring office in downtown Kellogg and try to get on, because the mine was looking for guys. It probably sounds stupid but the next morning I had to start searching for the Bunker Hill hiring office.

"Hell," I thought, "I've been living in and around Kellogg for a couple of years now, here it is March of 1973, and I still don't have the slightest idea where Bunker's employment office is."

I told the fella living downstairs in my apartment building what I was looking for. He looked amazed, I assume because he probably figured everybody on the planet earth knew where it was.

He laughingly said, "Oh, you won't have any trouble finding it, just look for the long line."

I drove down Kellogg's main street—there was only one—looking for the long line that my neighbor told me about. I passed old buildings looking like they'd been there since the Renaissance, whenever that was. Sure enough, there it was, in between two bars and across the street from two more.

I sort of laughed and thought, "No damn wonder I haven't noticed it, it's in the YMCA building. I've been in all these bars that surround the YMCA dozens of times but haven't figured I needed any more exercise than I was getting in the mines. Besides, I must have been too busy drinking to notice it anyhow."

I parked the old jalopy and, taking my place at the end of the line, began a long wait. As I slowly moved

Bunker Hill incline shaft lift, 1957.
The Spokesman-Review

forward I remembered the lines in basic training at Lackland Air Force Base in San Antonio, Texas. There, before moving forward, we had to come to attention, take one step forward, then return to a parade rest stance—sort of stepping off to the left side and standing with legs spread a little and arms folded behind the back. Out of boredom, I tried moving forward in line the Air Force way, but then I noticed that the other guys in line started looking at me like I either had a screw loose or some highly communicable disease, so I went back to half staggering like they were.

"Oh… there goes the line again," I thought over and over again. About an hour went by and what seemed like dozens of "jump starts" before I finally made it to the top of the steps. It was kind of exhilarating, because I didn't really think I was going to make it that far, not in a single week anyhow. It was a very long line. My eyes had been yearning to see through the open doorway at the top of the concrete staircase. I tried to imagine what secrets lay within. I had visions of a busy headquarters with people scurrying to and fro carrying memos from some corporate big shot.

Finally my turn came. Leaving the brilliant sunlight I'd been standing in for a long time, I stepped inside into darkness. My eyes adjusted after a few minutes, and looking around I was sort of disappointed. The room was narrow, short, and filled with dense cigarette smoke and wall-to-wall employment hopefuls. After filling out the job application, and another hour's wait, it was finally my turn to see Albi Sinks, the hiring man. I showed him my application and told him of my schooling and experience in three mines, limited as it was.

He told me about Bunker's 30-day probationary period for new employees and asked if I understood. I pulled the Sunshine's letter of acceptance from my back pocket and told him about my experiences with probation periods.

He said finally, "Well, I guess you do understand about them then."

The next few days rushed by quickly. They were filled with doctor's offices, more X-ray machines, pretty little nurses, and finally this really ugly short fella who was sitting behind a desk that sported a sign declaring, "Mine Foreman."

Next I took the 50-cent tour of Bunker's engineering office building, or at least that is what I think they called it. As I walked through the offices, they showed me many wondrous technical things, like three dimensional landscapes and lots of charts and graphs.

I began to wonder, "Why are they showing me this place? Oh… I know, I'll bet they want me to sweep it out or something."

I was told by my "tour guide," the little short guy's helper I'll bet, to show up for work the next day with my diggers.

I was there bright and early the next morning, just like I was told. I parked my car down in the company parking lot, which was about 20 miles, so it seemed, from the dry building. I locked my car up after grabbing my heavy green "lumpy" bag. After adjusting it on my shoulder and sort of half staggering under its weight, I started off down the sidewalk.

As I walked along I thought, "Man this thing's heavy." I tried to remember all of the junk that I'd had so much trouble packing into it. "Let's see now, there are my rotten but clean old diggers, mine hat, safety belt, hard-toed boots…"

I always hated the first day of a new hire-out. I'd heard that the Bunker Hill Mine was really huge. As I struggled with my heavy load across the street and passed by a large electrical transformer station, I thought, "There must be a whole heard of guys working up here if the mine's that big."

Looking up ahead, I saw that the narrow road I was following suddenly began a steep upward climb. I was tired and stopped for a moment to catch my breath. I'd been laboring under my heavy load for at least three or four blocks—it seemed more like a mile. Then a wave of exhaustion induced anger swept over me and I unceremoniously dropped the lumpy thing that was hurting my hand. I stood there gasping for air.

A couple of fellas walked past and one of them looked down at the large lump that was laying on the ground beside me. He sort of chuckled, and as the pair walked on up the hill he mumbled something to his partner. They broke into laughter. I felt used… damn I hated the first hire-out day.

I heard more voices behind me and thought, "I sure don't want to go through that again." I quickly hefted the heavy green bag over my shoulder and continued on.

Following the two fellas who'd gone on ahead, I started on up the steep hill. I soon came to the bottom of an enormous staircase up a steep embankment. As I stood there looking up in awe at the long climb ahead, I dropped the bag again and thought, "Damn, there's more?" I barely noticed as two more fellas passed by. Then I looked back down the hill and saw a whole group of guys on their way toward me.

I gained courage again and began the long climb, dragging the bag behind me up each of the staircase's 72 steps. I was puffing hard by the time I topped the last step, and thought, "Crap, I'm already wore out and haven't even made it into the dry to change clothes yet."

I stood there catching my breath, and tried to get my bearings while gazing out across the mine's train yard. There were lots of rails, muck cars, and a couple of long man-trains that were much longer than the Sunshine's. I saw a few motors, overhead electrical wires, and lots of equipment, all surrounded by buildings.

"This," I thought, "must surely be the biggest mine in the world. I know it's the hardest one to get to that's for sure."

It was the heart of Bunker Hill. Peering around the corner of a large two-story brick building, I saw what seemed like thousands of men milling around in front. I'd been sort of standing off to one side letting guys pass as I rested. Then I thought, "Well, I guess I can't put this off any longer," so I picked up my heavy sack and joined in with the other men walking toward the building's front door. I knew the bag would be a dead giveaway to the rest of the crew that I was a greenhorn. I came up with what I thought was a brilliant idea. I would try to blend in with the group of fellas I was with, "Then maybe no one will notice I'm carrying a damned sack."

I very skillfully, I thought, worked my way into the middle and sort of behind "my" small group of miners. I was satisfied with my plan and even began to think, or

Miners going off shift at the Bunker Hill Mine.
Kellogg Public Library

hope, "Maybe they won't even notice me at all." Hell, it was just as I feared. As I marched along peering suspiciously out of the crowd, I was met with a sea of eyeballs. Talk about a guy feeling dumb. There it was: the curious, blank-faced stare that I'd seen in all three of the other mines. It was like I had an audience and was a movie star. By the time I walked in through the door of the dry I was almost embarrassed.

Just like outside, the inside of the building was full of pushing, noisy, busy men preparing themselves for the work day. They all seemed to be wearing the same face as the miners I'd seen in the other mines—one of anonymity. The diggers all looked the same—torn, weathered, and "scungie"—and their faces looked nearly the same too. Well… some were uglier than others, I guess. Every once in a while I caught a glimpse of a fast-moving new hat or a shiny new pair of boots and thought, "I wonder if he's new too."

After changing into my crummy looking, half-rotten blue jeans and grease-stained T-shirt, I felt better. Now at least I looked "really" bad like everybody else. (My

blue jeans had been new only a couple of weeks before when I was working in the Sunshine Mine. The jeans' blue dye bled onto my legs because of the hot dampness underground, and I wound up with blue legs. Don't think that didn't make me feel stupid on my way to the shower. One of the guys remarked, "New britches, huh?" I looked around and saw two more pairs of blue legs go by too, so I didn't feel nearly as bad.)

I still had about 10 minutes before the train pulled out, so I started reading a notice posted on a bulletin board near the door. It was a bid sheet for one of the stopes. The mines all honored a seniority system of contract bidding—that is, the longest-employed man according to his hire date got first choice at new jobs. The thing that caught my eye about this bid sheet though was its wording: "Surviving partner has his choice of bidders." I thought, "Now what does that mean… did his partner die?" I looked around for someone to ask about this, but I saw my train pulling in. For the time being, my question went unanswered.

I grabbed my lunch box and walked through the door heading for the train. Then I saw Rick, the little fella who'd showed me around the day before, standing by the incoming train. He waved vigorously at me, shouting "Hurry up pard." Everyone is known as "pard" in the mines.

I rushed up to his side wondering what all the excitement was about. A good thing too; as soon as the train came to a complete stop (company policy forbade boarding a moving train), a crush of humanity pushed both of us up against the side of a man-car. I was really surprised, and wondered what kept us from just rolling right on over the train and all, because they were pressing so hard from behind. Rick and I were pushed all the way through the car and nearly out the opposite door. I struggled to hang onto my seat, and in what seemed like a few seconds the train was full.

It took me a second to recover. Still in sort of half shock, I blurted out to Rick, my new partner, "What the hell was that all about?" He just looked over at me with a big toothy grin and said, "Fun wasn't it?"

I noticed excitement in the faces of all three of my fellow travelers and thought about how stupid his answer sounded. After a few minutes of thinking about it and just as the train was pulling out I said, "Yeah... yeah, now that I think about it that was sort of neat." The fire of the moment had drained from their faces again leaving them with blank stares.

Now my 6-feet 2-inch, 240-pound frame had a purpose in life beside beating on boulders with a 10-pound sledgehammer. I decided I was going to enjoy the loading-up ritual that seemed to "get the day going" for Bunker Hill miners.

As we moved on, the rails narrowed from the eight or so pairs of tracks in the loading zone to a single set of tracks, and the buildings closed in on us. Our motor was an electric trolley type. It had a bar that pushed a pulley up against a bare, overhead power line on its end, much like the cable cars I'd seen pictures of in San Francisco.

Ignoring the sign stenciled just inside the door which read, "Keep hands and feet inside car," I pushed my face out through the doorway. I chuckled and thought, "It didn't say anything about a face," and looked ahead toward the front of the train. Then I felt the rush of cool early morning air against my face and saw the portal coming up fast. As the train rolled along heading toward the blackness of the Kellogg Tunnel, I thought, "I'm going to like working here... this is fun."

Suddenly we were immersed in the familiar darkness of an underground mine. The squeaking of the train's wheels clicking along the tracks and the groaning of the straining cars echoed off the walls. As the bar from the motor rubbed against the trolley line, it gave off static buzzing sounds, showers of sparks, and eerie strobe-like flashes of light. A damp, musty smell surged through the air... Hell, I was home.

I thought, "This is really neat, I can use all the stuff I've learned in the other mines in this one, because all these mines are pretty much alike from what they tell me."

When I worked in Butte's Kelley Mine I knew that it was located in a huge mining area, but the Kelley itself didn't seem that big to me at the time. Of course, I wasn't there for very long either. When I got to the Lucky Friday Mine, I was pretty well convinced that it was bigger yet. Then when I hired out at the Sunshine, I was amazed because of the hugeness of the place. It looked big enough to put the whole Lucky Friday Mine in the back end of one of its levels. But the Bunker Hill was just flabbergasting because of its size. It stretched from Big Creek, about three or so miles east of the main drift I was in, all the way to Page which was just short of Pinehurst, about five miles to the west.

Bunker Hill was a really old mine and had been worked for a century or so. Reportedly, some 10,000 miles of workings had been driven into and below the mountain here. Most of these old workings had since been filled in with sand and waste rock, to keep the ground from "taking weight." This, of course, is standard mining technique.

The method of mining in all the mines I'd been in was "cut and fill." When the ore containing silver, lead, zinc, gold, or whatever, was mined out, the process left a hole. The hole had to be filled in again, either with waste rock (the old method), or with sand-fill (the newer method) left over from the milling of the ore. Think of the U.S. Forest Service signs alongside roads in the mountains bluntly demanding, "Pack it in, pack it out." Much the same theory, only in reverse, is used underground. Make a hole... then fill it back in (or Mr. Air Blast might fill it in for you, with you in it).

I was thinking about all these things and looking out at the different crosscuts as we passed, clickity-clack in our little buzzing, sparking, flashing train. It couldn't really be called a "choo, choo" I guess. After it seemed like we had gone miles, we finally slowed down, coming to a stop near the shaft station.

Bunker Hill's Kellogg Tunnel.
Kellogg Public Library

We got off the train a lot slower than when we loaded up, that's for sure. Then we walked over toward the shaft. As I looked around the station, I suddenly remembered the thought I'd had only a few minutes before, "All these mines are pretty much the same." But now I thought anxiously, "The same hell, this place doesn't even have a shaft, or at least I can't see one."

That was my first look at an incline shaft. It looked like what its name implies… a steep incline. The station was much like other shaft stations I'd seen, but instead of the "elevator look," with the wall and a door that opens, this sucker looked more like a roller coaster, at about its steepest pitch too. As I stood there in bewilderment, staring and thinking "this is going to be fun," the hoistman lowered the skip into place. The skip looked like a long, flat railroad car on a hell of an angle. Well actually there were three skips running on rails connected together.

I saw the skip's cable which took off up the shaft toward the hoist's cable drum. The hoistman lowered the skip down so the upper deck was even with the floor of the station. Then Rick said, "Come on." He pushed his

way through the crowd of seemingly bored miners toward the shaft, with me right behind him, then stepped out onto the skip's deck. Actually it was just a flat surface with what looked like crossways planks bolted onto it about 2 1/2 feet apart. The planks served as steps when the deck was being loaded up and seats when its passengers sat down.

I followed my partner as he climbed up toward the top of the skip. Then he turned and sat down facing the station and all the miners who were waiting their turn to load up. I quickly followed trying to do just as he had done and sat down beside him. Ah, but my style wasn't quite what his was. When I got to the top of the deck, I was about to turn and sit down when I smacked a steel I-beam with my hat. The beam was used for loading material onto the skip. Well naturally the hat took off over the side of the skip and on down the shaft somewhere. There I was, suddenly with no hat and the object of a sudden roar of laughter from a really attentive audience of miners down below.

Someone yelled, "Go to the hoist-room, old Barney's got another hat you can use." I looked at Rick with real distress and started climbing back down the deck again to get off the skip. Then he yelled out from behind, "I'll go on down to 23 level... when you get squared away come on down, I'll be waiting for you there."

As I stepped out onto the station floor again the crowd of smiling, gleeful miners parted like a wave and let me through. I could hear a chuckle of amusement here and there as I passed by. Someone told me where the hoist-room was and I headed off down the drift in that direction feeling like a real dunce.

That's when I got my first real look at the hoist-room, but I could hardly figure out what anything in it was. I thought, "Well let's see now, those huge drums are full of black hoist cable, and there is a great big one of those, and look at the size of that damn thing..." Then perched on a chair high above it all I saw Barney, grinning from ear to ear.

He said, "Lost your hat, huh?"

I was really shocked that he knew why I was there. It didn't occur to me that a new guy standing there with a stupid look on his face and no hat would be a dead giveaway. I was sort of irritated at being the center of amusement for the whole crew and I told him so.

I said, "Those guys got their laughs in for today at least."

Barney saw that I was mad and said, "They weren't laughing at you. The reason they were laughing was, everyone of 'em has probably lost his hat down the shaft the same way at one time or other. Actually they were just laughing at themselves."

Man, what a relief, and here I was starting to think that I was the biggest idiot that Bunker Hill had ever hired. Of course that very well might have been true, but anyway... I felt like I had been initiated into the crew.

Barney pointed out a pile of hard hats laying in one corner and said, "Go ahead and take one of those and when you get a new one, bring it back."

I gladly accepted his offer and picked up a really terrible looking one that looked as bad as the rest of my diggers, so I'd look like a real miner. Now I was all set. It only took me a few minutes to walk back to the shaft where some of the crew were still loading up on the skip. I heard the cager yell "Twenty three," and I rushed forward to get on.

I climbed up the deck again, as before, and sat down, only this time I watched out for the damned I-beam I'd hit. Safely seated by this really crummy looking fella... look who's talking... I waited for the rest of the crew to

get on. The idea was for the top of the deck to load up first—those were the guys who worked on the lower levels of the mine. The decks filled up from the top down. The object was, when the skip got down to the first level the bottom guys would get off first. It was the same as in the conventional "vertical" shafts; lower levels loaded up first... upper levels got off first.   Remember when I said the planks were seats? Well the backs of the seats were the guys' knees behind the sitter.

We finally were all loaded up and the cager pulled briskly twice on the bell cord, signaling the hoistman to lower away. Now that was an experience I'll never forget. The hoistman began to lower us slowly at first, then we started picking up speed.

My thought was, "Good Lord, what have I gotten myself into?" The caps (thick overhead shaft timbers that ran width-wise about 2 feet above our "leaning back" heads) whizzed by as fast as a picket fence does when viewed from the window of a speeding automobile. Once I was able to get over the roller-coaster, sinking feeling and saw that we were probably not going to die, I settled in for the duration. Then I thought, "This is really great. If we weren't in the mine, but in a circus or somewhere, this ride would probably cost some real bucks, and here I'm getting paid for it too."

The hoistman slowed the skip down as the cager's bell signaled him to do. When we reached 13 level, a few guys got off and we continued on down. We finally arrived at the 23 level and the bottom of the incline shaft. When the skips dropped down onto the station itself they rolled out flat, right up to what looked like a loading dock for trucks at a supermarket, and sat there in horizontal position.

Rick, true to his word, was waiting for me at the station. We set off on a tour of one hell of a big level. We must have walked for miles in both directions from the shaft. First one way, then another. I was completely lost, I'm embarrassed to say, as soon as we went through the station's air doors.

Silver Valley mines, and probably mines everywhere else, have installed a double set of doors near the shaft stations to control the exhaust and intake airflow from enormous ventilation fans. Most mines had someone who acted as an airflow engineer (I guess you'd call him that) who kept an eye on the ventilation system as a main part of his job. Every once in a while someone would leave an air door open, either accidentally or on purpose, and the mine's airflow would change. Doors might be left open intentionally by an uncaring soul so the air would be better where he was working, but it would, of course, lessen the airflow that someone was getting elsewhere. As the mines were enlarged and deepened, the air flow guy took a little checking instrument around from time to time, making calculations for recommended improvements (in the old days, an up-held wetted finger was the instrument of choice, I think). The temperature of rock underground is at least a zillion degrees; thus, in no time at all, so is the skin temperature under a miner's collar. I'm referring, of course, to the term, "hot under the collar."

Twenty-three level extended from Big Creek, three miles to the east, all the way west to Page. Out there somewhere, the Crescent and Lower Bunker Hill mines were connected by a drift named the YU Drift, but God only knows why. I suppose someone figured that if anyone made it out that far on foot, he must be worthy of a lot of respect, but he must not be too intelligent so they misspelled it "YU" on the sign instead of "You."

Some of the raises we passed as I walked along in my water-filled, feet-hurting rubber boots looked like they had been abandoned during the Civil War or thereabouts. I was trailing Rick with a vengeance, fearful that if we were accidentally separated I might wind up spending the rest of my natural life wandering around in this maze of old workings. I fully expected at any time to see a skeleton laying by a rotted post.

About lunchtime, we finally made it back to the station and I felt like I'd just climbed Mt. Everest and returned to civilization a hero, of sorts. I dumped the sweaty water out of my boots several times and settled in for a lengthy lunch. As I sat there, or should I say, "laid there," I suddenly caught the movement of something out of the corner of my eye.

Startled, I sat up on my elbows exclaiming to Rick, "What was that over there in the corner?"

He responded, "Cockroaches."

Then I thought, "Great… what's next?"

Rick went on, "Guys chew sunflower seeds down here by the case and these damned roaches live off their leavings and lunch garbage. Up in Wardner [a section of the Bunker Hill Mine above Kellogg], they've got rats … big ones."

He got up, dug into a bag of Miracle Lime with an old coffee can and sprinkled the powder out in a cloud up against the wall. Then I got up and sat on a bench for the rest of the lunch break. I sure didn't want any of those huge, Miracle Lime-covered "crawleys" climbing up my pant legs.

We sat there in silence, listening to the slight rustling sounds of roaches for the rest of the lunch break. Finally, I couldn't stand it anymore; I got up certain that whatever I would be doing next was sure to be better than what I had been doing, or listening to, for the past half hour or so. Rick got up too and after we rearmed ourselves with our web belts and self rescuers, pipe wrenches, battery packs, hard hats, rain coats, and lunch gear, we set out for the shaft. We walked out through the double doors onto the station again and belled for the skip. It took about a half hour for the hoistman to get it down to us, but only a few minutes for him to spirit us up to 13 level. That's where Rick said we'd be working the next day.

He was 13 level's motorman and I was going to be his helper. Our level was very old, one of the first to be mined as the shaft was being sunk. I could imagine its age too if everything below it—15, 17, 19, 21 and then the mammoth 23 level—was mined later.

After we got off the skip on 13 and as I was looking around I noticed a pitchfork leaning up against a wall. Confused as to what it could possibly be used for I jokingly asked Rick, "What is that thing doing down here? I don't see any bales of hay anywhere."

He said, "Oh really? Stick it into that timber [a 10-feet-long, 12 x 12 inch cap] and see what happens."

I thought, "Ah, that's stupid, if I do that it'll… well all right, I'll try it."

I picked up the pitchfork and tested the timber as he asked. To my surprise it went all the way through the sturdy-looking timber. That chunk of wood had been there so long that it was just like mush.

Then Rick said, "There are only three stopes left on this level that haven't been mined out already, and they are all a long ways apart." He waved toward the back of the level and continued, "I mean hundreds of feet apart, and back there thousands of feet from the shaft too. In fact it's so far that the batteries on the motor won't stand over about three trips before they go dead." (Electric powered motors in all mines have large "banks" of batteries under their "hoods" that have to be plugged in and recharged after so many hours of use. That is, of course, except for electric trolley motors such as the one I rode into the mine on.)

We sort of hung close to the station for the rest of the shift, talking about everything from the ladies he was seeing to what he felt the miners were doing to make his life harder. After not being able to make a space for myself in the conversation, I settled back and

A SILVER VALLEY HISTORICAL VIGNETTE—

Above left—Coeur d'Alene head-frame machinery at Number One Shaft in the 1930s.
Kellogg Public Library

Far left—Bunker Hill/Sullivan changing house in 1916. This view of the downstairs interior shows clothes hangers, steam coils for drying, a Stokes splint stretcher, a 50-gallon chemical fire extinguisher, and a corner of a lunch table. Drys look much the same today except for more modern equipment and they often are larger.
Kellogg Public Library

Above right—Two miners in the upper right assess the excavation for the Coeur d'Alene Number One hoist room. Note slusher and scraper bucket in the foreground.
Kellogg Public Library

At left—A view of the remains of the Frisco Mill in Burke Canyon following labor trouble in 1892. This state of the art mill had been the pride of the district. It fell victim, though, to a long brooding misunderstanding between labor and management. The labor "war" trouble became intense, and a handful of irate, gleeful miners armed with high explosives made short work of the mill.
Kellogg Public Library

listened. After a while I started to form an attitude about my new partner. The words that seemed to keep popping up in my mind that would best describe him were, "jerk" and "jackass." I hated to make judgments about anyone, especially a fella I'd only known for a day, but there it was, I couldn't resist the impulse.

I think the thing that stuck in my craw the worst about good old Rick was his statement, "These damn miners take their grizzlies off the top of their chutes and muck the boulders down 'em." (Bunker's chute grizzlies were just like those in the other mines in that they were used to keep the largest chunks in the muck down to 10 inches in breadth. That way the mill on the surface could process the ore).

Rick went on, "Then they expect me to break up their big damned slabs with a double jack out here at the shaft. I figured out a way to punish those bastards though. Their contract [miner's incentive pay—the more rock you break, the more you make] is set up here so that they're paid by the ore car full. When one of 'em slabs me good, hell I just cut him a couple of cars... it sure gets their attention."

I thought about it for a bit, while he went on about his wonderful love life. I decided that sooner or later he was probably going to get his butt kicked by one or all of the miners he was getting even with. It was sort of a rough call about how to deal with errant miners, if indeed they were sending boulders down their chutes on purpose. I had to give Rick credit for that, but I figured he should at least let the boss handle it. The reason that miners would do something like that, of course, was to save time because "time is money."

Finally, I heard the hoistman's skip come rumblin' back down the shaft to pick up the crews at the end of the work day. The bottom of the skip dropped down into sight and the cager scrambled off onto the floor of the station. He belled the hoistman to lower the skip slowly on down a bit further, so the top deck was even with the floor. Then six miners, who worked in 13's three stopes, and Rick and I got on. Before long we had gone down to 23 level, were fully loaded, and then we were on our way up the shaft... but, this time, going backwards.

I couldn't help thinking, "How great can this riding up and down the shaft business get? I wouldn't mind just doing this all day long."

A few minutes later we slowed down and topped the shaft on the 9 level station. That was really awesome, watching the "floor of freedom" drop down beneath us and our subsequent return to it as the decks beneath us discharged miners. Those fellas who'd laughed so heartily at my blunder in the morning looked much different now. Physically drained by the day's work, they now were a bunch of greasy, scumbag-looking guys, the sight of which only a mother could love, I'm sure... or perhaps a dog.

After "dismounting" at the shaft, and a short walk, we boarded the "buzz, flash train." The motor moved toward daylight slowly at first, and gradually picked up speed. Before long we were careening down the drift, rocking back and forth due to the irregularity of the rails. The train's wheels shrieked loudly from time to time as we moved toward "Bud-light and fresh air." Oops, sorry, of course I meant to say, "Daylight, and fresh air."

My morning's assessment of the length of 9 level's drift wasn't wrong. That was one hell of a long trip, especially if you were really looking forward to getting to the end. Finally I could feel and smell the freshness of unpumped air.

Our train burst forth into the daylight... "Uh, what happened to all of the sunshine?" All during the shift, I'd been looking forward to seeing daylight. It wasn't nighttime yet, but it was winter. For some reason, even though I'd worked in other mines, this was the first time I'd noticed the relative darkness on the surface as I emerged from the mine. It wouldn't be the last time I was aware of this; during the winter months the only time I saw sunlight was when I either dumped shift, so I'd be on the surface during the day, or on those weekends when it didn't snow. A few minutes later we arrived in front of the dry. After showering, my first day at Bunker Hill ended.

When I reported to work the next day someone handed my wayward hat to me. The shaft repair crew working on the graveyard shift had been told to look for it and they found it. As far as going on shift and down into the mine, the second day was much like the first. Only this time, as Rick had promised, we began our day on 13 level. Six miners, Rick, and myself got off the skip on 13. The miners climbed aboard a small motor (mancha motor) and its timber truck (a small car used to haul timber and materials), and headed off down the drift into the darkness. Rick and I planted ourselves down in our "good morning, have a cup of coffee" positions, and took a "fiver," or break.

A good long while later we heard the rumble of the skip as it again made its way down the shaft. We waited for Dale Adams, the shifter. Rick and I sat talking. A few minutes later, I glanced back out toward the shaft and saw someone's cap lamp jostling through the darkness toward us.

"It's Dale," Rick said.

Underground, everyone had their own "signatured" way of walking, or should I say, their lights moved in different ways as they walked. I guess it's a lot like being able to tell who's behind you because of the sound of their footsteps. After working around each other for a long time, it seemed everybody sort of knew one another by the way their cap lamps bounced.

Dale was oldish and set in his ways, but sort of a likable kind of fella. One thing about him I didn't care for, though, was his damned cap lamp. He had a habit of bobbing it up and down in the eyes of whomever he happened to be talking to, which in this case was me. I hated that.

There was a standing joke to holler at someone, "Here… catch," then hit him square in the eyes with the beam from your cap lamp. Blinded by the sudden light, it was hard not to be nervous about what was next about to impact your body. Well, I sort of figured that good old Dale must have done that—this flashing the light in the face business—out of a concern that his charges were probably losing their sun tans.

Reaching our lunch table, Dale proceeded to give me a bit of a pep talk, promising that if I did good on the motor, someday I might become his number one motorman. I was busily comparing the position of honor he offered me with my actual job of being his "lackey" when he walked off toward the stopes to make his morning rounds.

Rick had been pulling muck from the bottoms of the chutes in a "gravity feed" kind of situation. His running feud with the miners on 11 level (the level above us) about the size of the boulders in their chutes had been going on for quite a while… months I guess. That day it finally came to a head.

Rick and I sat there a little longer and decided to start back toward the stopes ourselves. The muck motor had been left "plugged in," charging its batteries, by the opposite shift's crew that worked during the other part of the day. Rick unplugged it and immediately sat down in the motor's cockpit behind the controls, where he pretty much spent his working day. Whenever we accidentally derailed one of the muck cars or even the motor itself, which seemed to be quite often, guess who

the monkey was who fought with jacks and blocks of wood to crib up whatever went off the tracks? I hate to say it, but after a few hours of that I began thinking my new partner was lazy.

Thirteen level, like everything else I'd seen in the mine, was long, probably about a mile or so, and narrow with many turns. It reminded me of a really long worm hole I suppose, because it was so old, narrow, and windy.

After dumping our trainload of lead/silver ore onto the grizzly, I climbed into the empty muck car at the end of our string of nine cars. Rick's motor would push the whole affair back into the level again to the bottom of the chutes for another load. At the end of the day I was busy "tallying up" the number of cars we'd pulled from each chute when Rick snatched the paper from my hand.

He loudly declared, "All three of those stopes had bigger muck in 'em than what they should've had. Now it's my turn to play their silly game. Those damned miners are going to learn once and for all…"

He walked off down the tracks, mumbling to himself and scratching out the numbers that I'd written down. A short time later we were on the skip riding up the shaft. It just so happened that, after we reached 9 level, I got into the man-train already occupied by "those damned miners," as Rick so eloquently called them. They knew I was working with Rick that day pulling their chutes. They asked, "How many cars did we get?"

What a fix. I knew that Rick had screwed them good again, but, on one hand, I felt a little allegiance to him. On the other hand, here were miners who looked like they would really be mad if they knew what he'd been doing to them.

All I could think of to say was, "I don't know, you'll have to talk to Rick, he's got the paper."

The two greasy, burnt-out looking miners became sullen, moody, and, after a bit, they began unloading their pent up frustrations on me.

One said, "That damn Rick is screwing us. He don't mark down all of our cars. We've bitched to Adams about it quite a few times but Dale doesn't seem to give a crap about it, or us either as far as that goes."

Then the second miner, who hadn't spoken yet, looked at me with a wry grin, and said, "Don't be surprised if you've got a new partner tomorrow." Nothing more was mentioned. The rest of the ride out of the mine was peaceful, if not a bit inhibited.

Another night passed, and almost before I knew it I was again on the man-train heading back into the mine. I didn't see Rick get on the train, but that wasn't unusual. There were just so many guys, and a few gals, milling about the train yard that I figured I must have missed him. I happened to catch sight of the miner who'd told me the night before about the possibility of my having a new partner that day. He was looking straight at me laughing heartily.

I thought, "Well at least they're in good spirits today, anyhow."

After I was deposited onto 13 level alone, I finally decided that something must have happened to good old Rick. About 15 minutes went by. Dale finally came down to the level and my suspicions were confirmed.

He said, "Rick got his butt kicked last night by someone… here probably." He motioned with his head and an upturned eyebrow up toward 11 level, as if he knew who it was but just couldn't prove it.

He went on, "Then Rick called in this morning and quit. I'd sure like to know who it was. I'd fire 'em right on the spot. Well anyway… think you can handle the motor by yourself?"

His pep talk of the day before, encouraging me to do good so I could be his number one boy, still echoed in my mind. I thought, "This is my big chance" and said, "Yeah… hell, how hard can it be. Just ride around and look busy right?"

I don't think Mr. Adams really understood my answer from the bewildered look he gave me, but he didn't question it either. He just said, "Well, there you have it then," turned and walked away down the drift on his appointed rounds.

After he'd gone I got to thinking, "Crap, what have I done? I've never even sat in the seat on a motor before, and I don't have the slightest idea of how to run one. Guess I'll just turn handles and see what happens next."

After many nerve steadying shots of caffeine from Columbia, or wherever, I approached the strange yellow monster, offering up a silent prayer to whoever might be listening. Then I deliberately unplugged the power cord and positioned myself above the motor's seat. I felt like one of those bronco busters you see in the rodeos on television who's about to see if his butt is more resilient than the horses' legs. Then I slipped down onto the well-worn wooden seat.

There was a short power cord dangling on the dash in front of me, so I plugged it into what looked like the appropriate socket. The only controls I could see were a handle, which pivoted from one point and turned in both directions, and a foot pedal. (This was a deadman pedal. Shortly, my misuse of it nearly sent the train flying down a shaft. More about that in a minute.) Then of course there was a brake handle too, or at least that's what it looked like. I stomped down on the pedal, grabbed the end of the shiny brass handle, and shoved it forward. Lo and behold, the whole thing started moving. And the further forward I pushed the handle the faster it went. I figured that if I pulled the handle backwards it would probably make the motor go into reverse.

Then I thought, with more than a little exhilaration, "Hell… this is great, no wonder Rick didn't want to get out of this seat." I was on a roll.

I ran the motor back into the crosscut where the muck cars were kept when not in use and hooked the motor up to them. Then, after a little switching so I could get back out onto the main line, I continued back toward the stopes. I now was on my way. I have to admit, if there'd been bugs flying around in the drift they would've wound up staining my teeth from all the smiling I was doing.

I then came to the chutes and met the first real challenge. It was time to get off the motor and fill the cars. I tried hard to remember what Rick had shown me.

I stopped the train so that the car nearest the motor was positioned directly under the first chute, and I set the motor's hand brake. I got off and pulled the chute handle open. There was a rumble, no problem there, and in no time the car was full. I closed the chute's gate, and got back into the motor's seat to move up the second car. I did this over and over, and soon the train was full and briskly moving down the tracks out toward the station. Feeling proud of what I had just done, I jerked on the cord of my warning bell, clanging it for all to hear. Federal law requires that all underground motors be equipped with warning devices such as bells, horns, or whatever.

I was surprised at how quickly the train picked up speed, and before I knew it, I was really humming down the tracks. I went about three quarters of a mile or so and I started thinking, "Guess I'd better slow this sucker down because I'm not really sure where the station even is… gotta be sure that I can stop this thing."

About then I turned and looked back toward the rear of the train to see how the ore cars were doing. I was shocked; there was only one car connected to the mo-

At the Bunker Hill, miners going on shift had to make a long walk from a parking lot (located several blocks to the left, out of view) and up the street and the long staircase at left center leading to the dry.
Kellogg Public Library

tor. The other eight must have come loose somewhere back down the drift.

I looked up and down the drift feeling a sudden rush of "God... I hope nobody's watching," and pulled hard on the brake handle. The motor slowly ground to a stop and I just sat there dumfounded, wondering if maybe it wasn't all a bad dream.

Then a memory flashed through my "empty" mind about an incident that had occurred when I was a policeman in Oregon. I was alone at night and had been patrolling for hours. I was sleepy and bored to death. To break the monotony, I started singing, stomping my feet, and looking at all the neat stuff in the car. I looked at the console and its radio that came to life every once in a while to cackle about some problem somewhere. Next I looked down expecting to see my 357 magnum Smith and Wesson pistol in my holster, but it wasn't there! I'm sure glad there weren't any other cars around, because about then I slammed on the brakes and nearly

went off the road. As the patrol car came to a screeching stop, I thought, "God, where is it? Where's my gun?"

I opened the door, stepped out, and looked all over the seats and floorboards, but still no gun.

"What happened to it?"

Determined that if I had to I would completely dismantle the car right there in the middle of the road, I grabbed my flashlight angrily thinking, "I'm surprised I didn't lose this damned thing too."

I opened the back door and shined the powerful light at the floor behind my seat. There, just peaking out from under the seat was the black barrel of my cannon.

"God, what a relief," I thought, "if this'd happened with a prisoner back here I could have... Forget the prisoner, what if I'd had another officer riding with me, that would have been even worse." I must have somehow hung up the gun on the seat when I'd gotten in.

Another stupid thing I did later in my mining career occurred while I was working on the 3,000 foot level of ASARCO's Galena Mine. I was actually working as a miner then and my chute seemed to be "hanging up"—that is, muck wouldn't run out the bottom very well because of some kind of obstruction. It was a 120-feet-deep, 4-feet-square hole that had crib sides.

I had the motorman pull all the muck out of it that he could and then I put my plan into action. I'd ordered down a "boatswain chair" from the boss. It was a sling kind of an affair with a "D" ring at its top for connecting to a hoisting cable. My idea was to sit in the chair—I had never even seen one before—and let my partner lower me down into the chute with a small cable hoist called a "tugger." That way, I could find the obstruction and get rid of it.

The plan seemed simple enough and started off great. I rigged up a block, or pulley, over the chute, and hooked up the chair to the tugger cable and got into it. Positioning myself over the open chute, I yelled down through the 120 feet of open chute to my partner, "Lower away."

After only a minute of being suspended in the chute on the cable, I started thinking. "This can't be right, I shouldn't be going down head first."

Because of my ignorance of the proper hook-up technique, I'd put the chair on over my shoulders instead of my legs. There I was, upside down, and I couldn't do anything about it. I figured that if I told my partner about my predicament, he probably would have laughed so hard that I could've been seriously injured. I guess I should have asked how to put it on right, but then what kind of question is, "Duh… how do you sit in a chair?"

The straps pushed hard against my chest and lungs, and by the time I got to the bottom of the chute, I was gasping for air. I was sure that every ounce of blood in my body had settled into my pea-sized brain too. But… you know? I let him pull me all the way back up that chute again, still hanging upside down and I never said a word about it either. After all, I sure didn't want my partner to know that I'd done something stupid.

Now to return to my main story. There was no question as to the whereabouts of the missing ore cars. They had to be somewhere between the chute and where I'd stopped the train. The question that remained though was, "What happened to make them come loose from the train?"

I pushed my way back into the level looking for the cars while cautiously approaching sharp curves. I half expected to ram into them sooner or later. After retracing the entire route back to the chute, I finally found them. They were sitting right where I'd filled them. I parked the motor and checked the hitch on the front

car. It was broken. Rick hadn't told me about that one. After chaining the separated cars together, I set off again. This time, I looked back once in a while. Again, the ore train gained speed and soon was at full gallop heading toward the shaft and the ore pocket.

I clanged the warning bell as I approached the corners. After going about three quarters of a mile and passing by the same spot where I'd stopped before, I decided to be cautious and slow down. About 500 feet further down the line and around a curve, I saw the grizzly pocket coming up fast.

I took my hands off the throttle control and grabbed the brake handle. I had to time it perfectly to stop the train in just the right place beside the pocket. I cranked hard on the brake handle and the train slowed down a lot, but it didn't stop completely. I looked at the pocket as I passed on by it and figured that I must have misjudged the weight of the ore cars.

I thought, "Surely it will stop any time now."

As the train creeped on around the corner, I saw something that just scared the hell right out of me… the shaft. The tracks went right up to the gates of the shaft, and I couldn't stop. I was getting desperate and pulled so hard on the brake handle that I'm sure the motor must have been in pain. The brakes were "drum tight"—so tight in fact that they were smoking. That didn't help, the train was still inching toward the shaft. I couldn't stand it anymore. My last thought as I rose up from my seat and stood in the motorman's compartment preparing to jump was, "To hell with this damned thing."

I turned and hung one leg over the side to step off, when suddenly the train ground to a halt. I couldn't believe it! Why did it suddenly stop? I sat there shaking and trying to figure out what had happened. After a while, I regained a little courage and climbed into the motor again. I released the brake and put it into reverse … nothing happened. I then stomped down on the pedal, and the motor lurched to the rear so suddenly that it caught me off guard. I nearly fell backward off the motor onto the floor.

Well, what I had done when trying to stop the train was pull on the brake handle while the throttle was still on. That is, the throttle had remained "on" because my foot was holding the "deadman pedal" down. I found out later that the deadman pedal actually was a safety switch. If an operator died, passed out, or somehow otherwise lost the ability to operate the controls, his foot would slip off the deadman pedal, popping it into an up position which disconnected the throttle. That way an engine rolled to a stop, possibly preventing a disaster. They had been used for many years by railroads everywhere, but no one had told me about them, not even Rick. What stopped my train, of course, was the fact that I had removed my foot from the pedal when getting ready to jump out of the engine.

I'll bet its inventor didn't consider the possibility of me using his invention. After all, it's hard to invent a pedal to prevent stupidity. I'd heard about the deadman foot controller before, but didn't really pay it much attention. Actually I'd forgotten all about it. I just figured that when the train was moving, the pedal had to be pressed down.

I worked hard for the rest of the day, rumbling the train back and forth between the chutes and the grizzly. Incidentally, I didn't tell anyone about how I almost stuffed 'er down the shaft.

After a few days, my operating skills became better and better, and in no time I was an old pro. The miners who worked in the stopes on 11 level were really happy about my work. I kept a correct accounting of the number of cars I pulled from their chutes, and their contract money went up dramatically. In fact, I even added a few cars worth to their total now and then to keep them happy. I didn't think there was anything wrong with it, after all Rick owed them a lot more than that. I was taking no chances in getting my butt kicked either.

The days turned into weeks, and the weeks into months, as I sailed right on through the summer and into the fall, 1973. It was getting close to Thanksgiving Day and I looked forward to the change of seasons, with all its good cheer. And then, "Bam!" Bunker Hill went down on strike. Talk about putting a crimp in the holidays. I thought about trying to wait it out, but I wasn't much for hanging around anyplace either. ❀

CHAPTER 5

Chased Off by Another Strike

Sunshine Mine… Again

The Sunshine Mine was hiring. They still needed people to stuff down into holes in the ground to kick out some valuable silver ore. I was hired on the spot. Of course there still was the little matter of a physical examination, but I was armed with my infamous "spot" letter that time, which I'd kept. The doctors decided that there wasn't any problem with me physically—I had a strong back and a weak mind, two things which were required, at least for me, to be a miner.

I liked Chuck Poulson, the hiring man at the Sunshine. He seemed to be a really nice guy, and made the hiring out process flow smoothly. Before I knew it, I was standing at the bottom of the long metal staircase leading up to the mine's dry. Incidentally, right after I'd made it through all the required paperwork for hiring out, the mine fired Chuck. I always sort of suspected that I must have been the proverbial "nail in the coffin" of his career. Once the big bosses found out that he'd hired me back, I guess they were so ticked off that they canned him. The last time I saw Chuck was about six months later; he was driving a Holsum bread truck and as good natured as ever.

Anyway, I struggled up the long staircase and into the dry dragging my wardrobe. I was sort of proud of my brand new green U.S. Army surplus laundry bag. I felt somewhat successful just from having it with me. Probably because, as I glanced around at the rows of hangers, or baskets, suspended on chains near the ceiling, all I saw were crusty old-looking pillowcases, like the one I'd thrown away the night before.

A miner operating a jack-leg at the Sunshine Mine in 1981.
Sunshine Precious Metals Inc.

I unhooked one of the chains, letting down an empty basket, and changed into my friendly old "funky" clothes. I kept a wary eye out for familiar faces and wasn't disappointed. Three or four miners passing by stopped to say, "Where the hell you been?"

Another guy asked, "Where's the shifters shack?"

Now that made me feel great. Here I was just hiring out and I looked so crummy that another new hireling mistook me for one of the regular crew. I thoroughly enjoyed my short stay in the dry as I "suited up" for battle. After a bit of a search, I collected my cap lamp and battery from among the hundreds of lamps in the lamp room. When not in use, cap lamps were left there in rows to charge their batteries.

I made my way back down the staircase to the shifters shack with a spring in my step. I was happy; it was as if I'd never left the Sunshine. Memories of the eight months I'd just spent on the motor at Bunker Hill faded right away. One reason I didn't mind moving from job to job, and mine to mine, was that I didn't really expect to live long enough to retire if I remained a miner anyhow. I think most of the other miners thought so too. Besides, I figured that I was "just in between jobs," and someday I would get out from underground and get a real job.

I pushed open the swinging door of the shifters shack and met a wall of darting glances from behind the long counter. It was almost the same as before, and there was Larry Hawkins, my old shifter, sitting behind his large gray metal desk way over in the corner. He gave me a shallow fleeting smile as we made eye contact. The smile faded into deep thought, and he returned his attention to the pile of papers laying in front of him.

That was the first time I met Tom Barton. He was a big man… I mean big. He looked like a force to be reckoned with and had a personality to match. I found out later that he had a son who turned out to be a boss at the 'Shine too.

Old Tom walked over to the counter across from me and asked, "You Dolph?" I figured right there that these guys weren't much on conversation. It seemed like the first thing they always said to me was the two word greeting, "You Dolph?"

I replied with a grin, "Yeah… I'm back."

I noticed Larry as he glanced up from his work again, giving me a genuine smile. That was the only time I'd ever seen him do that.

Then Tom said, "Go on down to 5,000 level and I'll see you down there when I make my rounds."

I said, "Okay," turned, punched in my time card, and headed toward the door.

Larry looked up from his papers again and yelled after me, "Ya gunna stay this time?"

I stopped just short of the second swinging door and turned to face him. All of the shifters stopped what they were doing and stared expectantly at me, waiting for an answer.

With a shrug and raised eyebrow I replied, "Don't know… depends on how good ya are to me this time."

I turned and as I pushed open the door I heard riotous laughter erupt from the room behind me.

I again walked into the concrete-lined drift as I'd done so many times before, and began the long walk toward the Jewell Shaft. That's when I saw Dennis Sykes again. He was one of the cagers for the Jewell Shaft. We'd been rivals for my lady's hand. I was the one who succeeded in winning her favor, so I guess I came out on the best end of that deal. Of course there are times… no, not really. I wouldn't have changed a thing.

Now Dennis was hard as nails and a real outdoorsman. In fact just to give you an idea, many years before a fella went nuts and vanished into the mountains during the winter. Rescue crews searched for the guy repeatedly, but to no avail. Then everybody just expected the poor guy to turn up sometime after the spring thaw and in general didn't really hold out much hope for him at all. That was till Dennis came on the scene. He went up into the snow covered mountains alone, was gone for days, but eventually brought the guy in.

Dennis loved to do things like go on 100-mile hikes taking only a safety pin (which he used as a fish hook),

Sunshine Mine's Ten Shaft.
Sunshine Precious Metals Inc.

six inches of hemp rope, and a dry pair of socks. Then he'd spend six months alone in the mountains sleeping with the bears in -40 degree weather. Well… that may be a bit of an exaggeration, but you get the idea.

About a year or so later I was walking through a hospital hallway on the way to visit my wife in her room when I happened to glance through an open door and saw my friend Dennis laying in bed. I was really surprised to see him there. I noticed that he had casts on both of his legs.

I walked into his room and asked, "What in the hell are you doing here, Bud?"

After making our greetings, he said, "I was working with my partner in the Jewell Shaft, it was wintertime, and we'd just belled up the skip so we could get on. We didn't know it at the time, but the damned skip was stuck in the ice that had built up at the top of the shaft. We both got in and I belled the hoistman to lower away.

"He began letting out the hoist cable, but since we were all jammed up in the ice like that the skip didn't move. The heavy hoist cable started building up on top of the skip though, and its extra weight broke us loose. We dropped like a stone and my partner and I went into a free-fall."

I could see that Dennis was reliving his ordeal and I was careful not to interrupt. He continued, "I couldn't believe it because it all happened so fast. My partner and I were both weightless and floating around in the skip as it hurled down the shaft. Then I looked over and saw that he was floating out toward the opening above the door where I knew he would be killed if he got tangled up between the shaft timbers and the outside of the skip.

"I reached out with one arm and grabbed him around his waist; with my other hand I took hold of a chain hanging on the inside wall of the skip. Then I drew him toward me. I managed to pull him up against me too, but right about then we hit the end of that damned cable. Then the skip stopped instantly, but we didn't. He came down on me like a hammer and I wound up breaking both of my legs out of the deal, but at least he's alive now and I'll probably heal up sooner or later."

Dennis's story of desperation and unsung bravery is just one of many thousands that could be told about the hardrock miners of northern Idaho and everywhere else as far as that goes!

Well, back to my first day again. I got into the skip and rode down the shaft, amongst many "Hellos" and "Oh, you're back again huh?" That was really fun. The fella who'd asked me where the shifters shack was at the beginning of the day happened to be riding in my skip. From the look on his face I think he was amazed at all the guffaw that was going on about my return to the mine.

We approached the getting-off level and sure enough, as we stopped at the station, I saw the man-train again. The skip unloaded and I headed over toward it to find a seat. As I approached a partially empty car I noticed what looked like a spray, or something, coming out through every door on the train.

As I got closer it finally dawned on me, "They're sunflower seed husks."

I'd picked up the habit of chewing seeds too and was happy to see spit, bits of seeds, and probably teeth as well flying out onto the ground. At least I wouldn't be the only one doing this less-than-civilized habit.

I began feeling warm all over with the familiarity of being home. The thing that makes a miner feel like he is accepted (other than the money certainly) isn't the dynamite or equipment that he uses to drill and blast his rounds. And it isn't the ground he works in either, since it poses such a hazardous environment to his health and life, what with air blasts and such. No, it's the other miners—the brothers who depend on each other when the need arises, just like when Dennis saved his partner.

I squeezed myself into a car, sat down, and pulled out a sack of seeds. I had to laugh, because before I could even finish tearing it open two of the fellas in the car reached out with their own sacks offering me a "chew."

The modern day sunflower seed "chew" probably has replaced the "slug of chewin' tobacco" used by folks in the Old West. I stuffed my cheeks full of the salty little critters and my fellow travelers nodded their approval. Before long, I added my own stream of spent sunflower husks to those already flying out the door.

My dad once told me about a mathematical problem that he'd solved, about filling Yankee Stadium full of ball bearings or whatever it was. I sat there thinking about this and began wondering how long we'd have to sit here spitting seeds before the train would be buried. From the way they were building up, almost like snow, it didn't look like it would take long at all.

I was lost in my thoughts about lots of dumb stuff like that when the train suddenly lurched forward. That brought me back to reality. I settled in for the long trip over to Ten Shaft. It didn't seem like long at all, however, before the train began slowing at the end of its one mile or so route and then stopped near Ten Shaft's station. I remembered Bunker Hill's incline shaft and how much fun it had been to ride in. Then I thought of the air blast in this damned shaft and how our skip had hung in it for what seemed like hours before we were rescued. As those thoughts flooded through my mind, I'd gotten onto the skip and we were quickly dropping down the shaft on our way into the guts of the mine.

During the 1972 fire the bottom levels became flooded because the pumps were put out of action. Suffocating, brackish groundwater seeping from seams in the rock eventually filled the bottom of the mine from 5,400 feet, or whatever it was, up to about 4,600 feet. This was the first time that I would be going deeper than the 4,800 level, which I'd worked in nine months before. After a few minutes we swooshed right on past 4,600, but the formerly water-filled shaft didn't look any different to me at all at the lower depths. Of course we were dropping like a rock and everything looked sort of blurry. I did notice that the temperature went up quite a bit before we finally slowed and came to a stop at the station on the 5,000 feet level.

I got off the skip and was left alone waiting for Tom to come down. The skip quickly disappeared down the shaft on its way to the bottom of the mine. I looked around and observed massive wooden posts that rose vertically along the walls topped by heavy horizontal timbers, with head boards between their ends and the rock walls. It looked much like most of the other shaft stations I'd been in. I don't know exactly what it was, but it just felt unreal to be there. I knew Ron Flores,

THIS MEMORIAL IS DEDICATED
BY THEIR FAMILIES TO
THE MEN WHO LOST THEIR LIVES
IN THE SUNSHINE DISASTER
ON MAY 2 1972 AND
PRESENTED TO THE SILVER VALLEY
BY THE STATE OF IDAHO ON
MAY 2 1974

SHERMAN ELY - SITE DESIGN
KEN LONN - SCULPTOR

WE WERE MINERS THEN
BY
SENATOR - PHIL BATT

who was one of the two fellas who'd escaped from the inferno that killed the 91 miners in 1972. He was on the 4,800 level—near the same level I now was standing on—when the rescue crews finally found him. I shrugged the weird feeling off and chalked it up to a full moon or something.

I sat there for a good 15 minutes in silence, alone with the thoughts of past events that had occurred there. Finally I could hear the skip rumbling down the shaft. It came to a stop, someone threw back the bar that held the gates in place, and Tom stepped out onto the station. Then the skip continued on its way.

I was glad to see him. It had been sort of spooky sitting there alone in the heat, listening to the snapping and popping sounds the ground made, and smelling the rotten gaseous odor of decaying timber. I wondered when it was all going to be ripped apart by air blasts like the one that hit when I was in the skip.

Tom, like all the other shifters, carried an aluminum clipboard with him wherever he went. Or at least it seemed like it. He sat his clipboard down on a pile of 6-feet-long lagging and we began to talk. Turns out that he'd been a miner over at the Star Mine up in Burke, which is about a half dozen or so miles northeast of Wallace, for many years.

He said, "Yeah, got so I couldn't mine much any more so I turned to doing this," meaning bossing.

We talked on and it turned out that he'd put in some time in a mine in Tibet, or Peru... well, it was really high country that didn't have much oxygen to breathe.

He said, "You know how chickens have that red floppy thing on their necks? Well up there it's blue... no air." That still sounds a little fishy to me, but I'll accept it as a truth. After all he was the boss, right?

Another fella named Russ had gotten off the skip with Tom and we were all deeply involved in a bull session for quite a while. Finally Tom rose to his feet, grabbed his fancy clipboard, and headed off down the drift on his rounds. He told me to work with Russ for the day.

Ninety-one men perished after being trapped by fire in the Sunshine Mine on May 2, 1972. The disaster was a blow to Silver Valley residents and the mining industry. Two years later to the day, this memorial constructed by miner Ken Lonn was placed near the I-90 freeway and the mouth of Big Creek, which passes by the Sunshine Mine. The "eternal flame" in the miner's lamp bears mute testimony to the challenges that miners must endure.
Shoshone News-Press/Photo by Don Sauer

After Tom walked off into the darkness, Russ and I took an unsupervised fiver. As we sat there talking and sharing experiences, I started sizing him up and it didn't take long at all to decide that I really liked his carefree attitude. Russ had quite a sense of humor too. Well just to elaborate on that a bit, this is the story that he told me.

He said, "I was walking through the drift back there once..." He stopped and gestured into the darkness after Tom with his hand. Then he went on, "While I was walking along, an air blast hit somewhere in the wall beside me. Then the damned wall collapsed right down on top of me too and I was immediately pushed down to the tracks and buried completely. It all happened so fast that I didn't really have a chance to do anything.

"As I laid there, I didn't feel any pain, I didn't feel much of anything... just tremendous pressure, from the weight of the rock that was on top of me. It was really weird. I could still see, sorta, but couldn't yell out for help or anything. I laid there for quite a while like that struggling to get free but the rock just got heavier. I finally started getting dizzy, damn it was hard to breathe."

Suddenly he stopped his story, looked over at me, and said, "If you don't believe how hard it is to breathe like that with half a mountain lying on your lungs, just try having someone sit on your chest and then try to get some air."

He continued, "Well anyway, there I was, startin' to stiffin up and couldn't get any air. Then I saw some light. Hell... I thought I was dead, you know with the bright light, the tunnel, and like that? The way it turned out, Ol' Jeff was working back toward the end of the level that day, and he just happened to be walking out toward the shaft to get somethin' right about then. It was about five minutes or so after I was hit.

"I still couldn't holler out at him or nuthin'. And by then everything seemed like a dream anyhow, I was going out."

Russ stopped his story, sort of coughed right then, and poured himself another cup of coffee. Then he cleared his throat and continued: "That's when it got to be sort of funny. Old Jeff saw the color of my hard hat laying in the muck pile when he got to it and stooped over to pick it up. Our faces weren't but an arms length apart then and when he pulled my hat off I was laying there with my eyes open, staring up at him."

Russ then broke out in laughter... after he was able to contain himself again he continued, "When Jeff saw my face he let out a scream that sounded like something my wife would have done. I guess he expected to find an empty hard hat instead of one with me in it."

We laughed about what had happened to him and thoroughly exhausted every angle of his story.

Then Russ said, "Every once in a while, I'll wait till there's a lot of guys around and catch Jeff off guard. Then I like to holler out at him, 'Hey Jeff… find any good hard hats lately?' Boy that pisses him off. He's really embarrassed about his little girly scream."

Russ and I got up from our long fiver and he showed me around. The 5,000 level, not unlike the rest of the Sunshine, is nothing short of enormous, and it took us quite a while to cover it all. It has long drifts, big bore holes, and lots of "worked out" stopes that were abandoned because there wasn't anymore ore left in them.

I was going to be a motorman's helper again, for the time being at least. Most of the contract miners there in the 'Shine—and every other hardrock miner in the U.S. and Canada too—probably were making really good money compared to the "piddley" little bit I was getting. I felt embarrassed about my "day's pay," an hourly wage instead of being based on contract. It was December 1973 and I made an early New Year's resolution right then and there that I was going to "go mining" as soon as possible.

The rest of that day went by fast and, almost before I knew it, I was getting into my car and heading home. The night went quickly too—it seemed I'd no sooner closed my eyes to go to sleep than I was awake again and heading for work. I found myself putting on my only partially dry diggers and climbing down the long staircase to street level again and on into the shifters shack, ready for the new day.

Tom looked up from behind a large pile of papers that were scattered across his desk. He saw me and said, "Go up to the Mine Safety Office today for safety orientation," which was a fancy name for a long coffee break. That's when I met Gordon Burdick—the Sunshine's safety man. He was, if you'll forgive the expression, a "hippy looking" kind of a fella… well no, actually with his easygoing demeanor and happy-go-lucky style he reminded me more of a game-show host. There were three of us "new hires" in his class. Each of us settled back into the worn wooden chairs with, what else, a cup of steaming hot coffee.

Gordon began his little talk by saying, "In the mines of northern Idaho, as in all deep mines, there are hundreds of little chores that need to be done to prepare for the next round [or blast]. And without exception the most important one is barring down [prying down loose pieces of rock from the back and walls with a scaling bar]."

Then Gordon began telling us a story about barring down: "This fella, Frank, had a farmer friend named Bob. And one day Frank went to visit Bob on his farm. Bob stopped long enough to let Frank get up onto his tractor with him and then continued on plowing. All of a sudden Bob stopped the tractor, grabbed a shovel from behind his seat, and leaped to the ground. Once Bob had run about 50 feet from the tractor he stopped, raised the shovel over his head, and swung it hard to the ground several times.

"Bob returned to the tractor and continued on plowing, as before. The two friends began talking again and soon Frank had forgotten all about what had happened with the shovel."

Gordon sort of chuckled as he stopped talking and poured himself another cup of coffee. Then he continued with the story: "Then it happened all over again. Bob stopped the tractor, grabbed his shovel, went out into the field, hit the ground with it a few times, then returned to his seat and continued on plowing again.

"Unable to contain his curiosity anymore, Frank, shouting over the roar of the tractor's engine, laughingly asked, 'What's with the shovel?'

"Bob replied, 'Snakes… I've got lots of 'em out here.'

"Frank responded, 'But why do you kill them? They aren't bothering you.'

"Bob looked Frank squarely in the eyes and yelled back, 'Yeah, but now there are two less that could.' "

Gordon ended his story by saying, "No matter what you do, be sure and bar the loose ground down if you see any. Even if you aren't a miner."

I enjoyed his story; it contained a message. Loose ground is, always has been, and probably always will be, one of the biggest problems for miners. I once made a safety suggestion when I worked in the Lucky Friday. Well, actually, I made quite a few. At that time the mine awarded real neat things like belt buckles, flashlights, trading stamps, and such to whoever made the best safety suggestion of the month. The one I was talking about, though, was a slogan I made up.

I suggested that the Lucky Friday would be a safer place to work in if they put up a series of signs like the old Burma Shave highway signs. I suggested, "Bar down the walls… bar down the back… or they might carry you out… in a rubber sack." The beginning would be placed near the mine's dry, so the guys would read part

"Bear" Hunter drilling a round.
Hecla Mining Company

of it from the day's "git-go." The rest of the message would be spaced out across the mine's yard and up to the shaft. I thought that curiosity alone would surely lure the miners into trying to find out what the next sign would say. I know I'd really be looking around, myself, trying to find out what the rest of the message was. Sort of like Paul Harvey's, "and that's the rest of the story." Unfortunately, I didn't win a belt buckle with that suggestion. One of the other guys proposed something stupid and unimportant like: the need to close the gates on the shaft so no one could accidentally fall to his death.

Gordon filled the day with stories and information about safety stuff, most of which, I might add, I thoroughly enjoyed. It was late in the afternoon when he finished and there wasn't enough time left in the shift to go underground and work. Then came one of my favorite things… we were sent home. But we had been inspired to do a great job underground, and we were aware that doing something like getting blasted to bits wouldn't really be in the best interest of our mining careers. He fed us a lot of information that was really basic, and treated us like we were teenagers. I suppose he had to because there was no way he could have known how much, or how little, we actually knew.

Federal Bureau of Mines regulations required miners to receive safety training updates each year. Instead of all-day sessions, most mines broke the training into periods of a couple of hours each month. That way I

could look forward to another "day in the sun"—or at least part of one—from time to time. That probably sounds ridiculous; sunlight is something that most people take for granted. For miners, though, it's a special treat to get a sunburn now and then. Most of the time it's "dark when you get to work and dark when you go home."

The next day I worked with Russ and his motor on the 5,000 feet level, but I was "fired up" with a desire to actually mine (i.e., drill holes in the rock and dynamite the hell out of it). Tom was a great shifter. If he hadn't been the "boss" I could have very easily regarded him as a friend. Of course that wasn't possible because of class distinctions, the separation of brains and brawn. Well actually, he had both of those too. I didn't really have a lot of either, but I did have the need to drill and blast. Once that fever gets into a miner's blood he is afflicted permanently with the condition known as "once a miner, always a miner."

I worked with Russ for only about a month when Tom gave me a promotion, a chance to move up—or was it down?—into a stope. However, my new partner, whose name was Rex, and I weren't really mining yet—we were assigned the job of repairing timber in the raise. Mr. Air Blast had really been feeling his oats when he visited that place, I can tell you that. One of the two miners who was working in it at the time was killed. Both of the miners were buried by the blast, but rescue crews were able to save one of them. Let me say right here that there is no warning when an air blast hits. Working in a stope was sort of like playing Russian roulette. A fella just had to hope that he wasn't in the wrong place at the right time.

Our "new" stope had such rich ore that we probably were the "umpteenth" crew that had been in there working it. The mine really wanted that high-grade silver ore. Whenever one of the other places had to be shut down for a day or two for whatever reason, the bosses pulled the guys out and had them work in "my" stope.

One miner, after he found out where I was working, said, "Our place was totally wrecked by an air blast once, too, and my partner and I were put into your stope. We worked in it for a couple of months, while the timber repair guys fixed ours up again."

Some of the Sunshine miners figured they had a premonition of when an air blast was coming. One of them told me, "When the hair stands up on the back of your neck and you break out in a 'cold' sweat, you'd better damn well get under some good solid timber someplace 'cause all hell is going to break loose."

Rex must have subscribed to his theory because most of the time he'd sit down and lean up against a "good solid post." He was in so much fear, I guess, that it'd just knock him right out—and he sure snored a lot. He'd been mining for many years there in the 'Shine and was just about to "call 'er quits," as he said, when he came in with me. Rex was in his early 60s and didn't talk much; it seemed he was always too busy gasping for air and struggling to stay awake. The main thing he said to me was, "Wake me up if you see anybody coming."

Our job title classified us as timber repairmen, which didn't require the furious activity that being a gypo, or contract miner, did. I was having a lot of problems with the "hurry up" of our days. I felt a lot like some kind of damned guard or something, as I sat there staring into the quiet darkness, watching for light… any light… while I protected my own private fool from "the wrath of Tom." I could hear the muffled rattle of jack-legs, or drilling machines, coming through the rock and thought, "Well at least someone is busy working and making a lot of contract money… hell everybody is, but me and this jerk. They're gettin' rich and here I sit, just gettin' stupid."

Here I was, "all fired up and ready to go," and there he was, snuffed out and ready to go too, but the other way. Something had to give and it did. My partner's days of hide and seek were numbered—that is, "hide" in the

Pushing stick explosives into holes with a wooden powder pole.
Hecla Mining Company

darkness from the boss and "seek" as much rest as possible. It happened near the end of one of our more grueling days. We were climbing up the ladders in the man-way on our way out of the stope at the end of the shift. The day was no different than any other in that it was hot as blue blazes. There Rex was, on the ladders just above me, and he was struggling to reach the top of the man-way. I was climbing along, slowly I might add, thinking about Jason, my one-year-old son, and how neat it was to be his dad. I heard a really deep sigh and I looked up and saw that Rex was hanging onto the ladder with only the "crook" of his left arm and standing on his left foot. His head was down and his right side was limp.

I thought, "He's going to take us both out."

I quickly climbed up to him and just had him cradled between me and the wide open spaces when he passed out completely and let go. Damn that was close! I was just barely able to catch him. Okay, there I stood, with his limp body between me and the ladder, with another 15 feet or so of ladder rungs between us and the top of the man-way. It was 40 feet straight down to the next landing, a little floor at the base of the ladder.

I shouted at him, trying to get him back to consciousness. Then I shook him and, after what seemed like an eternity, he finally started coming around. It was a good thing too because we'd been hanging there doing our "dance" for just about as long as my arms could hold out. I felt his strength come back to him. What a relief. The only thing I could've done with him next was to somehow "walk" us both back down the 40 feet of ladders to the next landing.

Normally, man-ways have landings, or floors, every 10 feet. But our damned place was lucky to have a man-way at all, after the hit it took from Mr. Air Blast. All the ladders were temporaries and sort of cobbled together, at best. They were just barely hanging in there. We started climbing up again and a few minutes later sort of spilled out onto the floor at the top. Man it was hot. Rex and I laid there for quite a while trying to get air. We finally got to our feet, and walked out to the shaft and the end of our day—and his mining career. He quit the Sunshine that night and I never saw him again.

Tom didn't put me back down into the stope after that. "Now we'll try you on the jack-leg," he said.

The next morning I was given a brand new partner and a different job—drift repair. Tom told me to watch out for my new partner because he was green as a new dollar bill and hadn't even drilled with a machine yet. Lonnie was this kid's name, and he was just the opposite of good, old, easygoing Rex. Whereas Rex was calm, almost to the point of rigor mortis, Lonnie was fast moving and high strung.

I sort of laughed and thought, "Hell, he's like a French poodle with hemorrhoids."

Our new job entailed barring down the loose slabs of rock hanging on the walls and rebolting the drift with 6-feet-long rock bolts. Lonnie, from the outset, begged me to let him drill with the machine. I spent the better part of the first day fighting with the machine in really rotten "air slacked" ground—i.e., rock that has become loose and crumbly because of rock bursts and its exposure to air.

Finally, I couldn't stand it anymore—Lonnie's mouth that is—I stepped away from the machine and waved him on. "Go to 'er buddy… it's your turn."

I stood well back from the excitement and lit a smoke. You ever heard the expression, "A monkey trying to love up a buffalo?" That's what Lonnie's relationship to the jack-leg looked like to me. Hell, the ma-

chine weighed almost as much as he did. Now I was pretty big and it was really tough even for me to wrestle the drill steel out of the holes once it had gone through into the crumbly rock. The holes filled up with "gravel," and a guy had to pull like hell on the machine to get the bulky drill bit out, even to the point of using a portable cable wench called a "come-a-long."

The powerful old machine was a Gardner Denver 83. As it faithfully pushed its spinning, hammering, water-squirting steel into the ground, Lonnie looked back at me as if to say, "See there, that ain't so hard." I just nodded and smiled at him in between drags on my cigarette, knowing full well what was going to happen next.

About then the drill bit bound up and the steel itself jammed, instantly stopping its rotation. Unfortunately for Lonnie, the jack-leg's rotation didn't stop. The torque that 90 pounds of drill air gave to it was really a sight to behold in a case like this. The hydraulic extension leg that pushed the machine forward flipped over and over, almost as quickly as an airplane propeller.

I had a hard time trying to keep from laughing. There was Lonnie, terrified, laying on the ground in front of me. He looked kind of like a barber pole for all of the hose wrapped around him. After I shut off the machine's air and helped him get untangled, I started drilling again, this time without the jabbering, accusing rhetoric from behind. I decided that it was indeed a good thing that I did let him try his hand at the machine. At least now I could drill in peace.

Alas, my blissful peace lasted only that day. We finished the "bolting," if it could be called that, by putting in only 12 bolts. Between fighting with my overly zealous partner, my own lack of experience, and the very stubborn ground, we didn't make much headway.

The next day was worse. Lonnie was hot after me again to let him drill. He must have forgotten all about the first round that he'd lost and was ready for a rematch. I saw it coming too, because, as soon as I started drilling he started in on me. I immediately shut down the machine and we both took time out. I set him up with his own machine on down the drift a bit from mine. Without really telling him as much, I had decided to let him satisfy his urge to drill and to get him off my back at the same time. After all, I figured, "Out of sight, out of mind." Well actually, to honor Tom's order to "keep an eye on him," his new drilling station was only about 15 feet away. I figured that way he was at least out of earshot.

Actually, I couldn't help but keep an eye on him as I drilled with my own machine because there wasn't much else to see. He strained and cursed, and just generally climbed all over his machine. He was giving it his all.

I thought, "Well at least this guy is no pansy anyhow. He's getting into the grease of the thing with both feet."

I'm glad that I sort of kept an eye on him like Tom had asked. After he'd struggled with his machine long enough, he finally got frustrated and pushed the machine away, hurling it to the ground. I saw what he was doing just in the nick of time and it scared me to death. I dove to the side.

When his machine hit the ground its leg suddenly shot out because of the air pressure on it, and the "Crow's foot," a three-fingered stand welded to the bottom of the leg, "jabbed" past my belly close enough that it left a red mark on my side. If I hadn't seen it coming, I don't know how the hell that would have turned out.

When I finally made eye contact with him, his look said to me, "Ha, ha, I win."

I could have killed the little son-of-a-bitch, but by the time I stopped shaking it was time to go home. I finally calmed down and told him that as long as I lived I'd never work with him again. I figured that my anger would best be served by abstaining rather than breaking his neck. When I counted up our tally of bolts for the day I found that we'd only put in 17 new ones between the two of us. I'd never even seen ground that bad before, let alone try to drill in it. Man, what a day that was.

Later when I got back up to the top of Ten Shaft, I noticed that a lot of the guys were sort of mad about something the company was doing, or had done, to one of the union members. I heard mutterings of discontent during the train ride all the way across 3,700 level to the bottom of the Jewell Shaft. After I'd gotten topside and showered, I saw small groups of fellas scattered out in different places in the dry. The small gatherings were growing into larger ones. They looked sort of like football huddles where guys all face each other and talk in low tones. Every once in a while someone would stick his head up and look around as if to watch for any unwelcome intruders.

The Sunshine's crew was made up of mostly strong, young, hot-blooded men who could get their hackles up to the point of rioting in no time at all. By the time I got to the bottom of the staircase, I could hear the discontent turning into screams of indignation. Angry curses floated in the air as I got into my car, and the winds of "war" were looming behind me as I drove down the hill toward home.

The next day, as I pulled into the 'Shine's parking lot, I was amazed to see dozens of men standing in a crowd facing the small bridge that spanned a creek and led onto Sunshine's property. A row of shifters stood shoulder to shoulder across the bridge. Tom was among them.

I heard Tom, who took up at least two places in the line of bosses, yell out, "If you want to work, come on across the bridge, if you don't… go home."

As soon as I heard that I thought, "What in the hell am I doing here? After all, I sure don't want to fight with that stupid machine today, or that idiot I'm working with either."

My pulse quickened and so did my steps as I turned and headed back to my car. I was laughing like a hyena by the time I got the door open and was almost blinded with happiness as I drove down the hill enriched by "Old Tom's" words. No more profound a statement was ever made. I reflected on those words for the rest of the day. Damn, what a man, he hit the nail right on the head that time. That's what I needed right about then, some good sound advice.

I doted in my new-found freedom, and didn't even bother to pack a lunch or try to go to work either for the next couple of days. I couldn't have worked, even if I'd wanted to, because the mine was out on strike… again.

One of the fellas said later, "Everybody in the crew stayed away, refusing to cross the bridge. All but one guy. He isn't much of a miner. When he got off shift that day he found his car laying upside down in the parking lot. Then a couple of days later he got turned upside down too."

I finally got my head on straight and decided it was time to find another place to work. I sure didn't want to try and outlast a strike. ✾

Hunter's round has been loaded and the spitter cord ignited. As the spitter cord burns its way up it will "set off" the igniter of each fuse primer. In this manner, the explosives in the holes are "timed" to go off in sequence one after another. Meanwhile, Hunter and other miners have gone up the shaft and off shift.

Hecla Mining Company

CHAPTER 6

My First Stope

Crescent Mine
Kellogg, Idaho

Another one of my friends working in Bunker Hill's Crescent Mine said they were shorthanded and he'd put a word in for me. The next day I drove over to Bunker's hiring office, which was still in the YMCA building in downtown Kellogg. Sure enough, the long line was still there too.

I parked my car and took my place at the end of the line. Again it took over an hour to make it to the bottom step of the long staircase. I was there so long that it was getting on late into the afternoon and I actually saw a bat zip by my face.

That did it. I got to thinking, "It's getting late, I'll probably have to come back and try again tomorrow; just have to be sure that I get here a little earlier next time."

I stood there looking up toward the doorway at the top of the stairs, scoping the length of the line. Suddenly I was surprised by the sight of a familiar face that appeared from inside. It was Albi Sinks, Bunker's hiring man. He studied the men in line like he was looking for someone. Then I heard him say, "Are any of you fellas miners?"

Everybody began looking each other over. It reminded me of that old television show, "What's My Line?" I waited for the guys ahead of me to respond to his question. When no one did, I raised my hand and said, "Yeah, I am."

Albi looked down at me and I saw a glimmer of recognition cross his face. He waved me up with his hand, and without waiting to see if I was going to follow

turned and disappeared back through the doorway. Following him, I climbed up the stairs, looking into lots of discouraged faces as I passed by. That made me feel somewhere in between being a celebrity and a real bum.

I entered the familiar darkness of Albi's office. It was still completely full, standing-room only, with people busily filling out papers and waiting their turn in line. I wondered if these weren't the same folks who were there when I hired out the first time. As soon as I entered the room I heard Albi's voice from within beckoning me.

I then heard him say to the folks who were waiting in the larger room behind me, "That's all for today, come back again tomorrow." Now I'll tell you what… if stares could kill, I would have been murdered a bunch of times right then and there.

Albi said, "What are you doing down here Dolph? You should have gone straight up to the foreman's office this time."

I was really surprised that he remembered my name, considering all the people he dealt with each day, and the way he said "this time" was sort of comforting to me because then I felt like I wasn't the only fool who was tramping back and forth from mine to mine. After a short visit with the mine foreman I was sent out for another physical examination. Then I went through the hiring process again during the next day or so. But I quit the Sunshine only after passing Bunker's physical, just in case I flunked the examination and couldn't get on at the Crescent.

The Sunshine and Crescent mines were located just across a canyon from each other, which created a situation that I thought was sort of funny. The parking lots

Belly dump ore car at the Crescent Mine portal.
Shoshone News-Press

weren't all that far apart, and I had to drive past the fellas I'd been working with only a few days before who were out there on the picket line.

The Crescent Mine was small by Silver Valley standards with only about 60 workers. Twenty or so were miners, while the rest were motormen, shaft repairmen, nippers (or helpers), hoistmen, and so on. We worked a split shift: half in the morning and half in the afternoon. I liked the small mine, small crew operation. It made me feel like we were mining back in the late 1800s—some of the equipment we used added to that feeling too.

My first shifter at the Crescent, June Lawley, had an unusual first name I thought. I use to kid him about it, reminding him of the Johnny Cash song, "A Boy Named Sue." I don't suppose I scored many points with June, but it didn't seem to matter because we got along really well.

Gall, or heat rash, is a condition that miners routinely experience on the job. The environment underground is hard on the human body because of the terrific heat and the constant abrasive action of dust and small rocks in the underarms, thighs, and the like. The skin is usually rubbed raw, as if by sandpaper. I've had it so bad that my skin looked like a dried-up lake bed, all cracked and bleeding. And talk about hurting!

One day at the end of the shift, I was crawling out of my diggers in the mine's dry and overheard June talking to one of the new guys, a young fella who had just worked his first day and was badly galled.

June saw that he was in a lot of pain and said, "Come on into the office, I've got something that will fix you right up."

I was interested in what kind of "cure" June had come up with because, as usual, I was galled too. The kid went into the office with him.

A short while later I heard June say, "Now lift your arm up a little."

A few seconds afterward I heard a blood curdling scream. I noticed the whole crew, who also had been listening, make grimacing faces like, "Man that must hurt, he'll never use any of that stuff on me."

It was some kind of a new salve or something that June had picked up down at the drugstore that day. I guess he was a little disgusted with it, because later as I was leaving the dry one of the guys pointed out its partially used container laying in the trash can. I didn't say anything to June about being galled that night and neither did anyone else. I just went home and put on

the old corn starch as usual. Baby powder worked for me too, but I liked corn starch the best. It seemed like more of a miner's thing to use.

I had only been working there a little over a month on the motor when June offered me my own stope. I thought, "All right, I am a success. It may have taken me longer to get my own place than anyone else on the planet but the way I figure, better late than never."

The stope had been sitting idle for quite a while, maybe a year or so, and was badly in need of repairs, which my new partner and I undertook during our first days there. The stope's back and walls were partially caved in, its timber had been jarred loose from air blasts, and the ground had taken a lot of weight. I think the corker, though, was that there were no tools. Oh they were there all right, but buried under tons of rock (eventually we did find them, one by one, and all thickly rusted). That was really good in a way because we received brand new pipe wrenches. The rest of our replacement tools were rebuilt, retreaded, and overhauled equipment that probably had been buried in other stopes at one time or another and, after being salvaged, were cleaned off and repainted.

In all of the other mines I'd worked in, I had noticed that the "old hands" barely worked up a sweat, while I perspired like a pig while working alongside of them. I thought, "Man, these guys must really be in great shape, they're like well-conditioned athletes."

My theory didn't make sense, though, because many miners actually were overweight or didn't look like athletic types at all. After working awhile in my new stope, I finally understood why this was so. Up to then I'd only worked in the stopes from time to time, as a temporary replacement. I hadn't worked steadily at mining much, and found out that I didn't really know much about anything. Oh, I knew how to drill, blast, and such, but a lot of situations came up where a miner had to improvise to make things work. Old hands knew how to do these things. Skills like that were learned only after a considerable amount of time on the job.

I took solace in the thought, "At one time, these experienced miners all went through this crap too."

My partner wasn't any more adept than I was, so it took us a bit of time to pull our act together. I wondered why June put the two of us together into a stope like that with neither one of us being a lead man (good miner). It was sort of like the blind leading the blind. Then I discovered why.

The Crescent's stopes were very hard to mine. June had to rely on the Lower Bunker Hill's labor pool for replacement miners, but very few of those guys wanted to work in the Crescent because of the terrible heat and air blasts that came with the job. For the same money, or maybe even more, they could get work elsewhere. So that left poor old June recruiting new miners most of the time.

It didn't take my new partner long to decide that he hated the mine's intense heat in general and our new stope in particular. One day he said, "That's it, I've had enough." He quit and went back to Arizona or somewhere.

That left me without a partner. I had to get one or I wouldn't be able to work the new stope. I thought of my friend who'd put in the good word for me at the Crescent in the first place, but he'd quit too. Then I thought of my younger brother Gary. At the time he was working for Bunker Hill too, only over in the company's zinc plant. He'd never been underground before, but he'd been bugging me about getting him on at the mine.

That night I called him on the phone and said, "My partner quit today. I talked with the bosses and they told me that I could have you as a partner if you can pass the physical. I told them you were working for Bunker Hill already and they said, 'Good, there won't be any problem then.' "

Gary went down to the office next day and took his physical examination. And, after a day or two of safety training, there he was standing alongside of me on his first day in "our" stope. I spent the next few months teaching him the basics. It was only a beginning for him, but he was a fast learner and I figured that he could handle things pretty well.

As I said before, June was always looking for miners to work in stopes. At night, he must have dreamed of ways to lure unsuspecting bodies into the mine. One trick of his, I found out later, was to let an experienced hand work with a greenhorn until the new guy was ready to go on his own. Then he'd do some sweet talking and tell the new miner how gifted an employee he was, and get him to work in a different (and usually more difficult) stope.

Well, it worked. Gary was flattered by June's compliments and was assured that he'd make some "really good money" by moving into a new stope. So Gary said, "Yeah, that sounds great, I'll take it."

Stairway leading to Bunker Hill's hiring office. Silent now, but the steps still beckon to miners from the past.
Jerry Dolph

Gary's new place was on the 4,100 level, located 200 feet lower and directly beneath my stope. Needless to say, I wound up with another new guy to work with the next day. I had to laugh and thought, "Damn, I'm running a student stope."

Something good old June had neglected to tell Gary, though, was the reason his new stope had been sitting idle for a year. The place had been "blowing up," or air blasting, so badly the year before that the mine's decision-makers had no choice but to shut it down. The closure would, they hoped, give the ground a chance to settle down. June probably hadn't told Gary about this because he didn't want to scare him off.

Now, an air blast is like an earthquake and, well… you just haven't lived till you've ridden one of those suckers out. That's exactly what happened to Gary in his new stope.

After he'd been working in it for only about six weeks, Mr. Air Blast made a visit. At the time, Gary was working in his raise, which was a 10 x 12 feet timbered 210-feet-deep hole, 50 feet down beneath the floor of the main drift, or tunnel. Heavy timbers had been installed in the vertical shaft to keep the ground open. It laid over at quite an angle and looked sort of like a small 210-feet-high elevator shaft that had gotten tired and was about to lay down. Gary and his partner, Jim, were working in both directions following the vein of ore. It had a two compartment raise. The man-way, of course, was the compartment where the ladders were located. The other compartment was the timber-slide, used to lower materials down into the stope. Below their work floor, the timber-slide had been converted into a chute for the muck to be transferred on down to the next level.

Mr. Air Blast brought with him a tremendous, bone-jarring explosion that shook even my stope 250 feet away. I staggered from side to side with arms out-stretched trying to steady myself as I dodged falling rocks and heard timbers groan and snap. Finally, standing there in the violent dust storm that seemed to appear from nowhere, I had a sense of dread.

I thought, "Damn that was a bad one. Someone must have gotten it that time."

At the end of the day, as we rode out of the mine on the man-train, I talked to Bill who was Gary's motorman.

He said, "When it hit I just about crapped my pants. I happened to be standing in the drift looking down Gary's man-way. I couldn't think. As I watched, the sides blew in. And for an instant, I saw muck roaring down the raise, mixed with broken posts and timber. The sound was terrible, sorta like the roar of a crowd at a big football game, it was so loud. Then dust gushed up out of the hole so hard that it nearly knocked me down. Everything turned so dark that I couldn't see any light, even from my own cap lamp which was right over my nose."

Bill continued, "I sure's hell thought that Gary and his partner were both dead, especially since they were supposed to be working out in the raise today."

Thank God he was wrong. After we'd showered, I talked with Gary about what had happened. As we were putting on our street clothes, he told his story in detail.

"I was slushing from the raise when it hit [a slusher is an air-operated, wench-type machine that pulls a heavy scraper bucket to and fro, scraping muck from the stope out into the raise where it falls down a chute to the level below]. I had two floors [six-inch thick barriers of wood used as protection from debris falling down the raise] over my head," he began.

"My thermos full of coffee was sitting on the floor beside me, and I was looking at it because I was just about to stop and have a cup. About that time, all hell broke loose. It happened so fast that I couldn't believe it... I froze. Concussion from the blast knocked me right off the block of wood where I was sitting. Then came muck roaring down the raise above me sounding like a freight train.

"It blew out the first floor and almost instantly hit the second one right over my head. It broke out the side of that floor, too, and some of the muck ran through. My thermos took off down the raise somewhere, and I never saw it again.

"It all was happening so fast that I just had enough time to glance up and see the muck hit the floor over my head. The wooden floor sagged down from the sudden weight of the falling muck and I was instantly engulfed in darkness. The dust was so thick, it was as if someone had just switched of the lights. All I could think of was 'Oh, God.'

"At first, when the sound of the blast exploded in my ears, it was deafening and seemed like it would last forever. Finally I could hear myself screaming. The sound of my voice was drowned out by the overpowering, constant roar of the muck caving down onto the floor above me. Listening to all of that in total darkness and not knowing what was going to happen next gave me a fear that I'll never forget."

He stopped for a second, remembering, and continued, "I crouched there on the floor, covering my mouth and nose and tried to breath through my sweat soaked T-shirt for what seemed like a long time. Then the sound of falling rock finally died out and everything was quiet except for the muffled sound of more muck running, and the faint sound of splitting wood coming from somewhere. My chest ached from trying to breath, also because my heart was pounding so hard, I guess. I was scared to death that the floor above me would finally give way to the tons of heavy rock that was on it, and sweep me right on down the raise with it.

"Finally, the dust cleared a little and I could see faint light coming from my cap lamp. Damn, that little bit of light looked good. Until then, I thought my lamp had been broken by the falling rock. After a while, I could just barely make out a small hole between two broken posts out in the raise, so I eased myself between them and started softly calling for Jim, my partner. I was surprised to hear him suddenly yell back. He was somewhere down below me in the raise.

"We both agreed to get the hell out of there, and began making our way down 160 feet of broken and twisted man-way ladders. The further down the raise we got, though, the clearer the air was of dust, and after we'd climbed down about 30 or 40 feet, we could see pretty well.

"Before the blast, our raise was in really good shape. It was straight and none of the timber was broken. As we climbed down, though, we didn't see anything that wasn't broken, or mashed. Of course, I didn't spend much time looking around either."

Gary continued, "We finally made it down to the level and walked the 1,200 feet out to the shaft. When we got there, I called the hoistman on the shaft phone and told him that we were all right.

"The hoistman replied, 'That's great, I just this minute called June and told him that I just finished talking with your motorman, Bill, and he thought that you and your partner were probably both dead.' The Hoistman continued, 'Man that was a bad one, I heard it all the way out here at the shaft. Oh, June is on his way down... I'll call him back and tell him that you're okay.' Then he added jokingly, 'Say... calm that motorman of yours down, will ya? He was just babblin' over the phone. I could hardly understand him.'"

Coming to the end of his story, Gary said, "After I'd finished talking with the hoistman, Jim and I headed back toward the top of our stope. It took a while—it's about a quarter of a mile—and when we got there, we saw Bill."

As Gary was talking to me, Bill had walked up and was standing there listening too. At that point he interrupted Gary and said, "When I saw you coming I could have kissed you both. I don't see how anyone could have lived through that."

It was amazing that there wasn't a single casualty from the entire incident. The day after Gary's big air blast, June asked my partner and I to go on down and help repair the stope. Man, now that was spooky. The ground was still popping and snapping, and every few minutes we heard another little thumper. Often it's sort of hard to tell the difference between a littler thump and a full-blown boom. Little thumps keep a person a little disturbed and possibly even shocked a bit. When one of the big boomers hits, of course, stark fear paralyzes the central nervous system and the body's thinking system shuts down completely. Its probably not unlike the absolute terror that a cave man (who was one

Bunker Hill motorman pulling down the handle of a chute gate while filling muck cars.
Kellogg Public Library

of our earliest miners, I'll bet) must have felt as he looked up and saw that a cave bear was about to gobble him up.

There were six of us in the repair crew. Two of the fellas climbed through the man-way hole and down into the raise. They were standing there on some broken timbers about 10 feet down talking about something, when a damned "boomer" hit. The ground shook, rocks dribbled down from everywhere, and dust belched up out of the hole.

Something else belching up from the hole was the two miners. I didn't think it was possible for two men to pass through a 2-feet-square man-way hole at the same time, but they did, and about beat each other to death doing it. The four of us stood there at the top of the raise watching all the excitement, trying to ride out the boomer ourselves. After it was all over, it took a long time for all six of us to stop laughing.

I was giving Gary a ride to work on a Monday morning about a week later, and as we drove along, he said, "Our motorman, Bill, has always been raving to Jim and me about how great it would be to win one of those big contests, like the Reader's Digest Sweepstakes, or something. It almost seems like he has constant updates on who's won, how much they've won, and all that."

Gary went on, "Well, I saw Jim yesterday and he told me that on Saturday night he had been out getting his snoot full again, down at one of the Wallace bars. He called Bill and wrapped a handkerchief over the telephone's receiver to disguise his voice.

"He said, 'Mr. William Carlson?'

"Bill answered 'Yes, speaking.'

"'I'm Ron Jackson with the Reader's Digest Sweepstakes prize committee. I am very happy to inform you that you've won our third prize. We will be sending a courier to your home in the next few days with your $100,000 cashier's check.' "

Then Gary said, "Jim was laughing so hard he could barely finish telling his story."

Gary and I arrived at the mine about then and went into the dry. As I went through the daily ritual of changing out of my street clothes and into my diggers, I kept an eye out for Bill to see if any excitement would develop because of Jim's surreptitious phone call. But Bill didn't show up for work that Monday… nor Tuesday, or even Wednesday. Finally on Thursday, he came to work… the suspense was almost unbearable.

Bill didn't say anything to anyone about the phone call or why he'd been gone for three days. There was only the usual small talk on the way into the mine that morning. I waited for our drive home that night to talk to Gary again and see if Bill had "fallen for it." It probably sounds dumb, but that is just about all I could think of all day.

Gary and I were on our way home when I found out the scoop. Gary said, "Bill complained bitterly all day about, 'Those damned sweepstakes gimmicks.' He told Jim and me about winning the contest and how he'd called Reader's Digest on Wednesday night, after giving them three whole days to make good on their promise to send a courier to his house with the $100,000 cashier's check. Bill said, 'You know those damned fools claimed to have never even heard of me or Ron Jackson either as far as that goes. Well, they'll hear from me, I'm going down tonight right after work and get me an attorney, we'll see…' "

A few weeks went by and Gary told me, "Bill hasn't mentioned anything about winning the sweepstakes to us again, or anything about an attorney either."

I knew that Jim felt terrible about the trick he'd pulled on Bill, but I don't think he ever fessed up. I don't know if I would have or could have either. After all, everyone is entitled to his dreams.

Following the big air blast, the decision to let Gary's stope "settle down" some wasn't made entirely by the bosses; we all refused to work in it. After a month went by, however, June must have sweet talked a few of the guys and repair work began again (which eventually took about nine months, giving the hell hole a rebirth.)

My partner and I served on a repair crew only that one time. Our stope had fair ore and the bosses wanted to see it keep producing. My partner and I were trying to do a good job for old June, who kept saying, "Now make me look good to Biearny Johnson"—our mine manager. I was proud to be a gypo miner, and my partner and I busted a gut to get the job done.

One day we'd finished loading the drill holes of our round with dynamite. I lit the fuses and we climbed down to the bottom of our man-way, where we waited for the charges to go off. I don't know… it gave me a sense of satisfaction, I guess. Here I'd slaved like a dog in really oppressive heat all day—slushing, timbering, pounding with a sledgehammer, and drilling, and it was going to all be over in a few seconds. I suppose I just wanted to wait for the climax. Then, "Oh… there it goes," and I heard the almost musical, rhythmic "thuds" of dynamite exploding. Dust shook in the air as each "shot" went off. I listened to our stope play out the

Miner drilling with a jack-leg. Note that the machine has two hoses connected to it—a large air hose to power the machine, and a smaller water hose for keeping down the dust.
Kellogg Public Library

music of my day's work. My partner had to go to the can, so he walked on out to the shaft. I was alone. Suddenly the blasts stopped.

I thought, "Damn, there were two rounds. I only heard 10 blasts and 30 of the holes didn't go off. I must not have lit all the fuses."

This meant that when we came to work the next day, I wouldn't be able to haul out much muck because I only had one heading, or place, to drill. And, company policy only allowed blasting at the end of the shift. About all I'd be able to do the next day would be light the missed fuses just before quitting time.

I thought, "Boy… old June's really going to be mad."

I stood there, my mind racing and searching for answers, and hoping that by some chance I'd hear more concussions. "Maybe it's just slow," I thought.

Still I heard nothing. A sense of dread set in as I nervously paced back and forth at the bottom of the raise for at least five minutes. I was tormented by the knowledge that the hoistman was going to lower the skip down to the level at any minute. Everybody had to be out at the shaft when the skip came. The bosses got really ticked off when some jerk was late and everyone had to wait for him.

I couldn't stand it any longer. It seemed like I didn't have a mind of my own; I was sucked back up the 110 feet of man-way ladders like they were magnetized. I climbed quickly, thinking "Crap, is this right?… Should I really be doing this?"

After reaching the top of the man-way and entering the stope, I met a wall of dust and thick, acrid smoke so dense that my cap lamp's powerful beam only played across its face without penetrating. Rock was falling somewhere, and I could hear and feel the distant "thumping" of other miner's rounds going off. It was a prime time for air blasts, which sometimes are triggered by shock waves from exploding dynamite. Incidentally, the Federal Mine Enforcement Safety Administration (MESA) requires that, "After powder is set off, a period of thirty minutes is to be observed where that blasted area is off-limits." This was a safety precaution in case a primer exploded late.

I pressed on with powder smoke and dust burning my eyes. I began coughing violently and held my breath. When forced to breath again, I pulled my sweaty T-shirt up over my mouth and nose to get a gulp of filtered air. I could only see a few inches in front of my face and I had to feel my way along the wall. Finally I found the fuses of the unexploded round. Working as quickly as

possible, I traced down the connections, making the necessary repairs.

Smoke and fumes from Hercules dynamite causes terrific headaches, sometimes after only a few seconds of exposure. Dust, smoke, and those awful fumes were getting to me by then; I had to keep shaking my head to fight back dizziness. It only took a few minutes to do the repairs, but by then I had a major, major headache. My heart pounded hard too… but I persisted.

It was finally ready. "Thank God for that," I thought.

Certain of my connections this time, I fumbled for my cigarette lighter and shakily relit the fuse. Now to "get out of Dodge" before the round went off. The air was still just as foul and blinding, and I now had about 120, 18-inch-long sticks of dynamite ready to explode in a few minutes. To tell you the truth, I hadn't considered the problem of finding my way back to the man-way hole through the smoke and dust after I'd re-lit the round. If I had, I probably wouldn't have gone back up into the stope in the first place.

Fear passed through me as I blindly felt my way, hands outstretched, along 100 feet of wall. I stumbled awkwardly over piles of loose muck and bumped into unseen objects on the way. Then I thought, "God it seems like this is taking a long time. Way too long. How much is left, a minute… a half minute?"

Then I finally reached the man-way gate, which I'll have to admit, made me one happy camper. I stumbled down through the hole and was only halfway down the first ladder when the dynamite started its timed, methodical explosions again. I thought, "Why was it going off so soon?"

I can tell you that being that close to exploding powder really clears up the sinuses. Each concussion "squeezed" me tight. I thought, "Hell, I've never been hugged by dynamite like this before." I guess I must have been hallucinating.

It didn't take long to climb to the bottom of the man-way and collect my lunch gear, and I made a real hurried walk out to the shaft. Just as I got there, the last man was stepping onto the skip and everyone waved and hollered, "Come on Dolph, let's go." They said a bunch of other stuff too but we won't go into that.

It only took a few minutes for the rest of the round to go off. I still to this day don't know what happened to the seven minutes it should have taken for the fuses to burn their entire lengths before the holes began exploding. The only thing I can think of was that I must have passed out somewhere between the time that I lit

These Bunker Hill miners of the late 1890s used the predecessor to the modern jack-leg. Their drilling machine had no water hose connected to it to cut down the dust. Miners did not last long once they were dusted (silicosis). Note soft hats and candle in center miner's hand.
Kellogg Public Library

the fuse and when I reached the first ladder. Surely it shouldn't have taken nearly seven minutes for me to get away from the drill holes and out to the man-way.

Working conditions for miners have been, and probably always will be, terrible. An old tale illustrating this still circulates through the mining regions today; it dates from years ago when mules were used underground to haul rock and materials.

One morning, so the story goes, a boss was talking to one of his men. He said, "Jack, take your mule down into the bottom of the mine and work with him down there today, but be damned careful because it's really dangerous. There are a lot of holes down there that he could step in, and there's loose falling ground too. It hasn't been timbered up in there yet either. And, oh… it's hotter'n hell down there too so be sure to give him a lot of water. I don't want him to get sick."

Jack listened intently to the boss. Finally, after he'd finished talking, Jack said, "Well if it's as hot and dangerous as that down there, what about me?"

The boss frowned and immediately snapped back, "Look here, we can always hire another miner, but we have to buy these damned mules."

Danger is an inescapable part of a miner's job. Only he can decide whether or not the return he gets for doing it are worth the risks. There are a lot of things for him to consider, like what I call the four *mores*. The

irony of mining is that the *more* dangerous the job is then the pay usually is higher—and the m*ore* taxes have to be paid, the *more* toys there are to be bought, and the *more* payments to be made. It's sort of like a dog chasing his tail: he stays busy, but doesn't get very far at all.

Let me stop here and explain a little bit about such mining terms as "round," "cut," and "fill." Deep hardrock mines of the Silver Valley, and probably everywhere else for that matter, are "cut and fill" operations. In a day-to-day sequence, miners dynamite loose the ore with "rounds" and then "slush" or scrape out the rock down ore chutes. That is, working from the center of the stope where the timbered "raise" is located with its ore chutes, "man-way," and "timber-slide," partners drill and blast out in opposite directions from each other following the ore vein. Miners utilize the ladders in the raise's "man-way" to gain access to the stope, and the raise's "timber-slide" is used for hauling equipment up and down). When after several weeks a miner has mined to the end of his side of the stope, usually 100 to 150 feet, he has mined out the "cut," or as some might say, "Cut out the cut."

This leaves a stope looking sort of like a tunnel, and for safety and other reasons it has to be filled in again. Sometimes the "fill" is waste rock, but sand is more commonly used. Sand is left over from the "concentration" (or processing) of the ore into metals in aboveground "smelters" (or mills), which may or may not be located close to the mine. Sand is hauled back to the mine portal and pumped through a pipeline back down into the mine and to the stope. One reason this is done is because the old, filled-in stope provides a new floor, usually about 8 feet higher up, for the partners to work on as they continue mining the vein in a new cut. The partners also have built their center "raise" up another 8 feet as well. Another reason stopes are refilled is because "rock bursts" (air blasts) and "air-slack" (ground loosened up from just sitting there exposed to the air) can cause empty stopes to collapse. The severity of air blast damage, in general, would be greater if the mined-out stopes weren't filled in.

The Crescent Mine wasn't endowed with really neat stuff like sand-fill (or breathable air for that matter!). It used the old method of "gob," or waste, fill. After miners blasted their rounds, the motorman decided if the muck was waste rock or ore. If it turned out to be waste, then the motorman dumped it into a waste pocket out at the shaft. Later, as needed, the waste was hauled from the bottom of the pocket, 200 feet further down in the mine on the level below, and taken to stopes located there and dumped in as fill. I've seen a lot of pipe wrenches, chunks of wood, and different kinds of junk in my fill before. I even got a hard hat once but never found out where it came from.

Standing on new fill which now becomes the floor of his new cut, a miner again drills and blasts, usually following the vein in a horizontal cut. Holes for the rounds are drilled in the rock with a jack-leg. These holes must be drilled in a pattern that will break up the rock when the high explosives are ignited. Having finished drilling the holes, a miner puts away all hoses and other equipment. He then loads dynamite and primers into the holes and lights the fuses. It is now the end of the shift, and the miners are on their way out of the stopes, down their raises, and onto the levels to get on skips to the surface. The next day, the high-grade ore is slushed out and then drilling resumes.

A miner only needs to break the ground just wide enough to work in, or, on the other hand, he can mine the full width of a vein plus about a foot on either side, which is the allowable width. The rules on allowable width of a round in miners' contracts are variable and determined by the mine management as work proceeds. It was sort of like playing poker with someone who could change the rules to suit the cards he was holding. If he saw that your cards weren't very good, however,

he'd increase your chances of winning so you would stay in the game.

After blasting the ore and slushing out the pile of muck, a miner puts rock bolts and metal mats in the back and walls for safety's sake. Rock bolts are 6-feet-long (or 8-feet-long if needed) iron rods, about as thick as a man's thumb, that are installed for ground support. It really gives a miner a sense of security to have a bolt securely in place about every two feet or so overhead and in the walls wherever needed.

So there I was at the Crescent, set up with a two-week contract (payments were set at 10 work-day intervals) and doing fine. I was cycling my round—i.e., a round slushed out and a round drilled in and blasted—every shift. Things were shaping up so I would be getting huge contract checks (in addition to the basic guaranteed day's pay that we all earned every week). That is "if" I was able to blast every shift, have no air-blast damage, and if I lost no footage, or advance, for one reason or another.

Now it was the turn of that sucker in the paymaster's office. I'm sure he saw from old June's daily reports that I was soon going to be a wealthy man. He undoubtedly called June into his office and said, "Do something." Next thing I knew, June insisted that I bolt up a wall that till then had been all right, or he'd put a crew in on the opposite shift for a couple of days to "eat up my contract" and slow down my progress.

I say that because sometimes it was really hard for a miner to go into a different stope and make an efficient series of rounds. The tools were different, the ground was different, and chances were that the miner himself was a little different—for instance, a miner like Tom, who was the oldest man in the Crescent at the time. Well, Tom was known to drink a few from time to time. One day, when working in a stope, the end blew off the "bull-hose," or large air hose. The hose immediately whipped violently around, blasting up dust and beating against the walls. Bull-hoses are colored with bright spiral stripes, like a barber pole, so they can easily be seen. Old Tom saw it all right and came flying down his man-way ladder scared to death yelling, "There's a giant snake up in there."

My partner and I had seen our chance, got greedy, and just worked our rears off trying to make more money, but we wound up fighting the company and the fella in the paymaster's office even more. Everyone knows that "the pen is mightier than the sword," right? Or at least his sure was. The mine would only pay just so much and was determined to stick to their guidelines. Oh, they paid the big check to my partner and me this time all right, but then arranged it so that during the next contract period we'd have to do all of the extra work again for less money.

I knew one crew at the Crescent that worked only until they got so much done and then they just sat down. The way they explained it to me was, "If the mine is willing to pay you a certain amount of money and you fight with them trying to get more, you're either going to have trouble with the relationship between you and them, or you'll see your contract cut so that you'll have to take more chances and work harder to make the same money. It's like fighting with an ocean tide, you can struggle against the current for just so long, but eventually it's going to have its way."

Kellogg, Idaho, is an old mining town dating from 1893 or whatever and full of old bars. One day when I was in the Rio Club, I met this fella and we got to talking. There was a gunnysack laying underneath his bar stool, so I asked him, "What's in the sack?"

He replied, "Oh, it's my diggers. I'm one of those poor Butte miners. The rich ones came away with Budweiser boxes." This was in 1981 just after Butte's Anaconda Mining Company had shut down their operation and laid off thousands of miners. He was out looking for work.

I suppose there have been miners who were able to invest their money wisely and became "well off," although I personally don't know of any. Of course, I only worked the mines for 16 years all told. How does the old saying go? "You make what you spend, and spend what you make."

I once heard about a miner named Bill who took the "good stuff"—high grade ore—home with him. Just a little each day, in his lunch box. It wasn't much at a time, but over the years he'd wound up with an enormous pile of "potential wealth" out behind his woodshed.

As the story goes, Bill took his coffee cup in hand and would stand for hours, looking at his hidden wealth. He dreamed of far-off places and the good things he would soon have. After all, he did need a new house. He hadn't been able to move out of the one he'd been in for the last 30 years because of his "treasure out behind the woodshed."

Then the day of his well-deserved, and planned for, retirement finally arrived. He and his wife Susan had been making arrangements to move and sell their pile of high-grade ore to Cominco, a Canadian smelter in Trail, B.C., and the only one on the West Coast. Finally the results of their many years of planning came together. They'd hired a local dirt contractor to load up and ship their ore to the smelter, and it took a huge front-end loader and five very large dump trucks to move the pile.

Once the job was done and as the last truck was pulling out, the contractor approached Bill and Susan. Complaining bitterly, he said, "This stuff is so heavy that I couldn't fill the trucks full. Hell, if I had, I'd a blown out all of their tires." Bill and Susan choked back their happiness realizing that the price of metal was up and "the heavier the better."

Then the still-moaning contractor gave them his bill for $2,500 and said angrily, "I'm losing money on this one. Next time I'm really going to check out the loads before I make a deal."

Many weeks went by and finally an envelope from the Canadian smelter arrived. Bill saw the brown business envelope first and pulled it gently from their old tin mailbox that hung on the front porch. He yelled at Susan and they both went into the kitchen and sat down at the table. For as far back as either one of them could remember, whenever anything really important happened they always talked about it over the kitchen table. They both knew that their pile of ore must have been worth a fortune and, after sitting there for a few minutes, staring at each other and the envelope, Bill finally took it in hand and very carefully tore it open.

There was a green check inside. Bill wasn't able to see the amount yet, but he could see the lettering typed neatly in its upper left-hand corner: Cominco Smelting and Refining, Trail, B.C. He looked up at Susan again and slowly said, "This is it." All the while thinking of the hundreds of times he'd come home and gone out behind the woodshed in the summers and winters… slowly he pulled the check from its envelope. He saw the numbers and began reading them aloud, "One million, three hundred thirty thousand and four dollars."

Bill looked up in astonishment at the beautiful little lady sitting across the table who'd been with him for all these many years. They both suddenly cheered wildly. Jumping up from their chairs, they ran into each other's arms, sometimes laughing, sometimes crying. Finally, with tears streaming down his face, Bill reached down and picked up the check from the table to look at it again.

A 1956 view of the Consolidated Mining and Smelting Company of Canada, Ltd., located about 100 miles north of Spokane at Trail, British Columbia. The plant included a lead smelter, zinc plant, refineries, and sulfuric acid plants. Cominco also operated a fertilizer plant on this site.

Suddenly he fell silent, and slumped down into his chair. Bewildered, Susan asked, "What's wrong?" Thinking, "What could possibly be wrong enough to get such a reaction from my new millionaire?" He couldn't talk, and with trembling fingers, he handed the check to her. She took it, and saw the name Cominco Smelting and Refining, just like he'd said. Then she read on to see those wonderful numbers, "$1,330,004."

Bewildered, Susan glanced back up at Bill. He saw her confusion and said, "Look at who it's made out to." She glanced quickly back again at the check and saw her husband's name, and the name of the mining company from which he'd retired. Susan stood there, stunned and finally said, "What'll we do?"

Bill got up from his chair and called the Cominco Smelting and Refining Company. "Why is my check made out to me *and* the mine? I sold you the ore, they didn't."

The voice on the other end of the line immediately replied, "Wait just a minute here... We refine that mine's ore, and our assay department says that the ore you sold to us belongs to them. How did you wind up with it? I thought there was something funny going on here... there's no way that we're going to pay you, alone, for something that belongs to them."

The voice continued, "All you have to do, though, is get them to endorse the check and everything will be all right, won't it?" Bill slowly hung up the telephone receiver, knowing that if he asked the mine to endorse the check, they would know that he had stolen their "good stuff."

That's all of the story I'd heard. I can only assume that Bill tried some other way to get the check cashed, but, knowing mine paymasters, I doubt that he had any luck.

We miners stuck together in a brotherhood requiring the purchase of big, shiny toys, the best of which were brand new, 4-wheel-drive, pickup trucks. Our attitude was "If you want it, then you'd better get it quick, because you might not be around to enjoy it tomorrow."

It was a big game between us and the mining companies, played like this. First, we'd make good money and buy the good things in life, like new campers, boats, etc. Then it was the companies' turn; our union contract would expire, so we'd strike for whatever seemed appropriate at the time. After a few months, finance companies would repossess a lot of our toys, we'd be rested up, and we were ready to go back to work again. In the meantime the company had taken care of problems in their shafts or whatever that probably would have forced them to shut down operations for awhile anyhow. Of course, it was a lot cheaper for them to have us walk off voluntarily than to pay for our unemployment benefits after laying us off. Then, after the company's "dead work" was caught up, the mine operators were ready to open again. They made us an offer, we accepted, and it was back to work.

A bit of time would pass. The well-used look in the parking lot soon was replaced by the shine of new paint and the smell of new upholstery again. The company knew we would work hard to pay for the things we wanted. They must have been glad to see us, one by one, replacing the cars and trucks repossessed by finance companies with new vehicles. After our resting period ended, I'll bet the wives were glad to see us go back to work too, at least my wife Jo Ann sure was … that way she got her 1949 Ford station wagon back.

The need to win the game drives a contract miner to the edge of his endurance and he keeps coming back for more. What else could entice someone to tempt death and, seeing that he'd survived, go back to work again the next day? This probably sounds stupid, but, I felt sorta like a Gladiator as I "suited up" in my diggers, getting ready to do battle deep in the bowels of the earth— a fight to the end.

I heard one time that a Butte miner received bad news from his doctor; he had incurable cancer and only

a few months to live. As he was drilling out his last round one day, he probably was thinking about the future of his many children. While loading the round, he undoubtedly remembered that his mine's insurance paid double if he were to die underground. Considering he only had a few short months to live regardless, he lit his round and sat down under the face to meet his maker. Of course, no one can know for sure what the poor guy was thinking, but it seems logical considering what happened. I'm glad I didn't have to slush out his round for him.

The Crescent's oppressive heat was caused by a combination of poor ventilation and high rock temperature, and I routinely had to take seven or more salt pills a day. I swallowed three before going underground. Then, after a couple of hours, I'd usually begin to get sick and took two more. Then, every couple of hours, I'd need another "fix." I'd never seen such a pathetic crew at the end of the work day. We had to hold each other up on the way out of the shaft. While on our way up one day, my partner got a cramp in his gut and doubled up. I gave him a couple of salt pills to chew and after a few minutes his pain eased up.

I hated the "back of the thigh" cramps with a passion. Talk about hurting! The muscle felt like a big knot. I sometimes got them at night while I was sleeping. Jo Ann must have just about had a stroke, too, when I'd suddenly sit up in bed in the darkness, grab the back of my leg, and howl in pain. Eventually she got use to it and without saying a word she'd get up, rush to the kitchen, and return with a big glass of water and a salt-shaker. After downing about half a saltshaker and a gallon of water, the pain finally went away. I'd get up a few hours later and go back to work. She worried that I had too much salt in my system—bad for the old ticker and all, you know. So, I went to the doctor for a checkup. His report was that my salt level was right on track.

In the Crescent we played "duck" as the man-train was on its way out of the mine. We were, of course, hot and exhausted from the day's work. Some of the guys who still had ice water left over poured it into plastic bread bags. After tying off the ends, we hurled our wet "missiles" at each other. Once in a while, someone's hat would get knocked off and go flying. The motor would stop, and the miner who'd lost his hat would retrieve the "skid lid," usually out of the piss ditch, then we continued on. I can tell you that when one of those bread sacks hit against my super-heated face, now that was a thrill for sure. We were already soaking wet, so the extra water didn't make much difference.

In wintertime the sudden difference in temperature as the man-train exited the mine could be awesome, sometimes maybe a drop of 100 degrees or so after moving just a few feet. The last 50 feet of the drift, just inside the mine's portal, usually remained shrouded in fog, and we'd brace ourselves to meet the winter atmosphere. When we came out of the tunnel, frigid air blasted our hot bodies, shriveling us up inside our wet rubber slickers. We then "speeded" across the frozen ground, heading toward the dry. As we ran I'd usually hear someone's voice—muffled by the flap of a warm coat—say, "Man that's the fastest I've seen you move all day." If a stranger happened to be watching us when we came out of the mine he probably would have noted, "Man, look at that crew move, they must be real money makers." All I can reply to that is, "yeah… right."

We all knew exactly what to do, and that was to quickly get out of those frozen, wet, slimy diggers. The Crescent's "dry" pretty much looked like all the others in the Valley. It was a large, wonderfully heated room with a high ceiling. Inside were rows of benches; and, about six feet or so off the floor, shelves were suspended on chains and pulleys hanging from the ceiling. When a chain was loosened, a basket dropped down about chin high. The idea was to strip off your rags, which sometimes were all that was left of your diggers, and shower as soon as possible so you could go home. We didn't run in the dry, though; it was too dangerous.

We had this one real slob working there who chewed tobacco. After he got a big cheek full of "yuck" he'd spit it out onto the floor, the walls… in fact, he spit on just about everything, even the bowl of the drinking fountain. Everybody begged him to stop, even the bosses. One time I saw the jackass spit on the wall of the skip, then lean up against it and keep right on talking, and chewing his cud.

June and the other bosses finally had some signs made up reading, "Don't spit on the floor," "Don't spit in the water fountain," and so on. They waited… the first time he spit on one of the signs telling him not to, they fired him. He filed a grievance with the United Steel Workers Union, but they hated him just as much as the company—we all did—so I guess he went someplace else and spit on them after that.

I smoked cigarettes at that time in my life and was able to do so while working in really wet conditions. I've since quit, thank God. Taking a shower and smoking a cigarette at the same time was something that I and the other smokers didn't give a second thought about. Pranks occurred, of course; one time after getting the soap out of my eyes, I looked up and saw the end of a fire hose sticking through the shower room door. There was shouting and running, and lots of empty space in the shower for the next batch of guys.

Another time, while I was dressing and talking to my partner Tom, who was drying off, the outside door suddenly opened and in walked two very drunk young ladies, appearing to be in their 20s. One of them was Tom's next door neighbor and she promptly sat down in his lap. I know this embarrassed the hell right out of him. He had nothing on at all except an astonished look. One of the fellas there that night had just hired out and was taking his first shower with us. It was his last; he quit the next day. I guess he thought we were all nuts. Sometimes I would have agreed with him too, but we needed an outlet from the severe conditions under which we worked.

All miners, of course, have to deal with the hostile environment underground in one way or another. One time I talked to one of the guys at the Crescent, who said, "I hired out once at the Lucky Friday and the foreman took me around, showing me the layout of the mine. We went into a stope to watch the miners drilling out their rounds and I saw one of those poor bastards standing in water clear up to his butt. I figured that he could get some other monkey to perform for him because I sure's hell wasn't going to."

The old, mined-out workings under the Kellogg area's new Silver Mountain Ski Bowl are truly enormous, stretching miles up and down the Valley. As I mentioned in an earlier chapter, the Crescent Mine, situated on the western edge of Big Creek, is connected to the Lower Bunker Hill Mine which is under Kellogg, located about four miles away. The two mines meet on the Crescent's 3,400 feet level where Bunker's eastward running "YU Drift" comes in. I once heard on KWAL, the local radio station, that since the late nineteenth century Bunker Hill miners had cut 10,000 miles of tunnels underneath Silver Mountain. Nearly all of this, of course, has been filled back in with sand or waste rock.

The mountain overlooking Kellogg was, for many years, named "Jackass Peak," in memory of Noah Kellogg's jackass. Noah is credited with the discovery of the Silver Valley mining district. The story I heard is that, in an effort to escape from him, his wayward jackass stumbled and kicked loose some silver ore, uncovering the richest silver mining district in the world. The name "Jackass Peak" was changed in recent times because, as I was told, "Tourists wouldn't understand."

The Bunker Hill complex includes the Shay Drift on its 23 level, which has been driven underneath Smelterville and extends all the way west to the old, abandoned and waterlogged Page Mine near Pinehurst, a distance of nearly five miles. When I first heard that, I had visions of some miner accidentally driving a stope up into the bottom of the Page, which is filled with groundwater. When mines are abandoned and their pumps are closed down, they naturally fill up with groundwater, and that's actually a good thing. By having the water in them, the timbers supporting the shafts, drifts, and stopes are protected a lot against the air, which causes dry rot. Of course, if someone accidentally mined up into an abandoned mine containing millions of gallons of water, he'd die instantly. Even though it was a long ways away, my stope in the Crescent was lower than the YU Drift by many hundreds of feet.

Between the Crescent and Sunshine mines, there was an area only about the length of a football field that wasn't "holed through." I asked June once why that was, and he said, "We wouldn't want those guys over here stealing our stuff now would we?"

I could hear and feel vibrations from the Sunshine guy's rounds going off sometimes, and I wondered about the logic of June's answer for a long time afterward. Because, as I figured, if the drift was "holed through" between the two mines, then the 'Shine would have had another potential escape route. That is to say, when the Sunshine Mine's tragic fire occurred in 1972, the fellas trapped in the blaze might have had an escape route they could have used. The other side of the coin, I suppose, is that maybe the ventilation somehow would've been screwed up and everybody who happened to be underground that day in three mines, all the way from Big Creek to Page, could have died. Of course, there probably were unscrupulous people over there wanting to come over and steal the Crescent's rusty old garbage that passed as tools.

I experienced the effects of an underground fire one time in the Crescent while we were riding down in the skip at the beginning of a shift. Old June happened to be riding down with us that day. Some of the fellas who didn't smoke cigarettes began smelling smoke, and a few seconds later we all smelled it. The stupid thought that immediately passed through my mind was of a pig roast-

Split timbering is evidence of a visit by Mr. Air Blast to the Galena Mine's 2874 raise. This view is looking down the raise's ladder. ASARCO Inc.

ing over a fire. There was no way at all to communicate to the hoistman about what was happening and that we wanted to come back up. Hell, he could have been up there sleeping in the fresh air for all we knew.

We continued dropping like a stone down the shaft right into... what? When we finally reached 3,400, June reached out and grabbed the bell cord. He signaled for the hoistman to take us right back up to the top station again. June had to do it twice; I guess the hoistman didn't understand why. By then thick black smoke permeated the air and the beams of our cap lamps cut through it like knives.

The skip started up the shaft while I thought hard about the Sunshine fire of the year before. Then something happened that I thought was really dumb. The fella standing right behind me sort of put his chin on my shoulder and quietly said, "Gotta smoke?" Everybody heard him and we all roared with laughter as we sailed back up the shaft through clouds of smoke.

By the time we reached the top of the shaft, coughing was about the only thing that I heard. No laughter … just coughs and an occasional curse, some coming from me. We rushed over, climbing back onto the man-train and the hoistman got on too. We high-tailed it down the drift, headed toward that small speck of daylight that we knew was there, but couldn't yet see, about a mile away.

Our train finally rushed out into the bright sunshine, chased by choking clouds of black smoke. The mine manager and the rest of the top crew were all standing there near the portal, staring in disbelief as smoke rose like a cloud into the sky as we came shooting out through it. We were sent home with four hours show-up pay. Later that day, I heard on the radio that one of Bunker Hill's big rubber-tired muckers had caught on fire and burned up completely. It was on 21 level in the main Bunker Hill Mine, about four miles or so from us.

The communication gap between a moving skip and the hoistman is an ongoing concern. A few of the mines, such as the Lucky Friday, and the Homestake, of Lead, South Dakota, worked hard to try and eliminate that "dead spot" in communications. The Lucky Friday put high-powered walkie-talkies in their skips for just such emergencies, and the Homestake installed an intercom set-up.

Like I was saying, we got the exhaust air from Bunker Hill. If anybody even belched over there, the Crescent sucked it up like it was made of gold. Once a federal safety inspector from the Bureau of Mines came through our stope. He wasn't looking for safety violations, but was only interested in measuring the dust in the stope's air. He brought little dust particle counters with him that my partner and I had to wear as we worked that day.

I'll have to admit, when I turned in that neat, little clicking machine at the end of the day, I felt sort of sad. It was like having a little living thing hanging on my chest keeping me company as I worked. We routinely kept the place wetted down with water as much as possible, and passed his check okay. Oh, by the way, my partner took his little machine apart and stuffed it full of fine muck. When he turned it in that night it wasn't clicking anymore.

After the federal guy made a few more tests in the back end of our place and was on his way out, he turned

to me and with an incredulous look on his face said, "You actually work in this?"

I just gave him one of my best greasy smiles and replied, "Yeah, great isn't it?" He shook his head and climbed on down the broken ladder in my man-way. For some reason or other, it seems as if visitors frequently asked me if I "actually worked" in my pretty little stope.

The next time I mined across the stope (one floor higher up), I timbered it all the way across. I had a replacement partner do something here, though, that was really raw, or at least I sure thought it was at the time. My partner dumped shift one day and I was given a replacement. About midway through the day, the new fella complained about needing to go "potty."

Now my stope was around 150 feet above track level. So for him to go find the little sawdust filled bucket—which had its own house standing out near the shaft—he would've had to climb down our man-way that far and walk about 1,200 feet out to the station, then he would have had to retrace the same route back. One of the important things to do before going down in a mine for a shift was to appease mother nature's calling. I didn't tell him so, but, in emergencies like his, a lot of fellas "went" in empty dynamite bags. Then they sealed them off and carried them out of the stope at the end of the shift.

I had to go to the end of the stope and repair my "slusher's" cable. Coming back a few minutes later I was really surprised to still see him there. I can only guess he must have done it in my stope that day because he only mentioned his need once.

Incidentally a "slusher" is an air or electrically operated machine. It looks a lot like a tugger—the small, single-drum cable hoist used in the raise—but a slusher has two cable drums on it. They are geared to rotate in opposite directions, with one handle for reeling the scraper bucket in, and the other to let it back out again.

The cable for the slusher's let-out drum was called the "haul back" cable. This cable was strung out into the "cut" to a block, or pulley, hooked to the face of the rock. The "pull in" cable, on the other hand, was strung from its drum on the slusher directly to the front of the scraper bucket. When I reefed back on the "pull-in" handle, the slusher's 7 horsepower air motor pulled the scraper bucket in, bringing with it the muck that I was scraping out. And, of course, if I pulled on the "haul-back" handle, the scraper bucket was hauled back to the face again for another scoop. In normal operation, a miner uses the slusher to pull ore from the stope's face, where it has been broken loose by dynamite, back to an ore chute located right in front of the miner in the raise.

Well, about two weeks after I'd had the one-day replacement, I was doing my final "cleaning out" with the slusher, and we were getting ready to refill the stope with waste rock. Incidentally, I should probably stop here and point out again that all of the other mines in the Silver Valley used sand to refill mined-out areas. The Crescent didn't have sand-fill; as I said before, mining in the Crescent was sort of like working back in the old days.

After I'd been cleaning out for quite a while, I started smelling something really foul. My regular partner was helping me that day and, as I was slushing, he stood just behind me and off to the side. As the odor became stronger I glanced over, giving him the evil eye and thinking the worst. He must have smelled it too because he held up his hands and, with an apologetic look, denied any slippage.

Then it hit me. Man look out… you're coming up on some poo-poo. I quit cleaning out that section of the stope, and left a 4-feet-deep pile of high-grade ore running about 500 ounces of silver to the ton. It must have been worth a jillion bucks or so, at least it sure looked like it. Sort of an expensive cover for what was left of my one-day replacement. But the way I figured, stopping that awful smell was worth every ounce of silver in that pile to me.

To refill the mined-out floor, we dumped waste rock from "belly dump" muck cars into a "bean hole" (a 4-feet-across shaft at the end of the stope that went all the way up to, and underneath, the center of the little railroad tracks on the level above). I can't for the life of me figure out how the name "bean hole" got into the mines, but I'm sure there must be a correlation with something there somewhere.

The way it worked, once the motorman parked his train of waste rock on top of the bean hole, he dumped the load out of the bottom of the muck cars and into the bean hole. I was sitting behind my slusher in the stope, and could hear the vibrations and see the dust from rock falling down through the hole and hitting the bottom. Then I cranked up the slusher and, pulling on the haul-back handle, the scraper bucket then pulled away from me towards the fresh pile of muck. Once the bucket hit the back end—I could tell by the sudden resistance on the cable—I let loose of the handle and "pulled in" with the other handle. That brought the scraper bucket and its load of waste rock out toward me.

After lots of pulling on handles and many cars full of waste rock, the stope finally was filled.

One major problem with this system was the fact that the slusher cable's block hung right in the bottom of the bean hole itself. Thus, when the motorman dumped his load, the muck fell directly onto the block. If the cable broke, it had to be repaired, fed back through the block, and hooked back up to the scraper bucket again. I had to repair the cable quite a bit, but this one time in particular was a real challenge. The stope was nearly full of waste rock by then and it was near the end of the shift. We were about to stop filling for the day. Well, sure enough, the cable broke again and the motorman had just gone out to the shaft with his train to get another load.

Now I just couldn't let him dump more muck down the bean hole onto the empty, dangling block and bury it. I knew that if he did that, then I'd have to crawl back in there on my belly and dig an entire train load of rock out by hand, and there'd be no place to put all of the muck since the stope already was nearly full. There was about 3 feet of room between the fill and the back, or ceiling, to work in.

Because of snags in the cable, I had trouble pulling it out from the slusher's drum and it took longer than I had figured. After I'd freed up the cable and was finally ready, I let out lots of slack and crawled back toward the end of the stope, dragging the end of the repaired cable behind me. I was trying to feed the cable back in through the block again before the motorman came back with another three car loads of rock to dump.

Working with old cable like that (another part of the Crescent's Old West way of mining) was really painful at times. The broken and frayed ends of the cable stuck out like the barbs of a porcupine. In all the excitement of trying to hurry, I accidentally snagged myself twice in the leg and once in the arm, giving me several deep, painful punctures.

There wasn't any way to signal the motorman that I was working down in the bottom of the bean hole either. Unless, of course, I'd climbed all the way up the man-way to the level above and stopped him altogether, and that would have taken time. The way I figured it was that contract miners just didn't quit; they just faced whatever it was that was wrong and made it work. I was still feverishly trying to finish before he returned, when I heard the rumble of the train coming. I thought I'd be through before he dumped, but I was wrong. I heard the squeak of the iron gate at the bottom of the muck car swing open, then followed the "swoosh" of muck falling. The muck we used was really fine, about as large as pea gravel. Finally finished, I retreated as fast as I could, trying to get clear before the muck hit the bottom of the damned bean hole. I didn't make it.

About then my partner just happened to walk back to my end, probably because it was near the end of the shift. His work place, of course, was on the opposite end of our stope and on the other side of the raise—nearly 150 feet away. This was the first time he'd been back on my end since lunch. He didn't see me when he crouched down, looking back toward the bean hole to see how I was doing. He then decided to crawl back in. When he got to where I was, all he saw of me was my boots sticking out of the muck pile. I was buried completely, except for the bottoms of the boots. I guess he didn't want to have to look for another partner because he grabbed my heels and pulled me, struggling for air, out of the fine muck. Except for a few cuts and bruises, I was no worse for wear. A friend in need is a friend indeed, right? I didn't tell June about that one either because I didn't want to look stupid.

We did our final clean-out by "hand" with what is known as a "Fin hoe." According to the story I heard, this tool's name originated many years ago in Butte. Butte had a lot of immigrant workers in its early days, and one of them, a miner from Finland, bent the end of his shovel over so that he could "drag" the muck out, instead of digging it out with the shovel's pointed end. As it turned out, his method of moving muck was easier so the name stuck. The Fin hoe has been modified many times since and the modern one looks like a long, triangularly pointed hoe.

A reason I mentioned the Finlander is that the Silver Valley, like every other mining camp, has seen many, many thousands of miners come and go. They have left behind colorful names that have endured these many years. For example, the poor guy who has to transport the honey (poo-poo) buckets is called the "shit nipper," unfortunately. I somehow can't believe that our inventor of the Fin hoe could in any way be responsible for that title. I was "that" kind of a nipper for a while once. Before I began working exclusively as a miner, I had to dump the honey buckets too. So I guess I had that less than distinguished title for a while myself.

Once in a while, when one of the other guys saw me "dumping the goodies," he'd say something like, "Man that's awful. Doesn't that bother you at all?" We nip-

A view of the drift at the bottom of 2874 raise. The rock burst squeezed the timber in towards the center, broke the overhead cap, and raised the rails on the floor up two feet.
ASARCO Inc.

pers really didn't have any choice in the matter; it was either do it or else. I figured out a really great comeback. Whenever someone would ask "How can you do it?", I'd answer, "Baby needs a new pair of shoes," and they'd leave me alone.

The behavior of men in the Crescent wasn't much different than in any other mine in the Valley in many respects. When it came time for men to get on the skip at the end of the shift, for example, there were those who "held back." They acted like they didn't know what was happening, but they were waiting till the skip was almost full. Then they'd rush forward and try to push each other out of the way so they could get on last. Their goal, of course, was to load up last so they could get off first. It was kind of a macho thing to do.

Speaking of macho guys, I want to tell you about Pete. He was one of the Crescent's old-timers, a really hard-nosed old guy. If you didn't do it his way, then you were doing it wrong. He would really get under your skin. I sort of liked his rough outlook on life, though, and he seemed to have a firm grip on things. Pete, in his early 60s, was the only miner I've ever known who was in such good shape at that age.

It must have been whiskey that kept him preserved so well. He told me once, "Ha… these kids really brag about sharing a bottle of whiskey and missing work. They carry on like they're real men. Hell, I buy a case of whiskey at a time and stay gone till it is too."

One day Pete was yelling at some of the younger fellas who were working down on the drift next to the tracks. He was telling them how they were all "know-nothing greenhorns," and how they should've never hired out at the mine. He shouted loudly too, that they should have gone to work digging a ditch somewhere instead, because that's probably all they knew how to do anyhow. Old Pete was a feisty old fella and was just giving 'em hell. That was his way.

As he was hollering, bless his heart, he stepped up onto the back coupling of a muck car in an effort to hitch a ride out to the station. We all did this from time to time. The train started moving forward, but Pete was highly distracted, to say the least, and didn't notice. About that time, he finished yelling at the guys and turned around to face forward in the direction the train was moving. By then the train passed under a chute lip (the bottom of a chute hanging down low over the tracks). Sure enough, old Pete got peeled right off the back of that muck car slicker than anything—got knocked cold he did. You should have heard the cheer rising up from the guys he'd been hollering at too.

Oh, he was all right. Pete was much too macho to show his hurt and probably didn't want to mess up his image anyhow. We all gathered around to see if we could help out. When he came to, he got up and without saying a word brushed himself off, pushed his way through us, and staggered off down the drift toward the station.

As I mentioned before, a tugger is an air operated wench-type machine, more or less round, about three feet long and two feet high, with a single-cable drum. A tugger's cable, which is much smaller than slusher cable, runs from its drum up into a timber-slide. At the top of the timber-slide, the cable goes through a block and runs back down to the "skip" (can), to which it is connected. Miners move timber, powder, and other materials up and down the raise in this small skip, which is 5 feet tall, 18 inches deep, and 30 inches wide.

As the tugger's throttle handle is pulled back, it reels in the cable which in turn raises the skip up the tim-

ber-slide. And when the handle is pushed forward, then the skip comes back down the raise again, gravity fed. Once, I was running the tugger handle with my right hand and trying to force the cable to reel up neatly onto the drum with my left. I had a firm grip on the cable, a few inches above the drum. The tugger's motor suddenly jerked backwards and sucked my hand down in between the cable and the drum. The fella who was with me at the time saw what I'd done, turned white and looked away, as if noting, "Man you lost your fingers."

Fortunately, I was able to stop the tugger before the cable did tear off my fingers. Then I very slowly reversed the tugger's motor and my hand came out alright. That little episode still sends chills up my back—"Damn, that was close." I missed having a stump of a hand by only a fraction of a second.

A bell cord in our stope ran through and up to the top of our man-way. We used the usual signals when telling the nipper to stop, raise, and lower the skip: one to stop, two to lower, and three to raise. If we wanted him to do it quickly we would give him the signals faster (it was the same procedure used in all the shafts in all of the mines).

First thing in the morning, when our nipper came back to check and see if we needed anything, he started the tugger and raised our lunch buckets up to us. We usually put them in the skip before we went up the man-way, so we didn't have to carry them as we climbed. I should mention that we had "raised metal" (heavy mesh) type gates on top of our man-way and timber-slide for our own safety. They were kept closed, unless we needed the access, because it was a long way down. We had two slushers in our stope, as did most work places. A bad thing about them was their brake-bands. On each drum, there was a set of bands that looked like brake shoes on an automobile only much bigger. I heard they were made out of asbestos, which as we all know can be sort of bad for one's health, to put it mildly. I think that they were changed from asbestos to some kind of synthetic material, but I just don't know when the change was made, or even if indeed it was, or what they're made out of now. I sure hope it was before 1972 when I first hired out.

After slushing for a while, the brake bands heated up because of friction against the slusher's drums, and they smoked badly. After a while, I couldn't see anything due to the smoke. Then I usually had to stop and pour water on the slusher to cool it off.

People make mistakes, but when a miner makes one it tends to be critical. Once in mid 1974 when I was running late at the end of the shift, I accidentally left a case and a half of dynamite, about 150 sticks, lying on the tracks. I should have returned the unused powder to the magazine, but in my haste I forgot.

My opposite shift's motorman was pushing a small four-wheeled flat car called a timber-truck back into the level at the beginning of their shift. The two miners that worked in my place were riding on the timber-truck. When coming around the last corner to the stope, they suddenly met up with my little "land mine." The two miners saw it first and desperately hollered for the motorman to stop—he was pushing them right over a potential bomb. The motor was going so fast, though, that the two miners didn't have time to finish their warning. They did get stopped, but wound up smearing sticks of dynamite in between the rails and the wheels of the motor and flat car. Thank goodness I didn't leave blasting caps there too. Boy don't think I didn't catch hell for that one.

Another time, my nipper was carrying a nearly full box of dynamite back from the magazine to me and he accidentally dropped his lit cigarette into the box. He turned white, looked at me, dropped the box down in front him, quickly sat down cross-legged, and began picking out and hurling dynamite sticks over his back searching for his lost smoke. Every once in a while he'd look up and, I think, the term "abject terror" would be a good description of his look. He eventually found it. I figured he was either desperately afraid, or desperate for the cigarette he'd lost. Actually it was sort of funny. We know that dynamite will burn before it will explode… most of the time.

I heard about a more serious error in judgment that occurred when a mining crew was blasting something in their raise. They were supposed to watch all entrances, but they guarded only one of the two ways into their stope. Their shifter and a couple of federal mine inspectors walked right into it. The result of this error in judgement was one dead, one blinded, and another man screwed up pretty bad too.

I really enjoyed pulling tricks on the other miners whenever I could, though. Everyone else did too. Oh, I'm not talking about the kind of trick that a crew in the stope above me pulled once. They came down into my stope when I wasn't there looking to steal 40 feet of air hose. They found my new 50-foot hose and cut 40 feet out of its middle with an axe. I couldn't understand why they didn't just cut 10 feet off one end, but they severed 5 feet off each end, taking the 40-foot-long middle. They left me with two 5-feet-long pieces. Now that was just dirty pool.

No, I'm talking about the kind of trick that I once pulled on a guy named Pete at the end of a shift. I had just finished "loading out" (putting dynamite into the drill holes) for a big drift round. I had forty-five 8-feet-deep holes to shoot that day and I had put in nearly two cases of 18-inch-long sticks of powder altogether. My drift rounds typically were so big and I used so much dynamite when I blasted that one of the fellas 400 feet higher up in the mine told me, "You know, your rounds are so big that I can hear my timber groaning and taking weight when you shoot."

Well, it was blasting time; I'd already lit my fuses and was waiting for my round to go off. The spot I chose to sit it out was about 100 feet down the drift toward the shaft, and near the top of another stope. I didn't want one of those guys to accidentally walk back to my heading and get caught in my blast after coming up their man-way. That's when Pete, one of the fellas from the stope below the tracks, came up to the level. He saw me, stopped in the middle of the drift, and stood there gabbing about something.

As he jabbered, I thought, "Hell, here's my chance for a good one."

I kept the poor fool talking too. Now I was around a corner and figured that when the round finally did go off the concussion would go through the drift like a freight train, but I'd be out of the way, so I'd be all right. Man old Pete liked to tell tall stories. I was afraid that he would stop talking, though, and walk off, but he faithfully rattled on like a magpie about something and was really getting into his story good when the enormous round finally detonated. The concussion knocked him down immediately, blowing off his hat and generally making a complete mess of his composure. I stood behind the corner laughing like hell, and watched him roll around on the floor till the round finished going off. I didn't really expect the concussion from the blast to be that strong, but I guess we were a little closer than I thought. His frail body just blew all over the place.

I can tell you this, when that poor son-of-a-(you know what) finally did get back on his feet, regained his

Lucky Friday's Silver Shaft near Mullan, Idaho. Note the hoist cables running on sheave wheels at the top of the head-frame.
Hecla Mining Company/Van Gundy Photography, Spokane WA

composure, and got his hat back on, he was extremely irritated.

There was a rule in all of the mines: "Anyone caught fighting underground will be automatically terminated, no matter whose fault it was." So I didn't figure he'd hit me or anything, but he sure was excited. Pete was a good sport, and by the time we'd walked out to the shaft and stopped to wait for the skip, he was laughing.

That night, as we left the dry on our way home, he yelled out to me, "That was a good one Dolph, but you just wait, someday I'm going to get even with you." He never did because, I'm very sorry to say, he died of cancer about a year later.

Have you ever heard of the golden carrot? or at least that's what I called it. The mines paid us on a contract or incentive system—"the more you break, the more you make," referring to rock, of course. In my case, what complicated things was that I happened to have an opposite crew working my stope on the other shift. Well if I didn't get enough work done, they really got mad. The system was such that we all had to work like dogs to keep the routine going. I suppose they must've had beautiful baby boys to support too. Incidentally my son was growing like a weed by then and has been ever since.

Modern equipment, of course, has allowed today's miners to haul out a lot more rock than in the old days. Before the introduction of air operated drills, miners used "hand steel," which looked like long chisels, to drill holes. A miner held the hand steel in place with one hand, while hitting it with a hammer held in the other hand. If working as partners, one held the steel and the other did the hammering. Many miners were missing fingers, and hands too probably, because of this drilling technique. I heard that when air drills were introduced the mines offered contracts to a few of the miners and trained them how to use the new equipment. Then they canned the 20 or so other miners in each stope that were using the old hand steel method because they weren't needed anymore.

The new pneumatic drills were powerful and the dust they caused by hammering on the rock was deadly. It wasn't till quite a bit later that someone invented a way of squirting water into the drill hole. A stream of water ran all the way through the drill steel itself and out where the bit was cutting into the rock. Watering the drill holes pretty much eliminated the horrendous clouds of dust, but a lot of miners were already "dusted" with silicosis by then. That meant their lungs had filled with dust particles and they had difficulty breathing. A lot of them suffocated to death, or at least were crippled for life.

Being dusted in the coal mines was called "black lung" because of the blackness of the coal dust. On the other hand, I'm sure that being dusted in a hardrock mine back then was sometimes called, "gettin' fired." After all, what mining company in its right mind would keep someone around who couldn't produce anymore.

When I first worked in the Lucky Friday Mine, I told a guy that I was thinking of moving over to the Sunshine. He said, "Oh, don't do that, the dust over on that side of the valley has little microscopic barbs in it and if it gets into your lungs and sticks, you're done for... dusted."

I worked on that side of the valley for many years, however, and I'm—excuse me, cough! cough!—still here.

Dust remains a serious problem for miners. One of the things that is stressed in the mines nowdays is to keep the stopes wetted down with water so as to keep dust at a minimum. The dust sometimes still gets bad, though... can you imagine being in dust so thick that trying to breathe air is sort of like trying to breathe in water. Well, I shouldn't complain. I guess that's just part of the job. If you can't stand the heat stay out of the mine.

One day June said, "There are going to be some trailers parked down at the Bunker Hill Steel Worker's Union Hall in Kellogg, and we're all required to have our lung capacity tested."

I asked around and found out that the test was done by having a miner blow through a tube looking like the cardboard center of a toilet paper roll. The tube was connected to a machine by a hose. Now, I was never very good at tests in school, but thought, "Surely, I could pass this one. After all, how hard can it be anyhow?"

I was getting plenty of exercise every day, climbing up the hundred feet, or whatever it was, of my man-way ladders, and then back down again at the end of the shift. That's not counting all the work that I was doing after I got up into my stope either. Of course, I did have to stop from time to time, but I thought that was normal.

Anyway, back to the test. Have you ever blown your toe nails out through your mouth? Man, I sure did, or at least that's what it felt like. When I was finished, to add insult to injury, they told me that I'd flunked the test. I figured it was to be expected, after all I'd never been any good at taking tests anyhow. They told me I was "dusted" up pretty bad and to blow up balloons and jog down the street to exercise my lungs. If you see a bunch of people running around town early in the morning with balloons hanging out of their mouths maybe they're miners who took the same test I did.

The golden carrot was firmly in place. If one of us slowed down and for some reason didn't blast a round, then everybody—my partner and I and the two other guys working as our opposite crew—suffered. When contract pay was in jeopardy, we all had to work twice as hard to take up the slack. It made a fella damn near work himself to death so he wouldn't let the other guys down. The system was really ingenious. When it was first invented, I heard that the mines told their "new" contractors, or gypo miners, that they'd developed an incentive system so miners could make some really good money. That wasn't why it was invented probably, but it must have sounded good to the miners at the time.

The money that miners now make, considering the rate of inflation and wage and benefit cuts, has continually gone down compared to amounts they used to earn. Of course, the mining industry in North Idaho has fallen on tougher times, especially with the fall in the price of metals, particularly silver. Most guys disgruntledly believe, however, that if the mines chew away long enough at the cash they pay their contract miners, then the companies get to buy fancy mining equipment and don't have to pay much for it either.

If I were to take you on a walking tour of the most-recently active, major mines in the Silver Valley, I probably would start with the gigantic Bunker Hill Mine complex at the Valley's west end (see map pg. 29). Here, we'd be under the old flooded workings in Page, which is just short of Pinehurst. The Bunker Hill underground workings continue east under Smelterville, Kellogg, and Elizabeth Park, and eventually to Big Creek and the Bunker Hill's little sister, the Crescent Mine. Bunker Hill has closed down its operations in recent years.

To the east of the Crescent is the still-active Sunshine Mine, but the Crescent and the Sunshine are divided by a football-field-length section of unmined rock. On its east side, the Sunshine Mine is connected to the old Silver Summit workings, which run a couple of miles further east to the edge of Osburn. I might point out here that the old Silver Summit is just one of more than 40 "major" mines that once were active in the Silver Valley over the past century. When participat-

ing in fire drill practice at the Sunshine, I and other miners were directed to get out from underground by walking through the Silver Summit's old drift, which the Sunshine used as part of it ventilation system. I was really impressed at how well the old Silver Summit timber had held up over all those years; at least I figured it had to be an old mine considering how small the drift was. In places, there barely was room to walk through it.

Now to continue moving eastward in our tour of the Silver Valley. There are several more old mines under Osburn, which as far as I know aren't connected. I've never really heard much about them, either.

The Coeur Mine is located southeast of Osburn toward Silverton, and a mile or so farther east is the Galena Mine. Both are operated by ASARCO, Inc. and are connected by a ventilation drift.

Immediately east of the Galena is the Caladay Mine, but the two aren't connected. The Caladay is a newer operation that never really got off the ground. When it was being developed in 1975, my father was superintendent for the McKim-Kaiser Construction Company, one of the Valley's building contractors. McKim-Kaiser had the contract to put in the mine's hoist-room pad. It was a massive undertaking because of the enormous concrete forms and the many curtains of iron rebar that needed to be installed. The pad itself was designed with a walk-way inside, for continued maintenance and such.

When the iron work was being installed Dad asked one of the laborers to "go and get a bolt, and take these two guys with you to help."

The laborer replied, "Hell, I can do it by myself, after all it's only one bolt."

Dad looked at the young fella, sort of laughed to himself, and said, "Okay then, go ahead."

The strapping, proud young man strutted off on his way to do the job. After being gone only a few minutes, he returned and said sheepishly, "I guess you're right. Maybe I do need a little help with that bolt." As it turned out the bolt was 8 feet long and weighed 350 pounds. Big stuff.

Dad also told me, "One time we were working with the valve on the end of a concrete pump that we borrowed from the Hecla Mining Company's Star-Morning Mine. Someone accidentally left it closed and then started the pump. A few minutes later the valve exploded like a bomb and took off like a missile. When the broken piece hit the walls it ricocheted back and

View up the 6,200-foot-deep
Silver Shaft.
Bruce Baraby, Wallace ID

forth sending off big flashing sparks. We all ducked and scattered for cover."

He continued, "I found out later that the pump had the capability of pumping concrete straight up 12 or more floors in a building. What pressure. We made sure that the new valve was left open when the pump was running after that."

The lady behind the desk at Zanetti Brothers concrete company must have been tickled to death when my dad walked in and asked for 658 yards of concrete. This was the largest single order they'd ever sold. Concrete trucks from Osburn hauled the concrete to the mine where it was poured into "torpedo type" mining cars. A motor then pushed the cars into the mine, unloaded, and returned. This was done on a continuous basis during what is known as a "monolithic pour," which allows for the seamless concrete to set with maximum strength. The continuous pour lasted over 52 hours—from 8 A.M. on a Monday morning, until sometime on Wednesday afternoon.

The Caladay's developers, of course, invested millions, including the purchase and hauling in of a hoist. This was quite an undertaking because of the hoist's giant motors, huge cable drums, and massive hoist cable. The hoist dated from the 1930s or 1940s and had been in storage in a Wallace building for a long time. I think that everyone in the Valley believed that it was still a real good one too.

At the time—the mid 1970s—this new mine was more of a community development project than anything else. Many people were looking around for work (as usual), and there was a lot of public interest in the new mine. I later heard that the new company did a lot of exploratory work with diamond drills looking for ore, but didn't find much, or at least not anything really worth going after. Full-fledged operations never started, and the whole project just sort of petered out in the 1980s, I guess. It's a shame too. I can remember when announcements about the Caladay Mine hit the local news. Everyone in the Valley became excited, figuring it would be a real money-maker, like Bunker Hill or the Sunshine. There was even talk about hiring 600 or 800 men, making it one of the biggest in the Valley.

At this point we have traveled underground up to the outskirts of Wallace. The mountains from here on eastward are peppered with other old mined-out workings. One of the important operations in this locality is Hecla Mining Company's Star-Morning Mine (where my dad borrowed the concrete pump), located up Burke Canyon just to the northeast of Wallace. The Star was "the mine of choice" for tramp miners for many years because it was non-union and Hecla paid their men well to keep it that way. Or, at least, that's what the miners who worked there have told me. It must have been true, because every time I tried to hire out there I was turned away. No one would quit the damned place, and about the only way to get on was to wait until someone died.

The Star is deep—8,000 feet or better—and its bottom, of course, is well below sea level. Even though it has valuable ore reserves, it became unprofitable to mine because of its tremendous depth, and, of course, due to depressed metal prices as well. It was just too expensive to haul the ore from the stopes all the way up to the surface, and its drifts and shafts had to be rebolted and timbered constantly.

In 1972, I heard a rumor that Hecla had a master plan to keep the Star going. They proposed driving a drift from it all the way to the Lucky Friday. Then, with special motors and muck cars, they planned to tram the ore from the Star over to the Lucky Friday's shaft where it could be more efficiently hauled to the surface. As the rumor went, the Friday's hoist-room operation went much lower than the Star's.

The master plan, however, was never carried through. Instead, in the 1980s Hecla constructed a revolutionary new shaft in the Lucky Friday, appropriately naming it the "Silver Shaft." This round, concrete-lined shaft was sunk down to the mine's 6,200 feet level. Up till then, mine shafts usually were just holes in the ground whose sides were "framed in" with heavy timbers and boards. The Silver Shaft, on the other hand, utilized steel for "timbers" and the shaft itself is encased in concrete. Hecla set itself up for the long run. By the way, the Kelley Mine's shaft in Butte is concrete lined as well.

Generally, I suppose, most mining companies didn't have the resources to construct something like the Silver Shaft. Besides, they probably just wanted to "get in, get the ore, and get out" as cheaply as possible. They hadn't figured on digging all the way to China to get the muck they were after.

The Silver Shaft can be sunk lower, too. I've heard talk about its potential of eventually going down to a depth of 7,500 feet or so. Of course, miners might have to live in the mines then because it would take too long to commute back and forth to work every day—sorta like in the South Africa diamond mines where miners live underground for a week at a time. The mine might even have to use mules again, as in the good old days. Standard practice back then was to leave those poor critters underground for three months at a time. In some cases, I'll bet they stayed in the mines for the rest of their lives, never seeing daylight again.

Having now completed our tour of the Silver Valley, let's return to the Crescent where I'd worked for over two years, from January 1974 until May 1976. I finally had decided to move on.

"There must be better holes to work in than this," I thought.

I don't know if it was heat exhaustion or trampin' fever, but I got up one day and just figured I'd go out looking for another mine to work in. A new notice posted on the lamp room's bulletin board wanted a miner for the big Bunker Hill Mine. I put my name down on it. Oh, bid notices came up from time to time and I never gave them much thought, but this time it was different. I had a real jerk for a shifter at the time, so I was motivated. It wasn't good old June, either. The company clown I had to face every day actually gave me a warning slip for "littering the mine" when spitting sunflower husks onto the ground, just like the great majority of other miners in the Valley.

My name hung on the board for several weeks, like a flag, for all to see. I felt that by just having signed that bid I was getting even with that idiot shifter. ❀

CHAPTER 7

High Tapper

Lower Bunker Hill Mine
Kellogg, Idaho

Then one day in the early summer of 1976 I found myself climbing the long metal staircase to the train yard at the Lower Bunker Hill Mine again. This time, I'd taken time the night before to drive up the steep hill to the dry and dump my diggers off. That way I wouldn't have to carry them again. As I climbed the stairs, I remembered how I'd nearly run the motor down the shaft when I was there before, because I didn't know how to operate it.

My first day at the Lower Bunker was very interesting. After everyone had put on their diggers and grabbed their lamps, the crew punched their time cards and stood in a mob outside of the dry waiting for the man-train. As I stood there, I noticed a new guy carrying a sack full of diggers and walking toward us with a stupid look on his face. I glanced around and noticed a general, blank stare on the faces of my fellow "bystanders." Memories of my first hire-out at the Lower Bunker flooded through my mind.

When the man-train finally did arrive, I climbed through one of its car's small doorways. This was like boarding Amtrak compared to the old flatcar I'd been riding on for the last couple of years over at the Crescent. I thought, "Hell, this is like old, home sweet home." I recognized two fellas in my compartment from when I'd worked there before, and we talked as we waited. Our conversation put me in mind of someone who'd "left town" for a long time and just returned.

We soon were on our way, entering the Kellogg Tunnel and its familiar dank darkness accompanied by the screeching of the train's wheels as they grated on the tracks. It was the same intoxicating atmosphere, for miners at least, found in all underground mines. The long ride seemed to go by quickly, probably because I kept glancing around looking for things I remembered. After getting off the train at the shaft, I walked over to the ridiculous looking incline shaft. Looking up I thought, "Yeah, there it is—the damn, hard-hat grabbing I-beam up there."

A few minutes later, a loud cager's voice broke up our quiet "mumbling" and barked out the string of levels that we'd be stopping at—sort of like at a Greyhound bus station. My turn to load into a skip came and I climbed on. Only this time, after I sat down, I still had on my hard hat. Just to make sure of that, I'd tied a little piece of blasting wire from the back of my hat to my lamp's power cord which ran to a battery hanging on my belt.

As I have mentioned earlier, there wasn't much clearance above the skip between the riders' heads and the shaft timbers. About six months later, as the skip was on its way down the shaft, one of the guys sat up too far and hit a timber and died instantly.

The guy that was sitting beside me must have thought I was crazy because I was laughing most of the way down. I couldn't help it. It was just plain fun. My roller coaster ride ended at the 21 level, where my new stope was supposed to be. That's where I found Roy McDaniels, my new partner, waiting for me. We exchanged greetings and began walking from the shaft

---

Muck train backing into Bunker Hill's Kellogg Tunnel for another load of ore. Note the warm underground air turning to mist as it rises out of the portal.
Kellogg Public Library

back toward our stope. I told him about the first time I'd hired out there and how I lost my hat down the shaft.

He just laughed and said, "I lost my hat down there too once. We've all complained about that damned thing hanging out there so close to the man-skip, but the mine says, 'We know it's a problem but haven't figured out any other way to load and unload the skips without having it up there.'"

We'd been walking for quite a while when we came through a couple of air doors. Then I looked down and was surprised to see no rails for a battery powered motor and its train. It was the first time I'd been in a haulage drift that had no rails or trains. Then I remembered the diesel muckers and trucks on the Crescent's 4,100 level, but thought, "At least there were rails there, too."

We came to a well-lighted "mechanics room," which had been blasted out of the rock at an intersection. I was amazed at the number of upward and downward drifts that had been developed. Roy saw my interest and pointed toward the steep up-ramp. "We work up there," he said. Then we walked over to the top of the down ramp and stood there, looking down into its steep, silent, ominous darkness.

Roy said, "The workings down in there didn't amount to much. The mine was never able to find much ore there at all. The diamond drillers hit some color in their core samples, so the company had this drift put in and looked around down in there pretty good too, but it didn't prove up. It was all just a big flop."

This section of 21 level, past the air doors, used diesel equipment—diesel trucks and front end loaders—whereas the rest of the level used electric motors. We turned and walked back by the mechanics room and started up the steep ramp at a 20 percent grade or so. I looked up and saw an elaborate lighting system which warned of approaching equipment. I thought of how much it looked like the traffic control lights on streets downtown. It was a rectangular box with red, yellow, and green lenses in it, and beneath the box hung a cord. When one of the trucks, or big "swivel in the middle" muckers, entered this area, the driver jerked on the cord. This turned the first light to red, and the ones beyond that to yellow thus warning any crossing traffic that "further on" there was a piece of equipment on the move. An occasional safety space, or turnout, had been blasted into the wall so people could get out of the way of big oncoming machinery. After the equipment operator had gone through the area and came to the last light, he pulled its cord too as he went by. Then all of the lights turned green, signaling that all was clear in that area. This is the same lighting system that was used in all of the Valley mines.

Ore bodies in the Lower Bunker had more lead and zinc, and, I found out, Mr. Air Blast didn't like that kind of ground because it was softer and absorbed ground pressures. That's why none of the Bunker Hill miners would come over to the Crescent. Mr. Air Blast didn't visit Lower Bunker very much, and I can't say that I missed the old boy, either. But don't worry—he was still alive and well elsewhere. I think he was still looking for me, too.

At the Galena Mine, between Osburn and Wallace, two hapless miners died instantly in a ferocious blast that entombed them where they stood. It took about a week for the rescue crews to recover their remains. One of the miners had been carrying a 10-feet-long powder pole when the blast hit. The muck covering them was so deep that it took days of digging just to get down far enough to expose the top of the "straight up and down" powder pole.

When loading dynamite into a drill hole, a miner begins by inserting a primer, or blasting cap, into a stick of powder. Then he uses a wooden or plastic powder pole to gently push the stick of powder into place. Because it has a detonator in it, this first stick must be handled especially carefully. After a miner pushes the dynamite stick to the back of the hole, he then "snugs it up" a bit by tamping it gently into place with the pole. From then on, a miner doesn't have to be quite as careful when the rest of the dynamite sticks are stuffed in. Wood or plastic poles are utilized because they don't cause sparks when banged against rocks or equipment like steel does. For lack of a handy powder pole, foolish miners have used drill steel to tamp their powder into place. You can visit them on Sundays, up on Boot Hill.

That's one thing that's really screwed up about this mining game, too. You might have a friend go to work with you and later that day he'd be killed. You might even have been very nearly killed yourself. Miners have many close calls. When these things happen, it's really hard on miners emotionally and gets everyone to thinking. Some of the guys who take it the hardest, though, are the bosses. Management feels really terrible about employees who die on the job. The Silver Valley mining community is so closely knit that many of the bosses and the miners grew up together and, in many cases, were even partners at one time or other.

The author, 3,000 feet deep in the Bunker Hill Mine.
Jerry Dolph

But business is business, and after an accident the company tries to calm everybody down by shining up their golden carrot a bit, usually with a little more money. Then the game goes on. Most miners don't miss very much work after a fatality; they just don't mention the loss of their fellow worker and keet the memory of how he met his fate in the backs of their minds.

Not much tomfoolery takes place in the hazardous environment of a mine; it's just too dangerous. One unfortunate incident of this nature, though, resulted in tragedy for a seasonal employee in the Lower Bunker Hill. The public-spirited Lower Bunker, and all the Valley's mines as a matter of fact, had been hiring college students as summer employees. Roy, my partner, had some definite opinions about the subject.

He said things like, "The mines are actually just trying to provide themselves with temporary employees who won't be on the full-time payroll or be eligible for full-time employee benefits either. Actually they're just taking work away from us full-time, card-carrying union members."

Personally I thought that by hiring college summer help the mines had recruited employees who were motivated and likely to do their jobs intelligently and vigorously. Otherwise, the bosses would have had to hire people off the street whom they knew nothing about (and who might come to work from under a bridge abutment somewhere, like I did). It was all just good business sense, I guess. I thought too that these summer jobs would help young people decide what they wanted to do for long-term employment. After they worked underground awhile, all of the summer workers that I ever talked to "knew for a fact" that mining wouldn't be included in their list of career choices!

I was saying that tomfoolery was dangerous underground. One of the temporary workers, a college student, was trying to sneak out of the Lower Bunker Hill early on his last shift in the summer of 1976. From what I heard, he probably had his cap light off so no one could see him.

Bunker Hill, like all of the mines, used "air doors" to help control ventilation systems. The big doors were controlled by either mechanical or electrical switches; handles were "thrown" when someone wanted to open or close them. In this instance, the muck train was coming back into the mine through the Kellogg Tunnel to get another load of ore from the muck chutes. The train had 22 big muck cars, driven by a very large motor. The control handle, which the motorman used to open and close the doors, was located in the tunnel probably about 100 feet from the air doors. Evidently the youngster was right in front of the air door when the motorman, who was sitting at the controls of his motor, hit the switch to throw open the air door. When the door opened, it struck the young fella and knocked him down, possibly even out. Then, as the motor continued pushing the cars forward, the train ran over him.

The man running the motor wasn't aware of what had happened until practically the entire train ran over the body. Then, the motorman looked down on the tracks between his motor and the last car in line and saw the lad. There wasn't much left.

The investigation following the incident found no fault with the freaked-out motorman or with the way he'd been performing his job that day. The whole crew really felt sorry for the poor motorman, but that didn't help him very much. He had so many problems from the accident that he nearly had a nervous breakdown. I'm sure he still has nightmares about it too.

Miners usually are "cut from the same cloth," or at least are very much alike in many ways. They work hard and do their jobs as best they can, and try to get along with one another. There is an occasional oddball here and there, though, who makes life interesting. One of these was a fella who worked for the Crescent.

This guy was missing a lot of work and June Lawley was trying to find out if there was anything he could do to help. June knew that the fella had a lot of kids to support and he finally decided to visit the man at his home.

The next day I was talking with June and he said, "I couldn't believe the condition of that house. I walked in and there was a pile of dirty diapers in one corner and garbage and beer cans were stacked knee deep in all of the others. He had an old dirty couch that he invited me to sit down on and that's where we sat and talked.

"We'd been there for a while talking, and kids were running all over the place. I wasn't really paying much attention to them till I saw this one little fella, who only wore a dirty little T-shirt, run past. There was a dog running right behind him too licking the crap off his butt. I must have made a face when I saw that because my most generous host then said, 'Can't raise kids without a good dog.' "

June then said, "I decided that my visit was done and got up to leave. He got up too and must have felt sort of guilty about the condition of his house, because out of the corner of my eye, I saw him push a dog turd under the couch with the side of his boot."

Now to return again to my first day at the Lower Bunker Hill. My new partner, Roy, and I had been climbing up the steep ramp for quite a while and had gone about 300 feet when it finally leveled out to horizontal. I looked off to the right side of the drift and saw a tugger. It had been stulled, or propped, down from the back by four 6-feet-long wooden posts securely holding it in place. The tugger was immediately adjacent to the top of a down raise. A small sign had been nailed on one of the posts that read "21-15-23"—the number of my new stope.

I suddenly remembered what Jim Arnoldi, my instructor in the Kelley Mine in Butte, Montana, said, "Stopes' numbers stand for their levels, veins, and locations." I smiled; it was almost as if Jim were still with me, rattling around up there somewhere in my hard hat and I was still listening to him.

We'd finally arrived at the top of our raise. I handed my lunch box to Roy and, as he put our gear into the skip, I stood there looking around. The drift looked really bare; it didn't have any timber in it at all except for those four wooden stulls. But otherwise it looked much the same as any other similar workings, with its checkerboard pattern of rock bolts in its walls and back. Then I looked back toward the ramp we'd climbed to get there. I thought, "God that's steep" and a sudden flash of fear swept over me. I just shrugged it off, though, and chalked it up to being in a strange place.

Good job of timbering in Bunker Hill's 24-16-23 stope. Also visible here is a rich muck pile of many tons of high-grade lead/silver ore. Kellogg Public Library

Roy said, "Go ahead on down and I'll run the skip on down to you."

Then I shined the beam of light from my cap lamp down into the darkness of the man-way. It looked like any other in that it was 4-feet-square, wooden sided, and went down much deeper than my light did. I did as he asked and stepped onto the first ladder. As I climbed down I noticed that the man-way was "laid over" a lot more than any other that I'd ever been in. By laid over, I mean that it was pitched at a very steep angle, probably a grade of 50 percent or so. I thought of how the funny looking decline shaft was at much the same angle. Then it dawned on me that all, or probably most, of the veins of ore down here must also be laid over at the same pitch. I smiled and remembered how much fun it was to ride down the shaft on its roller coaster skip.

The shaft, the stope raises, everything, were laid over at the same angle as the veins of ore (they had to be so that the miners could follow the veins). Even when a miner blasted his rounds he had to drill in his holes and shoot them at the same angle. I'd eventually climbed down through 75 feet of the man-way before I finally stepped out into the stope's raise area. It was heavily timbered with posts and overhead caps, bulkheads, and floors. Roy sent the skip down as promised and after he climbed down we both sat down for coffee and began to talk.

Roy pointed into the darkness behind me, saying, "I've been in here for two years and no one has ever cycled this place on your side before. It lays over too much over there. Nobody tries. So the money hasn't been very good in here at all."

The term "cycle," of course, means that the miner comes in at the beginning of shift, slushes out the round that had been blasted on the previous shift, bolts or timbers the ground as needed to hold it in place, drills out a new round, and blasts it when going off shift.

"Aha… a challenge," I thought.

Then I got up, stretched, and said, "Man, you are looking at the bad-assed miner from the Crescent. I'm going to cycle 'every' round… starting today," and we both went to work.

The "hanging wall" hung over the top of the vein. Conversely, its counterpart the "foot wall" laid over at the foot, or beneath, the vein. Sort of like a cliff that hangs over would be the hanging wall, and one that just slopes away, like climbing up a steep hill, would be the foot wall.

I'd set out to prove myself, and "did" by blasting a round that first day. I don't think Roy believed I could do it either, because just before I started he said, "It'll take you two days to put in your round, so you might just as well take it easy."

My end of the stope laid over so much that it was a real challenge. Just to elaborate on that a bit: the foot wall was smooth and when I sat my lunch box down on it the box didn't even try to slide down hill. The vein on Roy's side was straighter—more up and down—and easier to work, and he insisted on keeping it too. I blasted a round and made my 6 feet advance every day after that, but I had to work twice as hard as he did to do it, too.

My side of the stope had what is known as a "blind chute" in it. My cut was so long and winding back in there (around 240 feet), that it was necessary to have two muck chutes to slush into, instead of just one as was normal. The second chute, or "blind chute," couldn't be seen from the raise because it was around a sharp corner.

During the first days in the stope, I used the first chute. But both Roy and Fred, our shifter, told me that eventually I would advance right over the top of the second chute. The second chute would appear after a blast from a round penetrated a layer of 3-inch-thick boards and burlap that had been left on top of the new chute for cover.

The day I finally "found" that second chute was really a thrill. I didn't really know where it was up till

then. Fred kept saying that I'd find it 150 feet out from the raise, and I'd kept looking for it too, half expecting my latest round's muck to have gone down it. The first thing I did each day for quite a while was to walk back into the cut and look for the much ballyhooed new chute.

One morning after I'd climbed down the man-way, I walked immediately back through the cut to look at the results of my last blast. Sure enough, just like Fred had been saying all along, most of the muck pile was not there. I very carefully climbed up on top of what was left of the muck and looked down for the chute.

That's when I got a real shocker. It was down there all right… a really long ways down there. It was way back under the hanging wall and about 8 feet beneath my feet. As it turned out, I'd unknowingly been climbing uphill a little as I blasted each round. I looked in awe and saw the back was no longer 11 feet high as it was supposed to be—it was at least 18 feet high. I stood staring in amazement thinking, "God, what a hole."

Fred usually came down into the stope about an hour and a half after we did on his daily rounds. Dreading what he'd say, I scurried around attempting to somehow make the cavern look less ominous. It wasn't any use, though—I couldn't really change much of anything at all. I knew that Fred would be mad, and sure enough, he came unglued when he finally got there. He yelled, "Hell, you took out two cuts instead of one." Then old tattle-tale Fred went right out and told on me, too. The foreman's attitude was much worse… well, I won't even tell you what he said after he got there. I weathered the storm, though.

After all the hollering was over, I spent the rest of the day bolting everything up and installing a few stulls "width-wise" from wall to wall where I thought they were needed. Then I unhooked the slusher's tie-down chains and got ready to move it back to the new chute. The slusher had two 4-feet-long, 8 x 8 inch timbers that paralleled each other mounted onto its bottom and together they were called a "sled." And that's just what it was too. I connected the slusher's air hose up and stood on top of the sled straddling the two timbers, with the slusher itself just in front of my knees. Then reaching over I pulled down on its "haul-back" handle. The cable from that drum was strung out back to a block that I'd rigged up near the second chute. I stood atop the sled like that and rode it back to the first big corner, where the blind chute was. Then I chained it down and slushed the round's muck down into the new chute. I don't know if that was the way it was suppose to be moved, but it sure worked great.

The next day as I walked back into the cut I thought about how I really liked this set-up, probably because it was so different from the normal routine. The sand floor felt cool and damp, and everything seemed sort of neat that day. I purposefully walked slowly back from the raise to the second chute, really looking things over. Both walls laid over at a steep angle, and I knew from my limited experience that the back of the stope should have been about 11 feet above the floor. But the further on back toward the second chute that I walked, the higher and bigger things were. Until finally, standing there at the second chute, with all of the muck gone and only the sand floor to look at, the view was really awesome where the back was at least 18 feet high!

I thought, "I would have been all right if I hadn't left so much muck on the floor for a road bed. But the further I got back the more muck there was on the floor, and it was all so gradual that I didn't realize that I was going uphill that much and making the stope larger."

That day, and each day thereafter, I mined 6 feet a shift, slushing the muck into the second chute, of course. About a week later, I faced a situation that was… well it really scared the hell out of me. The new chute hung up.

As I mined past the blind chute, slushing ore down it, I'd been extra careful not to drop any wood or old bent-up rock bolts into it. These materials could easily "hang up" in the laid-over chute, obstructing the flow of the muck. Or so I was told—I didn't want to find out for sure. Something complicating the situation even more was the really heavy high-grade lead/zinc/silver ore that I was mining. It was so heavy, in fact, I don't think an average man could've picked up a piece the size of a lunch bucket, and still keep his hemorrhoids in place. The heavy ore had a tendency to bog down on the bottom side of the chute, hanging up everything above it.

It was Monday morning, and the chute had been hung up since Friday. I'd left a water hose running full blast over the weekend, hoping that somehow water would wash out whatever was hanging up in there. I'd spent the entire weekend worrying about whether or not the muck had gone down.

Finally the waiting was over. After I'd made the trip down the shaft to the level, I grabbed the motorman and his muck train and headed straight back to the bottom of the stope. I hoped to find that the muck had gone down and my chute's lip, or bottom, was full. The motorman positioned a muck car directly beneath the chute, and I climbed up onto the little stand that he usually stood on when he pulled muck. I grabbed hold of the iron bar protruding from the side of the gate, lifted it, and let the muck run. Immediately, broken rock rushed down and I felt relieved, but a few seconds later the flow suddenly stopped. Then there was nothing but silence. I stood with the door open staring up into a black hole. Just as I'd feared, only about a car-full of "fines," or gravel-sized muck, had come out.

About the worst thing a stope miner has to face, as part of his job, is "climbing a chute." I knew this, and didn't want anything to do with climbing what would be my first chute. I sent the motorman out to the powder and primer magazine for dynamite and blasting caps. When he returned, I tied two sticks of powder onto the end of a 10-feet-long powder pole and shoved my bomb up into the chute. Then we stood off a ways and I touched it off. Suddenly, muck began running again. I could hear it hitting the iron gate at the chute's bottom as it fell and thought, "Thank God for that."

Then, just as suddenly, the sound of falling rock stopped. It was again deathly still. Only about another half-a-car of fines had come down. It is easy to tell if just a little muck is falling because of the "shallow" sound. On the other hand, if the chute really "broke loose" as I was hoping, the many, many tons of rock would sound like an oncoming freight train, what with its rumbling, vibrations, and all.

I blasted two more times, first with two powder poles tied together, then with three. But nothing else fell out of the blackness of the hole, except some fines. I couldn't feed anymore lengths of powder poles up into the hole, either, although I tried. They just kept hanging up on something up in there. So, there I stood. I'd used up everything in my bag of tricks… the water hose and the dynamite.

There was only one thing left to do, and I was really stressed out at the thought—"I'll have to climb up from the bottom of this damned thing and blast it in its belly."

In the Butte, Montana, mining camps, miners who climbed chutes trying to free them up were called "high tappers." They lugged heavy jack-leg drilling machines, hoses, and steel up into the chutes and drilled holes into the bottoms of the boulders that were wedged in above them. Then, after loading their drill holes with dynamite, they blasted their charges. High tappers were well-paid for their efforts, but, as a rule, didn't usually live long enough to really enjoy their money. Now here I was following in their footsteps.

I pulled open the chute's gate again and stared up into the blackness, thinking, "The muck has to be hung in there at least 40 feet up."

Under the watchful eye of the motorman, I set to rigging up two sticks of dynamite tied securely with blasting wire, onto the end of a 4-feet-long piece of powder pole. Then I pushed an electric primer into one of the sticks, all the while hoping that the chute would somehow, magically, come down... it didn't.

I turned to the motorman and said, "Stay right here at the bottom, pard, and I'll be back down again in a few minutes." I climbed up into the muck car and, reaching for a hand hold, pulled myself up into the chute. As I did so, I saw water running down beneath me, and the look on the motorman's face. It was a look of dismay and one that gave me serious doubts about what I was about to do.

He just shook his head, as if saying, "You'll never come out of it alive—you're a damned fool to be doing this."

But I knew it had to be done, and said a little prayer under my breath. "Lord, I'm either going to find you up in this chute or I am going to find out why this sucker's constipated."

I began to climb. The chute was pretty much straight up and down for the first 30 feet or so, but then it laid over severely on the same angle as the vein up in the stope. There wasn't any wooden crib in that first 30 feet, either; just bolted rock walls. Where the chute laid over, the crib began. I thought, "No damned wonder powder poles wouldn't go up any higher than right here. They were hanging up on this dog-leg."

After I'd finally climbed to the bottom of the wooden crib, I could see the muck. It was about another 10 feet higher up. A chill ran down my spine as I stood looking up from an outcropping of rock. I thought, "God, there isn't anything holding it up here at all." I'd fully expected to see a broken board or maybe even an iron rock bolt or two; something, at least, that was jammed in and holding the muck in place. But there wasn't anything there at all, just a gradually sloping pile of broken ore. I looked down between my legs and saw fines dribbling down the chute below me, running with the water that I'd left on up in the stope.

By this time I was shaking so badly that I could just barely hang onto my bomb. I didn't know why either—

Skips come in many sizes and types. This one has been refurbished.
ASARCO Inc.

I didn't feel like I was afraid... but maybe just a little stupid. I very gently reached up and wedged the powder pole in place at the bottom of the muck and was very careful not to touch anything. All the while I was thinking, "There's over a hundred feet of ore above me in this chute and I sure's hell don't want to move it in any way."

I'd tied blasting wire for the electric primer onto my belt and strung it out from below as I climbed, so that part was already in place. With all the shaking I was doing, my fingers would just barely work as I removed the shunted covers from the ends of the electric primer's wires and connected them to the blasting wire. Finally it was done, and all I had to do was try to get the hell out of there... very quietly.

I don't know, maybe I'd moved something, but it sure looked to me like the fines were running faster than they were when I'd first gotten up there. I quickly worked my way down the chute again, being very careful not to pull down on the blasting wire as I went; I was afraid of tearing the wires loose from my planted bomb.

As I climbed gingerly down, I felt the ominous presence of the million tons of broken rock above me and thought, "Almost, I'm almost done with this damned thing." I'd worked my way nearly down to the bottom of the chute before really looking for the hole below me, but when I did, all I could see beneath me was a muck floor. I was trapped... the gate was closed, and the mouth of the chute had filled with fines.

I thought desperately, "What the hell's going on?" Even though I didn't want to make any loud noises, I shouted down to the motorman, who was still supposed to be there, "Open the damned gate." Suddenly, I heard it open and the muck floor beneath me gave way, looking like someone had flushed a toilet.

Then I heard a deep rumbling sound and thought, "That's awfully loud for just a little bit of fines." My life flashed before my eyes and I was suddenly gripped with fear. I jumped down into the hole, landing on my back on the chute's protective wear plate, or floor, at the bottom of the chute. Then I slid down and out under the up-raised gate and landed in the muck car, on my back again. The motorman slammed the chute gate down just after I'd come out through it, and then I found out what that rumbling sound was that I'd heard.

The sound grew into a roar and, indeed, it seemed like one hell of a big freight train was coming... the ground actually was shaking. As I laid there in the muck car, and before even having a chance to get my wits about me, muck slammed into the iron gate above me. I saw the chute's supporting timbers jerk a bit and dust belched from all the joints. Everything instantly vanished into a thick pall of dust.

I was in shock, I guess, and couldn't see the motorman at all then, but yelled out jokingly to him through the roar of the still-falling muck, "Well, we got that one down, pard." It took us a good five minutes to stop laughing, and almost as long for me to be able to even see where he was because of the dust. I've heard that you aren't suppose to laugh at your own jokes, but I couldn't help it. I felt really stupid because, after I got out of the muck car, I stood there laughing like a hyena and shaking violently for a long time, so scared that the muscles in my face were actually twitching.

Luckily, we didn't have any more hung chutes after that. Well, actually it wasn't luck, because I told my shifter, Fred, "If you don't keep my muck pulled and it has a chance to set up in the chute and hang up again, next time, buddy, you're going to climb it."

Modern-day operations in a well-protected working area in the Bunker Hill Mine.
Bruce Baraby, Wallace ID

I don't know if he just hated to climb chutes or what, but from then on the chute was pulled dry all the time, except for a little bit at the very bottom to cushion the gate. I should point out, however, that the mines usually liked to have the chutes full because they held up better that way, rather than having the sides constantly battered by falling muck.

I got along really well with Fred, even after my ultimatum... except for once. It was at the end of a two-week contract period when he came in to "measure up" my end of the stope. Shifters did that routinely at the end of each contract period so gypo paychecks would reflect the rate of advance that miners had made in the stopes. Fred measured Roy's side too.

Well, Fred must have been a little tired that day because he sat down in the raise and handed me the end of a 300 feet tape and said, "You take it to the face." I grabbed the end of the tape and walked the 230 feet to the end of the cut where I had been mining. I held the end up to the face, then I felt Fred pull his end tight, and then it went limp. He'd gotten his reading. Oh... did I mention that I was standing on the tape and had it wrapped around my gut a couple of times too? I don't know how that happened but figured... "Whoops."

Returning to the raise, I noticed he had a sour look on his face. He said angrily, "How in the hell did you get 70 feet of advance in 10 days if you were only drilling with 6-foot-long steel? What did you do, wrap the tape around yourself a couple of times?"

I said, "Damn, I don't know boss… you want to do it again?" He declined, but from then on engineers, under contract, came instead on measuring day and those boys strung tape out so tight it looked like a piano wire.

All the fellas got along really well and were always pulling pranks on each other. There was this one little guy named Bill, who'd had malaria while he was in the army and had lost all the hair on his body. Bill was a devout Mormon and a really good, hard worker too. Everyone picked on him, though, trying to get him to cuss. In the shower room they'd snap at him with towels, spray cold water on him—you name it. He was sort of shy too… I could tell by the way he'd sit on a bench wearing nothing but a baseball cap while waiting for his turn in the shower. I think he was just self-conscious about having no hair.

Everyone else just pushed themselves in, got wet, and stood off to the side soaping up, while waiting for another opening under a showerhead… you know, we'd share. When the guys got together like that, they were like kids, but I don't think they were all that bad. One fella told me that the reason they snapped at Bill with towels and such was to see if they could get him to join them and act "normal." Finally, though, Bill would reach his breaking point and cuss like a trooper. Then, everyone smiled and left him alone.

One of the fellas, though, was after him almost all the time, until one day when Bill decided to do something about it. Bill was down in the mine driving his motor along the rails when he saw his "nemesis" up ahead working by the tracks. Bill took out his pipe wrench, reached out, and took a swing at him but missed. I guess Bill's nemesis looked up at the last second and ducked. I talked to the guy that night. He said, "You know that little shit Bill took a swing at me with his damned pipe wrench?" After that I don't think they harassed Bill very much anymore.

Another time, one of the summer workers walked up to Roy and held out his tightly clenched fists. Then he very carefully opened them, exposing two handfuls of iron pyrites, or "fool's gold." In a hushed voice, while looking around suspiciously to see if anyone was watching, he whispered, "Is this gold?"

Roy, thinking it was a joke, replied excitedly, "Yeah… that is gold. Where did you find it?"

The kid turned as white as a ghost and screamed, "We're rich!" Then the young high-grader showed Roy

his stashes. As Roy laughingly told me later, "The kid had a small pile of fool's gold hidden behind every damned post in that drift. There was so much of it that he couldn't have been doing anything else but prospecting. He wouldn't have had time."

Attendance at union meetings is a part of a miner's normal routine, and I frequently went to gatherings at the United Steel Workers Union Hall, located close to the Kellogg High School's football field. Typically, miners filtered into the meeting hall one by one, then stood around with coffee cups in hand, talking about whatever. Soon, the small huddles of miners grew into a crowd and then everyone just seemed to know it was time to get business underway. We found our seats and sat down among the squeaking of folding metal chairs and a few coughs here and there.

A speaker climbed up to the stage, and, tapping on the mike, said "Testing, testing." It was time to begin. He then greeted us with a booming, "Good morning." People driving by outside in their cars undoubtedly heard him too because the mike was turned up so loud. But it wouldn't be loud enough for some listeners in the back rows, who shouted, "What was that? We can't hear you from back here. Turn up the mike." Then everyone else, in small huddles, debated whether the sound really was too low.

(I had a friend there at the Bunker Hill who once told me, "I don't like to wear earplugs when I'm mining. If the ground wants to say something to me, then I sure's hell want to listen." I never could figure out how he could do it. The roar of the machines and the hammering of steel just about drove me bananas sometimes and actually hurt my head, it was so loud. During the union meetings, of course, my friend was one of those fellas shouting from the rear of the hall because he couldn't hear the speaker.)

Having decided to increase the volume, the speaker then hollered at someone off to the side to turn up the dial. There was a pause, and the squeak of a few more chairs being adjusted. Then, with a high-pitched squelch or two from the mike and a window-shaking base, the speaker again said "Good Morning" and everyone nodded their approval. It was time to get on with business.

Another union that held meetings in the area was the Wardner Industrial Union, which had been formed in the Silver Valley many years ago. It met in the bowling alley once a month. I wasn't a member for a long time, but it seemed like most of the guys that I knew were. They kept telling me, "You gotta join up, it's a good union."

I finally joined, expecting its meetings to be a lot like those of the United Steel Workers Union. I thought it was just an old union that many of the local miners had formed and kept going, even though the big Steel Workers Union had taken over. In other words, I thought it was a sort of place to just get together to air grievances once a month and generally talk things over.

Then came the day to attend my first meeting. As I climbed the steps to the second floor of the bowling alley, I thought, "The two dollars a month, or whatever it is, sure isn't very much for union dues. Steel Workers dues are a lot more than that. They cost me two hours' pay a month."

The first room I walked into reminded me of an old school house because of its high ceilings, stucco walls, and enormous windows. It looked like a large kitchen area and I couldn't help but notice that stacks of cases of beer lined the outside wall. I thought, "Okay, the bowling alley downstairs must use this room for storing extra beer," and I went into the next room where everyone seemed to be gathering. It was a larger room, with rows of metal folding chairs facing a stage at one end. There were already quite a few fellas sitting around, even though the meeting wouldn't start for awhile yet. I picked out a likely spot and sat down too.

One of the guys who'd been bugging me to join came over and sat down next to me. We began talking and he said, "This is a great union, I've been coming here since…" He couldn't remember how long, but was sure that it had been at least six years. I looked around the room as he talked and noticed a roll-up type movie screen on a tripod standing on the stage in front, and the room's windows were all heavily draped. We talked a bit more and finally the meeting got underway. By then, there were a lot of guys there who I knew worked in different mines.

A speaker climbed quickly up onto the stage, chattered off the minutes, new business, and whatever else it was, and climbed back down off the stage again. I was astonished, it was over in just a couple of minutes. Then everyone got up and started back toward the kitchen area. They were leaving, I thought, and I said to myself, "Well hell, it's over… what kind of a stupid union meeting is this?"

I expected to at least see some kind of movie or something, what with the screen being up there and all. The fella I had been talking to jumped up, waved his arm,

and said excitedly, "Come on, let's go." I was confused, to say the least. Why was he getting so excited about leaving a meeting that only lasted a few minutes? Then I found out what all of the commotion was about. The fellas who'd gone out to the kitchen now came back and most of them carried a beer in each hand. I'll have to admit, then I too felt the flush of excitement. I didn't want to be any different, so I joined in and got my two beers too. After everyone had made their trip out to the kitchen and returned again to their seats in front of the movie screen, the lights went out and someone in the back turned on a projector.

I won't go into details about the "movie," but let's just classify it as an educational film on anatomy. One which I'm sure would educate the most ignorant of us about the real goals in our lives. Goals that a few of us strive after and sometimes just have to pay for, in one way or another. After a rather lengthy stay at the movies and quite a few refreshments, I got up to leave. I noticed that a lot of the fellas carried out half cases of beer as they left the kitchen area and started down the staircase toward the street. Again, I didn't want to be any different so I grabbed one under each arm and followed along.

I had no car at the time, but I lived close enough nearby that I could walk home. That's when the well-known dangers of drinking and driving, or in my case "drinking and walking," came into play as I stumbled into the old section of Kellogg with its mile-high curbs. I took one step off the curb and wound up doing a lip stand on the street. I never let go of my beer though. I was proud.

The Bunker Hill Mine, of course, dates back a hundred years or so—long before the introduction of electric or diesel motors. For decades, they used mules and horses to move the muck out from underground. I was talking to Pape, a long-time Bunker Hill miner, who told me, "Years ago my partner and I holed through an old stope that looked like it'd been there for many years. I saw stalls where mules were kept, and old hand steel laying on the floor around the bottom of a chute." He went on, "There was even an old wooden wheelbarrow, that had about rotted away, sitting under what was left of the chute that was only about three feet off the floor."

The old way of mining without pneumatic, air-operated equipment must have been a real backbreaking way to make a living. I wouldn't say that the modern miner is spoiled, however, because he works just as hard, I'm sure. It's just that he moves about 50 times (or

These Bunker Hill stacks went on line in 1977. The nearby stack is 715 feet high; the one to the right stands 610 feet.
Jerry Dolph

whatever) as much muck because of his modern equipment. I really think that the miner—the man—has changed little over the years despite the technological advances. I'll have to say this, though, it must have been a real bummer for the old-time miner to swing a single-jack (a 5 pound sledgehammer) all day with one hand, while hitting a 2-feet-long drill steel held in the other hand.

I worked in the 21-15-23 stope for over a year and always was delighted with the antics of the Bunker Hill crew. My stope was coming along fine, once I'd settled down into the steady slushing, drilling, and blasting cycle, and this routine didn't change much for me, or any of the other miners either. The thing that brought special interest into our days seemed to be the antics of some of our more enlightened fraternity. For some of them, it was real challenge to outdo the other guy, either gag-wise, money-wise, or any other-wise that came up. The following little story is a typical example.

It was wintertime, and rainy and cold. At the end of another long day, the man-train was on its way out of the mine and full of worn out, greasy miners. The small compartments in the cars, of course, hold four people, and on this particular trip three occupants of one compartment did something that evidently needed to be done. They stripped the clothes off the fourth guy, and, when the train passed in front of the parking area outside, they hurled him buck naked out through the door and into a snowbank.

At that time, wives and girlfriends were parked in front of the office and the snowbank, waiting for their husbands and boyfriends to get off work. The guys who told me the story all laughed, and one said, "That was funny as hell, it was sprinkling a little and all of the cars' windshield wipers came on when he flew out through the door into the snow." After that little incident, the mine wouldn't allow wives or girlfriends to park there any more. It was a shame too, because it was a long walk down to the parking lot.

Another amusing incident occurred one day, following the word from the shifters that we had to "clean up the mine. The big-shots are coming down to make an inspection."

All of the stope miners, and well just about everybody, busied themselves cleaning up their respective work places. At the time, a crosscut drift on 9 level was being used as a latrine and had been for quite a while. Guys buried their leavings with sawdust and wood chips, and since it was in the main air flow, odor wasn't noticeable at all. But then a shifter said, "Take air hoses and blow pipes and get rid of this mess." Well they did a good job of it all right, at least in regard to cleaning up the floor. The only problem was that much of what had been on the floor then became plastered to the walls. The story I heard was that a few of the inspectors accidentally brushed up against the walls and took home unwanted souvenirs.

I had worked at Bunker Hill for three years and four months (January 1974 to May 1977), which, of course, included my days at the Crescent, when the time came for the United Steel Workers Union contract to run out. Another strike appeared imminent. At this juncture, Bunker Hill needed "down time" to complete two massive 715- and 610-feet smokestacks at the smelter complex. Interestingly enough, the stacks had been constructed using a "slip-form," whereby a section would be poured, and, after the concrete set for awhile, the form was moved up for another pour. It looked like an enormous metal Band-Aid that went all the way around the stack. I was amazed at how fast they were able to pour concrete, let it set, and raise the form up again for the next pour. The only smokestack that the construction outfit built that was taller than Bunker Hill's 715-feet skyscraper is a giant near Salt Lake City, Utah, that stands around a thousand feet high.

Bunker Hill needed to consolidate the old and new facilities, but could only do so when operations and equipment were idle. Or, at least, that's what we all figured, even though the mine swore up and down that it wasn't true. I heard that the Environmental Protection Agency was hot after Bunker to stop belching polluted emissions into the Valley. Consequently, some genius decided to put up the giant smokestacks and spread pollution out across the entire Pacific Northwest so everyone could get a little. After the new smokestacks were operating, persons living as far away as Montana complained that their normally pristine air sometimes showed a blue-gray pall of stinky smoke.

The Department of Fish and Game even had hunters bring in samples of deer and elk meat (i.e., the heads) which were checked for lead and other crud, and not just bullets either. One of the guys who worked at the smelter once told me, "That's a laugh; the EPA is really hot after the mine to cut their pollutants in the air right? So what does the mine do? Wait till after dark and open those babies wide so they can damper them down and run cleaner in the daytime when the smoke can be seen."

In 1968, long before I became a miner, I had worked on the Kellogg Junior High School building during its construction. One of the jobs I had was operating a compactor to "tighten up" the fill gravel in the excavations where concrete was going to be poured. The school and an adjacent sprawling housing complex stood on top of an old airport runway, which in turn had been laid out on top of an old Kellogg city dump. The dump, in turn, sat over the old riverbed. The construction company's tractors had to dig through 13 feet of

garbage to get down to something solid enough to lay a foundation on. At 13 feet, tractors dug out enormous 3-feet-thick tree trunks that had probably been there since before the 1910 fire that decimated so much of the forests around Kellogg. I've always thought there was something prophetic about the similarity between the story of the Phoenix bird rising from its own ashes and a new school, which would foster bright minds for our future, rising from the ashes of a garbage dump.

At the construction site, I had to hold my breath much of the time because of the acrid smoke from Bunker Hill's smelter settling down into the ditch with me. I couldn't believe it either when I actually saw a pale blue haze slowly flowing into the depressions in the ground, like a barely discernible waterfall. There was a joke going around the Valley then, and it went, "in the summer you could sit out on your front porch and watch your grass die." At the time area residents were disagreeing among themselves about whether it was better to have clean air or jobs. I think the people who wanted to keep eating were winning.

Later, when I bought a house down on the flats in Kellogg in 1976, the sales contract declared that I wouldn't be able to sue Bunker Hill for pollution. The only way I figured that the mine could have gotten that bit of trivia added to my contract, and to other contracts in the area, was to have sent someone around years before to pay the persons who owned the houses back then to legally waiver this right.

The day finally came when the Steel Workers contract was up. When I came into work that day, Fred told Roy and I to haul our slushers, scraper buckets, machines, and tools back into the raise area where they would be protected from ground fall, just in case the strike turned out to be a long one. Fred's directive didn't really set well with me, since Roy and I happened to be in a good contract period. I knew that if I shut down and didn't muck out a round, the company would dock our gypo check for that day. So I went ahead and worked instead. Well, at the last minute, I did go around and gather up a few tools to make it look better. Fred had a really sour look on his face when I turned in our daily progress report.

Something I neglected to tell him, though, was that my round was only about two feet wide. I just ran out of time and figured that advance is advance. I wasn't about to let the company screw me by tricking me into cleaning up tools, and thereby preventing me from blasting the money-making round I could have gotten instead.

If the strike didn't last very long, I'd just widen it later on. The next day the strike began.

During strikes all entrances to mine properties are posted with notices about the ongoing labor dispute. I suppose this is a standard procedure during "contract negotiations" in any industry. My first picket duty assignment was at the back gate of the smelter, near the base of the 715-feet-high smokestack. There were 10 or so of us picketing there.

About an hour after I arrived, a pickup truck suddenly pulled up. It was full of workers who had the job of connecting the giant smokestack into the existing systems. We, of course, advised them about the strike. Meanwhile, the pickup had been observed by other strikers in the Kellogg vicinity and these men went running to their vehicles. Consequently, as we talked, dozens of trucks and cars rapidly arrived on the scene, full of strikers. They thought the guys in the pickup were strike breakers. Now this wasn't the case at all, of course. These four guys were only going to work just like anyone else would have, and had been working on the smokestacks probably from the beginning of the project.

That didn't matter; word was spreading like a virus through the area: "Maybe the Bunker Hill is trying some of the old tricks again, and bringing in scabs."

From what I'd heard, back in 1960 the Bunker Hill Company did bring in bus loads of scabs in an effort to break the union's will. It didn't work, because the weapons of choice that the angry striking miners used to protect their "rights" were baseball bats, clubs, or whatever else could deal a "blow" for labor rights. I think being smacked up against the side of the head with a good stout hickory baseball bat would surely warn me to stay away, or at least it would certainly get my attention. Needless to say, the scabs were driven away.

In a matter of a few moments, there were 50 angry miners surrounding the construction workers' pickup. The miners had the same excited look as the miner who had beaten up good ol' Rick, the motorman I'd replaced when I first went to work for Bunker Hill. I couldn't believe what was happening—Bunker hill employed nearly 3,000 workers and I think most of them were on the road headed our way, speeding along in bumper-to-bumper traffic.

The poor driver of the pickup was white with fear and sweating too. When we told him that we would appreciate it if he wouldn't go through the gate, he nervously said, "That's good enough for me."

He turned to the fella sitting beside him and I heard him say, "To hell with this… I'm gonna go get drunk." They drove off in a cloud of dust heading for a bar. After that little episode, our picket-line duty stations were watched carefully by sheriff and police cars.

About that time, Bunker Hill's president publicly stated that the company wasn't waiting for work to be completed on the new smokestacks before getting really serious about negotiating a new contract, but we all knew better. I hope that my observations don't make me sound like I'm against mining companies. After all, I did work for them for many years, and they did provide much needed jobs. It's just that theirs is a really competitive, tough, difficult, and sometimes nasty business considering the occasional fatal accidents and the pollution problems inherent in such an industry. In regard to the evolving technologies and the ever-changing business and social attitudes that have occurred over time, I'm sure they have generally done their best to conduct their industry as safely and cleanly as possible according to the standards of the times.

I went home that day disillusioned, thinking that by the look of things we were in for one hell of a long strike. I told my wife that I didn't think we could afford to wait it out because it might last for many months. She agreed and I began making telephone calls. I was trying to get a lead on a fill-in job. I had 3 and 1/2 years in at Bunker and didn't want to quit and lose it all.

I called the Homestake Mining Company of Lead, South Dakota, and told them of my predicament. I said, "I am on strike from the Bunker Hill Mine and it looks like it will be a long one. Are you doing any hiring down there?"

Then, surprisingly enough, the man on the other end of the line answered, "Your being on strike doesn't really mean anything to us. And yes we are taking applications at this time."

I hung the telephone receiver up with a smile on my face knowing what was going to happen next. My younger brother Gary had been working in the Crescent Mine, but since Bunker Hill owned it too, Gary also was out on strike. I called him up and said, "I talked with a fella down at the Homestake and asked him if the mine was hiring and he said, 'yes we are.' I'm leaving in the morning. Do you want to go with me?"

At six o'clock the next morning we drove out of the yard heading east toward the Black Hills of South Dakota. ✿

CHAPTER 8

Pig Trucks and Pink Rock

Homestake Mine
Lead, South Dakota

Gary and I were excited about the trip. It was late spring 1977 and there we sat in my two-year-old station wagon, with a long stretch of blacktop and our futures ahead of us. We were free. In other words… money was tight and Gary and I were both nearly broke.

One of the things that's really constraining to a miner is the closeness of his work. This is not to say that claustrophobia bothers him, but most times he can reach out and touch the very edges of his world. In my case, though, the saving grace was that I knew there were other things just beyond that dumb old rock wall, like daylight for instance. Here Gary and I were outside again, and driving through the real world, not just some dark tunnel. It had been five years since I'd been away from the Silver Valley and I was loving every minute of this new experience.

As we neared 4,725-feet-high Lookout Pass on Interstate 90, we laughed about the massive 2,000-feet-high "hanging wall" on the right and the equally impressive "foot wall" to the left. As we topped the pass, we were leaving the Silver Valley and entering Montana. I looked in the rearview mirror, bidding ado, for now, to my wife and our ever growing six-year-old son.

We drove through the mountains of western Montana and eventually found ourselves passing through cornfields and sagebrush plains near Billings. There, we

turned southeast toward Wyoming. By then it was getting late, and the excitement of the long day had worn us down some. I began looking in earnest for a place to stop for the night.

Somehow I felt we were much like the prospectors of old, out and about searching for our fortunes. In reading history books, however, I'd never come across a single page describing how even one of those grizzled old-timers spent the night at a motel. I wasn't planning on it, either. I figured that the modern equivalent of an old-time prospector's camp would be pulling your car into a highway rest stop. Though we were following in the tradition of the old-time tramping prospector, I still wanted to take full advantage of modern day conveniences.

I finally located a likely looking rest stop and pulled off. Though still elated, but feeling exhausted too, we settled into our respective places out in the back of our "wagon." As drowsiness began clouding my mind, I wondered what new adventures the morning would bring. What wondrous new things would we find just ahead of us down the road?

"My God! What's that horrible smell?" were my first thoughts the next morning.

An acrid, pungent odor burned my eyes and hung in the air like a fog. I struggled to gather my senses, while looking out through the fogged-up windows of our little impromptu motel room for the answer. At first, all I could see were enormous tires alongside of us.

The night before I'd pulled off into a completely empty, desolate-looking rest stop, but here we were completely surrounded by tires. Then, hearing a chorus of snorts from both sides of the car, I finally under-

---

Miner inspecting a shaft sinker. The drilling machines hanging on the chains are fitted with drill steel and are used to drill blasting holes in the floor of a shaft. After the holes are loaded with explosives and the round is blasted, the large claw picks up the loose muck, loading it into a large metal container positioned nearby.
ASARCO Inc./Charles E. Rotkin, Photography for Industry, NY, 1969

stood the answer: two pig trucks had pulled in alongside of us and we were sandwiched between.

I clambered over the front seat and, as we sped out of the rest stop and back onto the highway again, I looked back through the rearview mirror. I wondered how those sleeping truckers, who probably still were sleeping, could ever get use to that awful smell. I concluded that they must drive fast and keep their faces near open windows a lot.

As soon as possible we stopped and filled up with coffee in a small roadside cafe. I asked the little, apron-clad waitress if there were any mines nearby. She took my question one step further, answering "No miners around here, just cowboys." We thanked her and soon were watching the parched Wyoming landscape slip by again.

An hour went by, then two, and I saw a sign that read "Hole in the Wall." I thought of the infamous Wild West desperadoes, known as the Hole in the Wall Gang, and remembered the waitress's comment about cowboys.

I turned on my citizens band radio and jokingly said to anyone who might be listening, "What happened to all the bad men and outlaws around here?"

I was surprised when someone responded almost immediately, slyly saying, "Some of us are still here."

We were indeed in cowboy country. I was hoping, however, to see a tell-tale scar on a hillside indicating that there were mines somewhere nearby too, but I saw none. I knew that there were mines near Cody, Wyoming, close to Yellowstone National Park, but they'd been mined out and then abandoned years ago. By now we'd left Buffalo, Wyoming far behind, and had turned left, heading to the Dakotas. We were on what I figured to be the last leg of the trip to Lead, South Dakota, and the Homestake Mine.

I thought we might just as well take in some of the sights as we drove along. We turned off the main road to follow a sign that beckoned us to "Devils Tower National Monument." It was an impressive sight indeed; I could see why the local Indians had given it religious significance. According to Indian legend, an Indian maiden fleeing from an enormous bear perched herself atop a large mountain. In an effort to reach her, the huge beast clawed enormous gouges into the slope, creating the impressive rock spire.

I very much liked the story which, incidentally, I heard when I pushed the button in the little tourist information center at the base of the tower. It brought to

mind two possibilities: I concluded either the Indians of old must not have had a nearby television set as a center of their community's home life, thus they had to make up their own suspenseful thrillers; or, the millions of gophers in gopher town might have had something to do with it too. Looking out on the gophers (or prairie dogs?) bobbing up and down nearly as far as I could see, I thought of how fearful my wife was when she even heard the word "mouse." I concluded that the Indian maiden must have been frightened up onto Devil's Tower by the grandparents of the hoards of gophers I was looking at. I left Devil's Tower with a new respect for Indian lore, and with a need to go underground like the lucky gophers.

After returning to the main highway, I saw a rock shop and pulled over again. When I asked the clerk if she had any gold samples from the Homestake Mine, she replied, "No. We can't get any samples from the mine…"

As she spoke on, I recalled something I'd heard over the news one day: some Homestake miners and a few of the bosses had been caught high-grading (taking home) raw gold nuggets from the mine. We thanked her and continued on down the sun-bleached strip of blacktop, heading toward the much anticipated Homestake Mine.

Finally, just after dark, we drove into Lead, South Dakota. We were exhausted and looked for another "cheap" place to spend the night, only this time without pig trucks next door. I thought back to my days on the police department in Oregon. I knew that strangers sleeping in a car on some side street in town might be considered suspicious by local marshals and it generally was unacceptable. Consequently, I phoned the police and told them that we were in town looking for work at the Homestake Mine. They allowed us to park right in front of the police station for the night, which we did. I drifted off to sleep again assured that no nightmarish pig trucks would sneak up on us during the night.

The next morning, we drove around Lead, looking the town over. I was impressed by how much it looked like Wallace, Idaho. It too had been built in the "crotch" of a canyon and the houses were built as far up the canyon walls as possible, just like in Wallace. I was also impressed by its "cowboy and miner" character. We parked and went into a busy local cafe to "coffee up." Somehow the busy, smoke-filled cafe seemed like it came straight out of the 1870s to me. Maybe it was the rough, ornate stone work on the front of the building,

Historic view of the Homestake Mine at Lead, South Dakota.
Black Hills Mining Museum, Lead SD

or perhaps its high ceiling and crowded interior. The long, narrow cafe was filled with rough looking, noisy men who looked like they too were straight out of the Old West.

A couple of fellas got up right about then, and Gary and I sat down at their still messy table. As I settled myself in, I looked around the room and suddenly felt as if I were in a mine and sitting down at a wooden lunch table. The occupants of the next table suddenly burst into riotous laughter. A pretty little waitress hurried over and, as she cleared away the table, I asked her about the place.

She said softly, "Everyone in here works for the Homestake in one way or another. Those fellas at that table"—she nodded toward the belly laughers—"are miners and were just paid their contract checks."

She suddenly lost her sweet, innocent, unknowing air and continued on with knowledge that I thought she could only have gained by having worked there for a long time. "The miners at the Homestake aren't paid any contract until they reach the end of their cuts. So their gypo checks usually run about three months apart." (North Idaho mines, on the other hand, paid their "contract" miners a portion of their contract earnings in every other weekly check; the contract miners,

of course, also received a guaranteed minimum hourly rate or "day's pay" that came in a check once a week.)

She continued, "Those fellas over there were each paid $9,000 today." I looked into her sweet little face as she talked and was in awe of this sudden outburst of knowledge. She brought us cups of steaming black coffee to ponder over, then hurried off about her chores.

I knew that we would need a place to stay if we got on at the mine. It was late May, the weather was just beginning to turn nice, and it was a good feeling too. Most tramping miners preferred to be out and about in the spring or summer months; that way the weather wasn't a problem if they had to sleep under a tree somewhere. We'd seen a couple of campgrounds on our way through town, and talked about staying there too.

When the waitress returned with a half-empty pot of coffee, I asked her if she knew of any place cheap where we could camp out.

I felt just like one of the crew when she replied, "A lot of the fellas live in board and room houses around town. And the people running the houses will usually wait for a new guy to get his first check from the mine to get their money."

She gave me the bill, quickly scribbled an address and phone number on a piece of paper for us, and hurried off again. I looked over at the doorway and saw two fellas waiting for a seat. So we got up, I left a "paper" tip, and we went outside into the bright sunshine.

As we drove through the rustic town, I thought about what our little waitress had said about whole families working at the mine, all the way from grandfathers, to fathers, down to sons. Suddenly, I realized we were in Deadwood, Lead's sister city. The two are only a short distance apart. As we passed through, I thought, "Now this place looks like a cowboy town." In fact, somewhere on our drive I saw a small historical marker indicating the spot where Wild Bill Hickock was shot from behind by a coward.

I drove up to the address the waitress had given us, but the lady who answered the door of the large, older two-story white house said, "We're full up." About then, I felt sort of like the floor mat beneath my feet.

We soon found a motel with an opening, however. I told the husband and wife motel managers that we probably were going to be working for the mine in a few days, which was wishful thinking really, and I asked if they had weekly rates.

She replied, "Sure. In fact there are two miners from Idaho staying in the apartment just two doors down from the empty one, and in the court [an RV park was just behind the motel] there is a fifth wheel trailer with three more Idaho miners in it. All of those fellas work at the mine too."

I told her that I had no way of knowing how long we'd be staying there and asked, "If we have to pull out sometime during the week will you prorate the rent money and give us back the unused portion of it?"

She smiled pleasantly and assured me that they would and there would be no problem. I was sold; we had a room and settled in for the night. Sure enough, after seeing my Idaho car plates, all five of the Idahonians came by later that night for a visit. I was sort of surprised by the fact that they were all Bunker Hill strikers too. In fact, I knew them. It was like old home week. During their visit they told us about the mine and where to go to hire out.

During our drive through Lead, Gary and I had spotted a sign on one of the buildings that read, "Homestake Mine Employment Office." The next morning, after we'd finished the last of the peanut butter sandwiches for breakfast, we went in search of the employment building. Following directions given by our beer drinking fellow strikers the night before, we soon found ourselves standing on the sidewalk in front of the Homestake's hiring office. It was an older building that

kind of looked like an old-time glass fronted clothing store.

It was early yet, but the door was open. We stepped inside and began filling out the work applications they gave us. As I sat there penciling in my employment information, I noticed that the room had been steadily filling with hopeful employees, and finally we were 26 strong. Looking into all of the blank faces, I thought, "I sure hope these guys aren't all looking for the job I want. If they are I haven't got a chance." Somewhat nervously, I asked the fella in the next chair about the mine.

He said, "I use to work here a couple of years ago as a logger. The company has its own logging company that cuts all of the wood used underground. I'm trying to get back on again." I was relieved that he wasn't a miner.

He continued, "The Homestake has been here for 100 years and is over 8,000 feet deep. And there are probably about 1,200 people working here too." I thought, almost proudly, about "my" own Bunker Hill Mine and its 2,500 fellow workers.

About then I heard my name being called from a different part of the room. I excused myself, got up from my chair, and as I passed by I looked into the teeming faces of the people around me. Suddenly the old saying about an early bird getting the worm flashed through my mind, and I smiled as I walked toward the beckoning voice. Gary had been called too, right after me. We offered up our personal sales pitches and were hired.

The next 1 1/2 days were hectic, to say the least. We passed through a large old-looking medical clinic that someone said was company owned. We took breath tests, ran in place, looked at funny-looking blurry letters (or at least the ones I was looking at were) on a wall chart, and left bodily fluids for someone to flush.

In all the excitement, however, I had somehow missed the part where I was hired as an "underground laborer second class." I sat there in my motel room, brooding over my demotion, as I waited for dark so I could go to work on the graveyard shift. Gary had been put on day shift. I was a little disgruntled about that piece of trivia too. As I came to the line on my employment form indicating the hourly wage, it read, "$4.86" per hour. Now that was really disheartening. My second residence, all of the extra food, and the wear and tear on the old station wagon was adding up to more than I would be earning. I figured, though, that I'd do whatever I had to and maybe I could get in with one of those big money boys.

Another workday at the Homestake.
Homestake Mining Company

Finally dark came and I drove to the mine. As I climbed down a stairway headed toward the dry, I saw a sign on the wall warning that no ore samples could be taken from the mine and that violators would be prosecuted to the full extent of the law. I recalled our stop at the rock shop near Devils Tower.

I hadn't been in a dry where I had my own locker before, but there it was. I changed from street clothes into my rotten old diggers. As I finished dressing "down," the final touch was to put on my hard hat to top it all off. I felt like a real man then; I was a hardrock miner and on my turf again. But as I walked toward the shifters office, I remembered the hire-out paper, declaring that I was but a miner's helper second class and only making four bucks an hour.

Then to top it all off my new shifter said, "You're going to be working in the head-frame tonight. Watching the conveyer belt."

Now that took me back a bit. In all of the mines I'd ever worked in, I'd never done that before. We walked up to the head-frame and he showed me what to do. At the top of the mine's shaft stood an enormous tower, maybe 150 feet high. In the tower was the "sheave wheel," which is a pulley for the hoist cable. The sheave wheel is placed high in the tower, allowing room for the man-skips and the muck-skips (deep square metal cans that rode above the man-skips) to be pulled completely above the ground's surface. At times, this is necessary because the heaviest and bulkiest pieces of mining equipment, such as large muckers or whatever, are much too large to fit into the bottom deck of a skip. Instead, large equipment must be chained onto and lowered down the shaft by hanging beneath the bottom of the skip assemblage.

Well anyway… we walked into the head-frame and he pointed out the conveyer belt. This is how it operated: muck was dumped into the cans by the cagers down in the shaft. Then the hoistman raised the muck cans up the shaft to the top and the muck was dumped into a containment area. There the muck was sorted, with the big chunks going straight into a crusher. Now that crusher was really something; it looked to me sort of like the enormous barrel of a washing machine. It could take a chunk of rock the size of a small Volkswagon and grind it down to the size of a large suitcase. Then the boulder was dumped into another crusher… and then another. By the end of the chain of crushers, the once massive boulders were reduced to beach sand.

The conveyer belt caught the smaller stuff, while a large magnet suspended above the belt picked up the pieces of metal mixed in with the muck—tools, rock bolts, mats, or what have you. The idea was not to let noncrushable metal objects get into the crushers because they would damage the inner workings.

The shifter left me alone and there I sat, watching the conveyer belt. I heard rumbling as the skips came by and then up the shaft above me and when the muck was dumped from the can into the "pocket" up there someplace. Then things got really loud. I pushed Styrofoam ear plugs that the boss gave me into my head, pulled down the Bunker Hill "gun-shooters" (a kind of earmuffs mounted on the outside of my hard hat), and went to work. Sitting nearby on the floor in the huge room was one large wooden box for bits of metal and another for pieces of wood.

That is the way I spent the first few hours… rumble, rumble, dump, grind, and toss, toss. One thing I did like about my new job, though, was that I was outside, sorta. Something I didn't really care for, however, was that all of the rock, dust, bits of metal, and wood were colored pink, I guess because the "rock" was sandstone. I'd heard once that a federal prison painted the walls of its cells pink because the color tended to subdue the inmates' anger. It "placated their temperament," so to speak. I could believe it too, because it sure calmed me right down.

During breaks, when the cager was down in the shaft, or asleep, or whatever, I was able to walk over to the big garage-type sliding door and look outside to something that wasn't pink. It was dark and Lead's city lights were really beautiful. I thought of all the people who must be huddled near those lights… uh-oh, rumble, rumble, dump, grind, and toss, toss.

A couple of boxes of wood, one box of magnetized bits of iron, and a few hours later, the shift ended. I went home to my motel room and, in no time at all, I was back again the next day, ready to go. This time, though, the shifter said, "I'm putting you down the shaft tonight. You'll be working in the pocket."

I thought, "Well at least I'll be underground where I belong."

My classification as a miner's helper second class and the pay rate of four bucks an hour had been weighing heavily on my mind, ever since I first read the employment form. Near the end of our conversation I asked the boss, "How long will it be before I'll be able to go mining?"

He looked at me with astonishment and only responded by asking, "Why?"

Then I said, "Well, because I'm a miner! I've been mining for five years up in Idaho. I've even worked in a mine in the Butte, Montana camp."

He only chuckled and replied, "Here at the Homestake everybody who works underground has to go through a miner's training program. Even the electricians. They have to be trained well enough so they

are qualified as miners. Mainly because all of the underground work is part of a miner's job."

Then I remembered the crowded room in the employment office. I hesitantly asked him, "How long do you think it will be before I can get into the training program?"

He quickly replied, "Maybe three months."

I walked down the drift disillusioned, and thinking, "There is no way I am going to hang around here for three months waiting to get into a student's stope to take training. Hell, the Bunker Hill strike probably will be over by then anyhow. So in other words I'll only be able to make four bucks an hour while I'm here. I have to support the wife and son back in Idaho, and with me galavantin' around down here in the Dakotas, I'd go broke."

I decided right then and there that this was going to be my last shift for the Homestake. I somehow felt relieved, maybe because I sensed the end of an endless stream of the color pink.

I waited with the crew, and when it was my turn walked into the skip. The shaft and skips had a nice feature; the motor rails were embedded in the concrete floors so that the tops of the rails were flush with all walking surfaces and weren't a tripping hazard. The skip was big enough to drive a motor right into it and still have room to pull down the garage-type door on its front. As I stood there in the crowd going down, I suddenly heard an "over the radio" kind of voice. Then I noticed an intercom hanging on the wall near the front of the skip.

I thought, "Man this is nice. None of the mines up in the Valley have anything like that in their shafts. They don't have any way at all for the men who are in the skips to communicate with their hoistmen while the skip is running in the shaft."

The skip stopped at a couple of levels, men got off, and then I found myself deposited in-between levels. I was impressed; I was in an enormous room—at least 50 feet wide, 30 feet deep, and about 20 feet high—that was immediately adjacent to the shaft. Located at the back wall were the bottoms of two chutes—one for ore and the other for waste. Immediately beneath the chutes were two troughs sloping down toward the shaft. A small booth stood in between the troughs nearer to the shaft. This all was just about as alien to me as anything I'd seen so far in the mine. Oh, I recognized the enormous pink boulders in the troughs, all right; and, I understood bits and pieces of the operations here and

Mucking in a stope. Note mats bolted onto the wall for ground support.
Hecla Minging Company/Photography Unlimited, Spokane WA

there, but I was sort of befuddled to say the least. I think the cager showing me around sensed my confusion because he explained the operation to me.

With an arm outstretched and pointing a finger, he began, "The muck comes down those chutes back there from the level above, and continues on down the troughs."

Then, still pointing a finger, he explained, "See those two gates right there?"—up until then I hadn't noticed the two heavy iron gates that looked as if they were thrust up from the bottoms of the troughs—"Well, in between those gates is one skip-full of muck. After you're 'broken in' you'll be running the controls and sitting in that booth."

I still couldn't get over the fact that the booth he was then pointing to looked like a well-built outhouse with windows, one on each side facing a trough.

He continued, "Then when the hoistman finishes dumping his loaded skip up on top and brings the skip back down the shaft, you'll spot the skip for him [signal to the hoistman where to stop]. Then you'll pull on the

first lever and that first gate will drop down into the floor. That allows the muck in between the two gates to slide down the sloped trough into the skip. Then you'll pull the lever again and the gate will return to its upright position. Next you'll pull the second lever, that gate will drop down into the floor too, and the muck above it will slide down from out of the bottom of the chute. That refills the empty spot in between the two gates. And when its full you'll pull the second handle again and that gate will return to its upright position too. Get it?"

I said, "Yeah, that seems plain enough." As I spoke, I noticed a large pile of broken and shattered wooden powder poles over along one wall. Pointing toward them, I continued, "What are those for? Do you blast down here too?"

He replied with a sly grin, "Oh sometimes the boulders are just too big so we loosen them up a little for the guys up above."

I remembered how the enormous pink boulders were ground down to manageable size by the crushers up

Miner "timing" his back stope round by pinching the flaps on the ends of his fuse primers' igniters over a spitter cord. Note that the wooden floor he is standing on is in his raise area.
Hecla Mining Company

above, but I had no idea that in the beginning some of them had been even much larger.

I said, "This is sure different from any of the mines of the Silver Valley in Idaho. Up there the miners are responsible for making sure that the slabs are reduced down to no larger than 10 inches in width so they can go through their grizzlies. Don't the miners use any grizzlies down here?"

He only shook his head no, replying, "They break the slabs up pretty good though." Then, as we headed for the ore trough, I heard him mumble under his breath, "That'd sure be nice."

I spent the rest of the day barring enormous slabs of rock around so that the gates would operate properly, and I blasted the pink right out of those chunks that refused to cooperate. Almost before I knew it, the shift was over. The closer we'd gotten to the end of the day, the better I had felt because I knew I was quitting. As we rode the skip back up the shaft I stood there in silence, thinking.

A thought passed through my confused mind: "Here I was on a tramp and about to tramp out again, but from the mine I had just tramped to."

I asked the other fellas in the crowded skip if they knew a miner who only worked in the Homestake for two days. The fella standing in front of me sort of twisted his head to one side and in an unmistakenly bored voice said, "Not since last week."

I replied, "Well you've met one this week too. This is my last shift here."

He turned to one side and then with an interested voice asked, "Why quit?"

I told him of having to support two houses and my little family up in Idaho. And ended by saying, "... and all on four bucks an hour. Hell if I'm going to go broke anyhow, I might just as well do it while I'm home. I thought I'd be able to go mining down here, but now I'm told that it will be at least three or four months before I even get a chance to go through the miner training program. And even longer, probably, before I go mining."

As our small iron skip sped up the shaft toward the early morning light, the conversation grew in intensity. The other fellas in the skip had been listening and suddenly our confined space was filled with opinions, disagreements, and conclusions. In the end, though, it was decided that I was doing the right thing and that I should leave. I didn't really know whether to applaud them for their decision or me for making it in the first place, because I felt sort of like I was being kicked out. I was confused, but determined.

After reaching the surface, I showered, changed into my "streets," and drove back to the motel. Gary was still asleep in his room and had no idea of my sudden change of heart. I knew that, and as a joke, I barged in and banged furniture around and hastily stuffed clothes into suitcases. I became so engrossed in what I was doing that I completely forgot about him. Then as I grabbed for the last of the dirty clothes, I happened to glance into the next room. He was up and also stuffing clothes into suitcases, and in no time we were out the door.

I walked into the motel office to get our prorated rental refund. All I got for my trouble, though, was a dirty look from the motel marm and these words, "You weren't here long enough for that. We thought you were going to be here for at least two months or so."

I countered with, "But I told you that we had no idea how long we'd be here. You agreed that if we did have to leave, and had it coming, we could get some of our money back."

The pitch of her voice grew higher by at least an octave, and I thought she was going to have a stroke. I don't know, I guess I was resigned to the idea of being screwed in the morning, but at least I figured I'd get a little dig back at her.

I said, "Well, we have to take off… we're leaving now for Idaho."

She held out her hand and the whole tone of her voice changed as if by magic. She meekly replied, "Well you should give me back your two keys then."

It was my turn to play her game. With my best "Oh you're trying to screw us, huh?" look, I said, "Well no… we might change our minds and come back between now and Friday. We still have three days left that I've already paid you for."

With that I turned and could sense her icy stare on the back of my neck as I walked back toward the car. I knew she was trying desperately to think of some way to get the keys because she knew that she'd probably never see them again if I left. But she didn't get them and we drove off.

Returning to the mine, Gary and I collected our diggers and goin' away checks. Soon after, we were heading south down the highway. About an hour or so later, we came to an intersection and sat there looking east, in the direction of Sioux City, Iowa, and west toward Casper, Wyoming. I think that putting a sign like that up in front of a miner on a "tramp" should be illegal because it causes terrible inner stresses. I finally made a decision and turned to Gary, asking him if he still had his motel key.

He said, "Yes," then handed it to me. I chucked both of our keys out the window. As I drove away, I looked in the rearview mirror and could see them laying in the gravel close to one another. Then laughing, I said, "There's your key's back."

I'd succumbed to reason and turned right back toward Idaho. We drove straight through, too, and a day or so later I pulled up into my yard in Kellogg again.

Not long afterward, I telephoned the Bunker Hill Company and "turned in my time." I'd decided I'd had enough of this damned mining life. It hadn't gotten me

anywhere at all. Here I was still stompin' around the countryside looking for a mine to work in to support my little family and I hadn't had much luck.

I loaded my wife and young son into the car and we moved back to the Oregon Coast, where I finally found a job. It wasn't in mining; instead I hired out with a logging company. My job was to run along behind a bulldozer setting choker cables. I followed the timber fallers, setting cables on the downed trees so they could be snagged out of the woods. A bulldozer dragged the logs to landing decks where they were loaded onto trucks. I worked there for a while, quit, then worked for another outfit doing the same thing.

I'd been in Oregon for about two months when I heard on the news that Bunker Hill and the miners union had finally settled the strike. The same report said the company's new smokestacks had been finished and were in operating order. I just laughed, remembering that the president of Bunker Hill had stated that the company wasn't waiting to finish its new smokestacks before finally getting down to business with the union negotiators.

I eventually wound up working for three different logging outfits, as well as Coos Bay's Weyerhaeuser lumber mill.

"Now this is the best of all worlds," I reasoned. "The company's mill has been here in Coos Bay for many years, and once a fella gets on he's set for life."

After a one-month probationary period, I was considered a full time "puller" on the company's green chain, an admirable, if not difficult, job if there ever was one. I always felt like there was something missing, though. I'd been working there for about eight months and finally wound up just feeling miserable. I guess it was the steady stream of boards I pulled off the chain. Each new one was exactly like the last one I'd pulled off and placed neatly in a stack. When the stack was just about how I wanted it and looking good, a big damn overhead crane would swoop down and snatch it up, leaving me with an empty hole to fill all over again. It finally got to me.

I'd heard that mining gets into your blood, but didn't believe it until then. I thought, "That just has to be what's wrong, though. It's the only answer, but how could someone miss an occupation in which you beat yourself to death?" ❀

CHAPTER 9

"Ya' Can't Hire Out Anywhere, Now"

Galena Mine
Osburn, Idaho

I decided that I'd had just about enough fresh air and safety to last for a while, so I returned to the Valley looking for another hole to crawl into. It was June 1978 and the mines were still hiring anything with a pulse. I planned to hire on with a mining company I hadn't worked with before, which might change my luck, so I rustled ASARCO (American Smelting and Refining Company, Inc.). Both the Galena and Coeur mines near Osburn and Silverton were operated by ASARCO. Their hiring office was in historic old Wallace (in 1978, Wallace's well-preserved downtown area was placed on the National Register of Historic Places).

After the paperwork and a physical examination, I was told, "Go on over to the Galena and see the foreman."

I had to stop then and ask him how to get there. I found out that the two mines were more or less adjacent to one another on the south side of the Silver Valley and just east of Osburn. It felt great being back. Now I was a member of the mining community again and didn't feel like an outsider anymore. It's hard to explain but… well Dale, one of my friends over at the Sunshine, had a similar experience once that he was telling me about.

He said, "I use to drink a lot, more than I do now, and one time me and a couple of other guys who were working here in the Sunshine decided that we'd had enough. It was a Saturday night, and we'd had a few. We were feeling like this was going to be our new begin-

ning, it was great. So we loaded up my car and lit out for the east."

Dale continued, "I think we about drained every bar we came to. Well anyway, I woke up on… I think it was a Tuesday, alone and almost broke. I guess my friends musta left me to go their own way, wherever that was. I had $3,000 in my jeans when we were together on Saturday night in that Wallace bar. But when I looked in my pockets there in that crummy hotel room, I could find only about 10 bucks.

"It took a while to get my senses together and get cleaned up. And, man did I need a cup of coffee. My mouth felt like I had been drinking out of a garbage pit. I got my cup of coffee out of the machine in the hallway and after finally getting myself organized, climbed down three flights of stairs in that old moldy hotel before reaching the street. I still didn't know where I was either. In what town I mean, but figured… hell this has got to be Billings, Montana, because one of the guys I was with kept talking about how great it was there."

Dale started laughing and said, "I pushed open the door of the hotel and walked outside into a really nice day. I can tell you one thing, after taking one look at the size of those damned big buildings, I knew right away that it wasn't Billings, Montana… that's for sure. But where then? My car was parked across the street. At least that was something. I walked over and got into it and sat there looking around for a while. Then I focused on the windshield and thought, 'Damn, a parking ticket.' I opened the door again, reached out and pulled it out from under the wiper blade. After slamming the door, I read Chicago, Illinois, right at its top.

The Galena Mine head-frame.
ASARCO Inc.

I couldn't believe it, and thought, 'How did… When did we… ?'

"It took a while for me to get over the shock, and then I remembered the 200 bucks I always kept hid under the seat. I reached down and sure enough, it was right where I'd left it. I crumpled up the ticket and threw it out the window, and drove for what seemed like a long time before seeing the countryside again. That was one damned big town. And about two weeks later I finally wound up back here again."

Another funny part of his story, I thought, was when Dale said, "The 'Shine saved my stope for me. The main reason I left in the first place is because of that hot, air-blasting, damned stope. It just sat idle all the time that I was gone too. I guess the company knew I'd be back.

"I was only gone for a couple of weeks, but when I came back it was as a new hire. I lost all of my seniority, spent all of my money, and to top it all off, the mine put me right back in the same damned hole that I'd quit. Hell my machine was even still standing up against the wall right where I'd left it."

I felt a lot like Dale must have as I drove up the steep, mile-long road that dead-ends at the Galena Mine, what with coming back to the mines and all. After I parked my car, I climbed the stairs into the largest building there. I figured it must be the office and I was right. I was home again. There was that same smell: odors from moldy diggers and old rotten socks permeated the air. I thought, "How could any miner resist that sweet aroma?"

I walked down the hallway and looked at the bulletin board. Every time I hired out at a new mine this was the first thing I did, just to see if there was anything different going on. I thought, "It seems like I've been looking at a lot of new bulletin boards in the past few years."

Something on the board caught my attention. It was a notice that had been underlined many times with bright red chalk. It stated, "All crutches are company property and must be returned when you are finished using them."

I thought, "What the hell kind of mine is this?" I don't know why that sign stuck with me, but I wondered, "What does a guy have to do around here to get his own crutches?"

I walked into the foreman's office and saw a fella behind the desk pondering over a pile of official looking papers. He was a thick-shouldered, middle-aged man who looked like he'd broken a lot of rock in his time. He glanced up with a half smile, and without speaking reached out his hand to me as if to say, "Where is your form?"

I thought, "Damn, they must have quite a turnover here if he knows that is what I have for him."

Then he introduced himself as Doug Jutila, the foreman, and yelled out through the door for one of the guys there to show me around. As I left, he said, "When you get dressed go on outside and look for Walt Yost before you go down the shaft. He's your shifter."

I was given a short tour of the dry and lamp room, then the little fella showing me around said, "That's it."

I was suddenly a member of the crew. I had my diggers with me, so I found an empty hanger and began to get dressed. The dry, with its concrete floor and high ceiling, looked similar to any of the others that I'd been in. Lots of baskets—and full of old rotten looking diggers—hung in rows up near the ceiling. It was the beginning of the shift and the dry was crowded with miners busily readying themselves for the day, but the men were silent. It was just like I'd seen in all of the other drys that I'd been in at that part of the day, except for the sound of a few showers running for the graveyard fellas who'd just come up from underground. I saw the same quiet, "vacant" look in the men's eyes that I'd seen in the faces of most all the miners I knew. It was that same "Damn I gotta do it" look.

I put on my trusty rags and the heavy "gladiator's" belt with its mine lamp battery, self rescuer, and old piece of air hose holstering a new, bright red, company issue, 8-inch pipe wrench. I topped it off with my old, orange, Bunker Hill hard hat and my lamp, which was attached to my belt by the lamp's cord. Now I was "armed" and stepped proudly outside.

Then I saw the shaft and its 50-feet-high "head-frame" out in the paved yard in front of the dry. The head-frame looked like an oil-well derrick, except for the two sheave wheels, or pulleys, spinning in opposite directions at its top. I felt a little self-conscious as I approached a group of about 30 men standing near the shaft's gates. They were waiting for the hoistman to spot the skip so they could load.

A few of them gave me that, "Oh, a new guy" look, as I approached. Then I saw Walt… surprise, surprise. I recognized him and thought, "Hell, I know this guy, he was my shifter once over at the Sunshine." I sort of chuckled inwardly, thinking "Doug didn't tell me that this was my Walt." Making our greetings, I noticed out of the corner of my eye that the suspicious mood of the

Wallace, Idaho, in 1929. The nearly barren hillsides are the result of the great 1910 forest fire that gutted the entire eastern half of town. The conflagration burned over three million acres in Idaho and Montana and killed 85 people. In 1978, Wallace's downtown area was listed on the National Register of Historic Places.

Collection of Richard Caron, Wallace ID

men suddenly faded, and I was being accepted as one of them.

Walt said, "Jerry, go on down to the 3,000 foot level and work with Teddy Nicholby today in his back stope." Then he stood up on his tip toes and looked around through the men, and with a gesture of a partially missing finger, jokingly said, "There he is, he's that little, short, ugly one over there."

I knew what a back was, of course, but had no idea what he meant by "back stope." But I figured that this Teddy fella would probably be just the guy who'd show me all about it.

Walt had only three fingers on his pointing hand. When we were at the Sunshine he'd told me how he'd lost the other two: "Never put your hand into something that you're not sure about. I was a motorman years ago over at the Star Mine, up Burke canyon, and was working on the bottom of a chute trying to get the muck free that was hung up on the door. I put my hand into the chute between two large chunks of rock and tried to pull them apart. About that time the muck settled a

little and shoved the rocks together. And as I stood there watching, these two fingers got pinched off." Whereupon he held the two stumps right up in front of my face. I still remember vividly what they looked like and the thought, "Yuck," that flashed through my mind.

The skip finally arrived and our turn came to load up. That's when I first saw Teddy. When Walt pointed him out before, I wasn't able to see who he was talking about. But I remembered Walt's descriptive, "That little, short, ugly one over there."

The shaft was cramped and jammed; all the mines seemed to use the same "suck 'er in" way of loading up the man-skips. Teddy's hard hat was only about shoulder high on me and we stood beside each other on the way down. That was funny—we were packed in so tightly that my shoulder shoved his hard hat up against the wall. He moved and his hat didn't. Then I heard him angrily say, "Damn it, give me my hard hat back."

The skip whizzed down the shaft, which was only a few years old then, and I stood there still not knowing if my new partner was as ugly as Walt had claimed because I still hadn't gotten a good look at his face. But I certainly knew what the top of his hard hat looked like, that's for sure. We finally arrived at the 3,000 foot level. Teddy, our motorman, and I got off. Then the skip's doors closed and it disappeared on down the shaft, while the black, dope-covered hoist cable sang and banged on the sides of the shaft to mark its passing.

Bill Steel, our motorman, was in his early 60s and a world class swimmer, or so I was told. He sure didn't look that old to me. His job as a nipper, or all-around helper, was to service Teddy's "back stope." That is, Bill brought in all the equipment, timber, and powder that Teddy needed, and hauled out the stope's muck from the bottom of Teddy's chutes and took it to the shaft where he dumped it into the ore pocket. We left the station and walked back toward Teddy's stope, which incidentally was one heck of a long way from the shaft—probably three quarters of a mile or so.

On the way, I thought, "Old feller, I sure hope that you're in good shape, because I am just going to work your tail off today." I'd never worked in a back stope before and, to tell you the truth, didn't even know what the term meant. But I vowed that whatever it took today, I'd do it. We finally reached the bottom of Teddy's raise, and he and I started climbing the man-way.

I thought, "So far this place looks almost exactly like all the others that I've worked in, so what's the big deal?" We finally finished climbing 150 feet up, and I followed Teddy into the stope itself. Then I found out what the big deal was all about. Back stope miners drilled their holes straight up into the back using a "buzzy," which is a drilling machine that looks sort of like a jack-leg, but points straight up and is permanently affixed to a hydraulic, or air operated, two-stage leg. The leg pushes out and down on the floor, keeping upward pressure on the machine as its hammering and spinning drill steel cuts holes in the top of the stope. A control arm with buttons sticks out the side of the buzzy, and looks very similar to the control arm of a jack-leg.

Teddy, who would be doing the drilling, said, "Your job today is to slush out as much muck as you can get." Whereupon he walked into the darkness on the other side of the raise and started drilling.

This was the first day that I would be working as a miner again in nearly a year, and I sure's hell was going to make a good showing. I sat down on a block of wood on the floor right behind the slusher that someone had been using as a seat, then interlocked my fingers, pushing my palms outward, and spoke into the darkness,

A miner drilling with a buzzy (or stoper) in a back stope. Note the container hanging below his belt. It contains a special filter-type respirator known as a "self-rescuer," for protection against carbon monoxide gas from underground fires. Miners have been required to carry self-rescuers in all U.S. mines after the 1972 Sunshine fire which claimed 91 lives.
Hecla Mining Company/Photograph by Ted Clutter

"Okay old feller here we go." That day, I had the slusher so hot that I had to stop and pour water on it from time to time. It was smoking so badly that I couldn't see anything.

About halfway through the shift, something happened that still scares me when I think about it. The slusher's twisted, brittle, half-inch thick, wire cable was very old. It had been repaired quite a few times by previous operators—by knotting together the broken ends—and there were a lot of backlashes in it too. A backlash is a "tail" that sort of flops out from the drum as the cable is unreeled. I'd been fighting this cable since the beginning of the shift, and I had just decided to get ahold of Bill down below and have him bring me a replacement cable.

About then I reached up with my right hand to wipe sweat out of my eye. Just as I touched my forehead, a 2-feet-long backlash shot out from the spinning drum and wrapped itself over the handle where my hand had been seconds before. The backlash bent the handle over, almost tearing it clear off. Before I could react, the motor lugged down and stopped because I still had ahold of the other, "haul-back," handle. If I'd still been hanging onto the "pull-in" handle when the backlash grabbed ahold of it I would have lost a hand right there.

At the end of the shift Walt asked Bill, "How many cars did you pull out of the chute today?"

And Bill looked down at his tally sheet and replied, "Forty nine cars." That was about twice the number he normally pulled.

I was instantly reminded of Tennessee Ernie Ford's song, "Forty-nine tons of number nine coal," and thought, "Now I think I know how he felt." My neck was killing me.

Walt looked back at me again and said, "Looks like we're going to have to keep you in here Dolph." Incidentally, Bill went swimming that night, whereas I, on the other hand, went home to bed. I guess Bill was a world class swimmer after all.

After the first few days in the Galena I figured the biggest battle I'd have would be with boredom, because either I drilled for days on end, or slushed, slushed, slushed. The crew kept things interesting though. Fellas like "Moe" seem to have something going on all of the time. Old Moe was the mine's "shit nipper." His job was to go from level to level throughout the mine replacing full buckets with empties in the outhouses.

A new superintendent had started working at the Galena a short time after I did. Doug, the foreman, was taking him around showing him the mine, and they happened to come upon old Moe lying on a board fast asleep. Sleeping underground was not only against the rules in all mines, it was downright dangerous. I've heard of people who were seriously hurt and even of one guy who was killed while sleeping underground when a train ran over him. Well anyway, the new superintendent instantly got his hackles up and was just about to pounce upon poor ol' Moe when Doug stepped in. He whispered into the new "super's" ear about the service Moe provided and that he was the only one who would do it willingly.

Well, old Moe woke up just then and sat up on his elbows. He was trying to shake off a hangover from the night before. His bloodshot eyes tried to focus on the two men standing in front of him. He uttered, "Wha…" but the new "super" interrupted Moe, introduced himself, and said, "Moe if there's anything at all that you need you just let me know. You're doing a great job. Keep up the good work."

I think poor old Moe was confused because then he laid back down and closed his eyes again, probably to ponder the situation some more. Doug and the "super" looked back as they walked away and laughed when they saw Moe lay back down on the board and continue sleeping. The guy who told me this story had been over behind a post sleeping too, but he awoke at the last moment when he heard the bosses approaching. He then hid there in the darkness, fully expecting old Moe to get fired right on the spot, a standard penalty for being caught asleep underground.

Months went by with boring regularity. It now was spring 1979 by then and I had moved my little family to Pinehurst, which was about 15 miles from the mine. I had a brand new motorcycle and I was itching to ride it, but cool temperatures and icy roads wouldn't allow it. Finally the seasonal weather moderated and the big day for my first motorcycle ride arrived. It was still a bit cool in the mornings yet, but I figured, "It'll be all right." It was a trail bike, but I bought it with the thought of killing two birds… riding it on roads, and on trails. The thing I hadn't considered though was its really stiff suspension. Every little bump in the road sent shock waves up into the palms of my hands.

It was then that I discovered the term "carpal tunnel syndrome," a wrist malady caused by the constant vibration of the hands. Some call it "miners hand," but I think there are many housewives and store clerks who'd disagree with that description. I'd been feeling numbness from time to time in my hands while I was drilling in the mine. Sometimes it got so bad that I had to stop what I was doing and shake my hands, trying to get back any feeling in them at all. I didn't worry about it much, because when I shook them a bit the numbness seemed to go away. It got so bad while I was riding my shiny red motorcycle, however, that I couldn't hold onto the handle bars. I had to finally sell it.

Teddy and I got so good at back stoping that our contract pay shot right through the roof. At one point we were making more money than anyone else in the mine, and the numbers were still climbing. That was when the

A miner blowing Prell from a loading can into drill holes in the stope's back. Note the fuse primer cords hanging out of the drill holes; he has used a fuse primer to prime a stick of powder in each hole.
ASARCO Inc.

In other words, instead of being able to just knock off dull bits and put on sharp ones, we now had to carry armloads of chisel steel into the stope and haul out dull ones all of the time. We coped with the situation pretty well, though, and it wasn't really too bad—just a lot more work. But then it became hard to get certain lengths of steel for some reason or other. I'll bet if we'd been able to keep up speed even without some of the different lengths we needed, eventually the only steel we would have gotten from the mine would've been one dull 8 footer for each of us.

The stope's back was 7 feet from the sand floor. The drill stood about 5 feet high, leaving 2 feet between it and the stope's back. The drill holes had to be 8 feet deep, because we were blasting out an 8-foot cut. We began by drilling holes with 2 foot steel, then changed every 2 feet, going to 4, 6, and then, finally, 8 foot lengths.

The ground was very hard in our stope, which was a blessing of sorts because we didn't have to put any rock bolts into the back to hold it up. Of course, the only place that a mine could develop a back stope in the first place was in good, hard ground. The only problem, though, was that our drill steel bits really took a beating in the hard rock and had to be replaced with sharp ones often.

Well, just as the mine must have figured, our production dropped off—along with the money and our spirits, too. Doug told us we had to use up all the chisel steel first; after it was gone, we could go back to using knock-off bits. We worked as hard and fast as we could trying to keep up, hoping that the mine would eventually run out of steel, but it kept right on coming. We knew that they were sending out dull chisels, having them sharpened, and shipping them right back up to us. That was how it normally was done and we expected that to be the case. But when we began receiving new steel with the factory tags still on them, we finally realized that we were in a contest. So then it was our turn to play the game, and we responded by burying chisel steel. I'll bet that section of the Galena has two or three hundred "chisel steel" hidden under floors, behind timber, and buried in the sand.

The steel kept coming, though. Teddy finally gave up and quit, and went over to the Lucky Friday Mine. I hung on, figuring that there just had to be someway or other to beat this problem. We still had been making around $200 a day, but that $270 a day range where we'd been before was more what I wanted. My replace-

man with the sharp pencil must have gotten together with the bosses and said, "What can we do to keep them from making all of this big money?"

They came up with a really diabolical plan. That's when I became really familiar with the term "chisel steel." Up till then we had been using removable, star-shaped bits that could be resharpened, and were carried around in an easy-to-handle wire rack. These hollowed-out star bits were pushed onto the smooth cone-shaped end of the drill steel. When they became dull, they were knocked off and replaced with sharpened bits. Chisel steel on the other hand was a permanently attached drilling bit, and that's what the bosses decided we had to use from then on—"chisel steel."

ment for Teddy was named Jerry Nordholm; since he had a first name like that I figured he must be all right. We worked even harder, but the system that the contract man and his cohorts had worked out just couldn't be beaten.

The first thing Walt did when he came into our stope each day was to look around and make sure we didn't have any knock-off bits. I thought of trying to sneak some in from other parts of the level and hide them, but then he had all the regular knock-off steel and bits taken off our level, just to make sure that I didn't. I'd just about reached the end of my rope and we'd slowed down considerably.

I didn't like installing blasting powder in the Galena's back stope system. When the time came to blast one of our stope's 150-feet-long sides, we had to fill hundreds of 8-feet-deep holes with explosives. After handling such large quantities of Hercules dynamite, I'd develop awful "powder" headaches. There were times that I got so sick I had to crawl out from the back end of the stope to the raise where the air was decent, then hang my head over the side of the chute and try to revive myself; I would almost pass out. After laying there for a while, sometimes throwing up, I would struggle to my feet, take off my hard hat, and turn a water hose over my head, which seemed to help quite a lot. Then I staggered back into the gas and hit 'er again. I had to finish loading out, because I didn't want that sucker with the pencil to get too far ahead of me.

Conditions underground made for some almost comical situations sometimes. For instance, mines have porta-potty type toilets—well actually they consisted of buckets with plastic bags in them. After each use, cedar chips were thrown in to "quench the stench." Once the container was full, the bag was tied off, the lid put on, and it was all transported to the surface and disposed of quite properly, I'm sure. Anyway, Jerry once told me this story.

He said, "It was payday and I was standing in line in the hallway that leads to the pay office. As I stood there I began looking outside and saw Moe. He was loading honey buckets onto the back of a company pickup truck. He'd stacked them in there three deep. The load was a bit unsteady already and then the wind picked up. The fellas in the line ahead of me started laughing and everybody was looking out of the windows then. The buckets leaned first toward the rear of the pickup then back again to the front. "And there was Moe, hands outstretched, but still not touching the buckets. He ran

first forward and then backwards and looked like a catcher in a baseball game. He wound up catching some of the buckets all right. But unfortunately a couple of them opened up during their fall. Moe was really messed up and looked quickly up at the windows to see if anyone was watching. We all turned away and looked toward the other wall. None of us wanted to hurt his feelings by letting him know that we'd seen his little boo-boo, but we laughed about it for weeks."

One day I was sitting at home in Pinehurst watching television when Jo Ann, my better half, came in the front door. My back was to her so there was no way I could have expected what happened next. She was having a reaction to an antidepressant pill and, standing there in the open doorway, she let out a real shrieker of a scream. It instantly sent cold chills up my back.

The last thing a miner who works around Mr. Air Blast all day needs is a sudden unexplained noise, especially one that loud. It just about scared me to death. Before the din of her scream died out, she uttered a growling sound and drop kicked her purse across the living room. It hit the wall in the kitchen. I'm surprised that I didn't wind up with a coronary or something. To make a long story short: she was treated for her condition and she turned out just fine.

Jo Ann and I had both decided we needed a change of scenery anyhow and that only speeded things up a bit. We moved 40 miles away to Post Falls, Idaho, a small town located a short distance west of Coeur d'Alene. I asked around the mine about other fellas living in the Coeur d'Alene area. I found out that Dick Jones, who was the lamp man, and several others commuted to work from that area every day.

After I caught up with Dick, I asked, "Is there any room in your car pool?"

He said, "Yes, we could use another rider."

He was a colorful sort, and I really enjoyed talking to him during our daily commutes. Dick was in his 60s and just about ready to retire from a long career in the mines. On the way to work one morning, he told me a story about the living conditions that were more or less commonplace in mining camps when he was young.

He said, "Back in the 1930s, the wife and I were expecting our first baby. It was wintertime and there was about two foot of snow on the ground. We lived in a 'Pole house,' or at least that's what I called it. The bottom of it was made of logs and looked like a regular log cabin. The top of the house up above the logs, though, was covered by a tent. It looked like whoever built it must have just run out of logs, so he finished it off with the tent."

Dick continued, "I took the wife into town one day to see the doctor about her bad cold, and while we were there it got dark. The headlights on my old car weren't very good so I had to drive slow on the way back home. When we finally got there it was about eight o'clock, but there was a full moon out so we could see pretty good. It was really crisp and cold that night.

"The cabin sat down off the road a ways and there was a rough road down to it too. My old car couldn't make it down there, though, so I had to park off to the side up on the and hill above the cabin and walk down. The wife wasn't due for about two months or so, but she wasn't in very good shape, what with her cold and all.

"But she was a good sport and as we stood there in the moonlight looking at each other she reached out her hand and said, 'Are you ready?' She'd been talking all day about sliding down the snow covered hillside to the cabin when we got home, but I thought she was only kidding. I could see from the look in her eyes, though, that she was serious and really needed to get settled into the cabin as soon as possible.

"I knew that the walk down that steep road would be hard on her so I decided to give it a try. The snow was deep and soft so I figured that it wouldn't be too bumpy for her. We sat down together in the moonlit snow on that steep hillside. I held on to her tightly as we slid down the hill and tried to keep her from being jostled around too much.

"It seemed like we no more than sat down in the snow before we were at the bottom of the hill, laughing and rolling around in it. I helped her get up and brushed the snow out of her hair. We both knew that she needed to be warmed up as soon as possible so I kicked the snow out from in front of the cabin door and pulled it open. Then I found a match and lit a kerosene lantern that I kept on the table. The only pieces of furniture we had in the pole house were just that old wooden table, one chair, a bed, and a pot bellied stove.

"I helped her into bed, built a fire in the stove and got into bed myself. When I opened my eyes the next morning, I looked up and saw icicles two feet long hanging from the tent above us. I felt bad… I was sick then too."

Dick ended his story by saying, "We made it through that damned cold winter, though, and the kid turned out just fine. Both the wife and I have been kidding our son about how he is a cold blooded skier ever since too."

Dick spoke with a Southern drawl, or at least it sounded that way to me, and the stories he told had an Old South flavor. Cliff and Jim, two other miners in the car pool, were sort of laughing one day about something Dick had them do.

Cliff said, "We were on the way to work one morning and happened to come up behind a potato truck. Well the truck was dribbling good Idaho potatoes out from the little door in its back. Dick had us get out and run along behind his little station wagon pitching in potatoes. We got one hell of a load of potatoes that morning too. And that night when we went home Dick let us out of his car without any potatoes. He didn't want to give them up. And to top it all off the old fool boxed the potatoes up that night and brought them back up to the mine the next day. Then he sold them to the miners up here."

Cliff went on, "Another time when we were on the way to work, Dick spotted an old white dog that had a patch of brown over one eye running along the road. He called it, 'An old one-eyed dawg.' We saw that old dog most every day after that and just figured that he was living off the land. Well, finally winter was coming and Dick just couldn't stand it anymore. When we saw it again he slammed his brakes on and stopped the car. Then we all tried to catch it."

Cliff stopped his story and started laughing. Once he was able to control himself again, he continued, "That was really dumb, here we were, four miners all running like hell out through the brush trying to corral 'the old one-eyed dawg.' Heck, that old hound could run three times as fast as all of us put together. Finally we all gave up. But not Dick. It took us another half hour to get him back. There he was, a 60-year-old guy running like a teenager out through the brush, gasping, and puffing… trying to overtake a critter who'd stop every once in a while and look back like he was thinking, 'I wonder what that old fool's going to do now?' "

Meanwhile the steady day-to-day grind in my back stope continued. Then came the end of the cut and time for the sand-fill. Jerry and I had cleaned out the valuable ore, and it was time to "raise the chutes," a necessary procedure in all "cut and fill" mines.

The wooden crib (4-feet-long, 8 x 8 inch timbers with their ends notched out) that we used was stacked like logs in a cabin when put in place. Their ends interlocked and overlapped one another. One layer of crib (or four pieces) around a 4-feet-square hole formed a "ring" of crib. Before we prepared to extend the two chutes, man-way, and timber slide up to the next level, we dug down and cleaned the sand away from around their tops. Fin hoes worked great for this. Then we laid the new pieces of crib atop the old, finally stacking 8 feet of new crib up on each of the four chutes. Thus, four 8-feet-high chutes protruded like giant fingers from the sandy floor of our mined-out stope up to the base of the next cut that we would be starting. We double wrapped them with burlap that came in rolls stamped "Made in India."

Then sand was pumped from the sand tank up on the mine's surface, down into the empty stope. The grave-yard shift began pouring sand into our stope that night and the sandman (who was suppose to control the flow of sand by keeping in telephone contact with the sand tank guy up on the surface) was visited by his own sand-man that night. He fell asleep and let our place fill up way too much in the back end. So much so that we wouldn't be able to mine the place as a back stope, at least on the next floor. The sand-fill wasn't suppose to be any higher than seven feet down from the new back, so we'd have room to work. But his pour ran uphill all the way in the old cut from the raise to the back, where it was nearly filled up. Man, ol' Doug was mad. The poor sleepy-eyed sandman kept his job only because of the power of the United Steel Workers Union.

Before the pour, I'd run the sand-line pipe out from the raise into the stope and hang it up against the back. I would connect its 10-feet lengths together with "vic" clamps as I went, and tie the suspended pipe onto rock bolts, or whatever I could find, with tie wire to keep it up there. This was common practice before a sand-fill.

The day after the sand-fill, it was necessary for me to walk, or in this case "crawl," the 150 feet back under the brow (i.e., the 2-feet-high space between the top of the fresh sand and the old back). It was time to discon-nect the 10-feet lengths of pipe and drag them back out to the raise where they were stored and used again on the next fill. Water had drained through the fresh sand, all the way from the back end of the cut and out to the burlap-covered chutes where it ran down to the level below. The process had dried out the sand right around the raise first, so the new sand wasn't too bad near the raise at all—it was actually kind of stiff.

I began by walking, but about halfway back I had to drop down on my hands and knees, and finally I laid on my belly and crawled. The further I crawled, the softer and soggier the sand became, and it was sort of like quicksand back in there.

Miners raising a cribbed chute. The raise is at an angle, which is necessary to follow the ore vein. Once the man-way, timber-slide, and two chutes are extended up, they will be wrapped in burlap when sand is poured to fill the mined-out stope. Then they will start mining all over again in a new cut.
ASARCO Inc.

I began thinking, "There isn't going to be anyone around to pull me out if I start sinking. I'm alone, but I should be able to disconnect the vic couplings and drag out the sections of pipe with me as I go. I should be all right if I hang onto the pipe."

I clung to the sand line, as I worked my way along. I finally made it nearly all the way back to the end of the cut, where the sand seemed to be very soft. There was only about 18 inches of room between the sand beneath me and the rock above me to work in. I felt almost suf-focated. The sand didn't act like it wanted to support any weight at all either, let alone my fat little body.

Working as quickly as I could, I began by disconnect-ing the end clamp and about that time I heard "snap." The damned tie wire broke. Man, talk about a scramble for a new foothold on life. The pipe that had been sup-porting my weight dropped immediately into the wet sloppy sand and in only a few seconds my upper body sank shoulder deep into it too. What really scared me, though, was that there was no way to turn around. It was too narrow. I was sinking head first into the sand. I couldn't pull my way out either... had to back up. Probably the only thing that saved me was the fact that the stope was narrow enough that I was able to reach out and grab the walls and struggle against the "sucking" sand. It was a close call. I backed up through the soft mire with all my strength.

After finally getting back out to the raise, I spent about a half hour cleaning off and having coffee. It just plain made me so mad that after I got up my courage, I went back in for the pipe. I left the 30 feet in the back end of the cut, but I dragged the rest of it back out to the raise.

Walt told Jerry and I that since we didn't have room to mine the next cut as a back stope (i.e., drilling straight up), we'd have to take it as a "breast down" cut (i.e., mine out the floor horizontally in the conventional way). Consequently, we had to raise the crib for all the chutes about 6 feet higher and topped the sand-fill off so it was level all the way from the raise to the back end of the cut.

Thus, we took the next floor as a breast-down cut, much to our chagrin. Because we were only able to blast a 6 feet of advance a day, the money just wasn't there. Finally, six weeks later, we finished the new floor and it was time to pour sand again. I talked with Jerry and we decided to give the sand crew bottles of whiskey to do a good job. We received extra special attention from them, and perfect results after that too, I might add.

The sand was in, and now we were ready to mine out the new cut… back stoping this time. I drug my buzzy, air and water hoses, the different lengths of steel, drill oil, and the rest of the stuff I'd need to the back end of my cut. Then I strung out and connected the hoses to the pipes out in the raise, and finally to the buzzy. And I began mining.

It was sort of nice to be drilling up again, and I drilled that way for the rest of the day and part of the next. Jerry slushed on his own side of the raise. I did hate the "eye-blinding" aspect of back stoping though. The business end of the buzzy was only an arm's length from my face, and the powerful machine forced everything upward—drill water, steam, oily mist, whatever. There I stood, working a roaring, pounding, rattling machine under a cascade of water and grit coming down on top of me from the drilling. While the machine was running, it wasn't possible to look up at the hole and see what was going on because of all the crap in the air. Safety glasses weren't the answer either; they were instantly covered by muck and acted only as blinders.

I played a kind of game with the drill steel. Standing there with my eyes closed tightly together, facing the end of the steel as it hammered away, I would just barely open one eye… just a crack. Then the stupid steel saw what I was doing and instantly sent gritty water gushing into the tiny little opening in that squinting eye. Then I had to shut the machine down and clean the gravel out of my eye by grabbing my upper eyelash and lifting it up and down over the bottom eyelash. That "scraped" the crap out pretty well.

Once I'd gotten myself squared away, I began round two and started the machine up again. Next time I held up a hand while hiding a barely opened eye behind it. It was the steel's turn again to gush "gritty" water in my eye. If that damned steel had been alive, I think… no I know… I would have taken it out of the machine and beaten it to death over a rock. But I needed it for the next hole, so I was trapped into drilling on.

Sure, mining companies wanted everybody to wear safety glasses to satisfy some fool in a safety department somewhere. We all knew they wanted us to keep our eyesight. But none of those safety people could give a definitive suggestion on how it was possible to wear those damned, foggin' up, falling-off-the-face blinders while we worked, and still get anything done.

Walt told me one morning before the shift began that a federal mine inspector would be coming through my stope sometime during the day. After getting down into the stope, I, like everyone else in the mine, tried to "spiff" up the stope and get rid of any obvious "ticketable" safety hazards.

Well, sure enough, just before lunch there he came. However, I was surprised to see that Dan, one of my old partners in the Sunshine, was the inspector and that he was in a position of such importance. We greeted each other and exchanged pleasantries… for some time. I think the Galena's safety man, who happened to be with him, was surprised too that I knew his fellow inspector.

Dan said, "I went into the Bureau of Mines, and after a couple of years of going through gravel pits, the coal mines of Virginia, and the like, I finally became a full-fledged inspector and was reassigned to the Silver Valley."

I asked him how he liked being in the coal fields. He said, "Didn't. A lot of them are one and two man operations and when I'd come around those fellas treated me like I was a government whiskey revenue man. I was even run off with guns a few times."

An empty stope being filled with sand. Note the burlap-covered wall in front of the sandman.
ASARCO Inc.

Then Dan said, "There's a rule in the bureau that if an inspector has worked in a mine before he entered the bureau then he can't inspect that mine." Then with a sly grin he said, "Something to do with gettin' even, I think."

The visit went well and Dan didn't take out his little black "gig" book to write anything down at all. So I figured I was home free. Finally he said his goodbys and left, with the Galena's little inspector in tow. After they'd left I sat down on a block of wood behind the slusher.

The mine's rule was that if a fella was operating a slusher and certain other types of equipment he was supposed to wear company-issued safety glasses. There was a general consensus among the workers, however, that the mine's warm, moist atmosphere caused them to fog up only a few seconds after they were put on, which was a real problem. Consequently, miners played "hide and seek" with the mine's bosses. Bosses tried to sneak up on the miners and catch them without their glasses on when operating equipment, and then the miners would turn their faces away, "hiding" while trying to put on the glasses.

I sat there remembering back to when Dan and I had worked together at the 'Shine. At the time, the Sun-shine bosses had a very strict policy regarding the use of safety glasses in the mine.

Dan had said things like, "They just don't work because I can't see well enough to be safe when I have them on."

I sort of smiled to myself, forgot about the glasses I was supposed to be wearing, and cranked up the old slusher. I remained sitting there for a few seconds, listening to the wine of the air slusher's motor and pulling on the haul-back handle. The heavy bucket crawled back into the darkness of the cut. A minute later Dan poked his head out from behind a post and waved. He hadn't really left at all, he'd just been hiding there behind that post.

"Damn," I thought, "He caught me, I wonder what he…" About that time Dan pointed his finger at me like he'd just fired an imaginary pistol, grinned and said, "You owe me one."

In that instant, when making eye contact, we both were drawn back to the Sunshine and the many conversations we'd shared there. Still smiling, he again disappeared behind the post and I knew this time he'd really gone.

The next day when I was drilling away, I thought I saw a string or something hanging from the back just above my hat. I immediately shut off my machine and stood waiting for the fog to dissipate so I could see what it was. As the air cleared, and after wiping stuff out of my eyes a couple of times, I finally saw my "string."

On the cut before, when I'd come across the floor "breasting down," I must have had a "missed" hole (i.e., dynamite in a hole didn't explode). Missed holes are commonplace. Many times during blasts, fuses are cut by flying rock, or whatever, leaving a hole that doesn't go off. Usually the outside of a missed hole is blasted away by exploding dynamite in adjacent holes, leaving only a few sticks of unexploded powder in place at the very end of the hole.

The string hanging down in my stope was the dangling end of a live fuse primer that was still firmly embedded into 1 and 1/2 sticks of dynamite at its other end. I'll have to admit, after seeing that my drill steel had ground its way dead center right up and through the missed hole, it just scared me to death. I remembered having heard only a few weeks before about a miner somewhere who'd drilled into a missed hole and died for his efforts. If a blasting cap is hit really hard, perhaps with the drill bit on the end of hammering steel, the impact sometimes causes it to explode. Sparks sometimes can ignite a fuse primer too.

After withdrawing my steel and then removing the old dynamite from the hole, I discovered that my drill steel had passed directly through the powder and just missed the primer by about an inch. It was a real squeaker. I then took a break from drilling and checked the back out thoroughly, all the way out to the raise. I didn't want to find any more surprises... accidentally.

The Galena, like all the other mines I worked in, used dynamite sticks measuring 18 inches or so in length. Another powerful blasting agent was called "Prell." Made of fish guts and diesel oil (or so I was told) and transported in 50-pound bags, it consisted of thousands of tiny little "pink" balls. Someone had finally come up with the bright idea of coloring blasting powder so that if a poor miner accidently drilled into a missed hole, like the one I found, he could see the unexploded charge and keep from killing himself.

I used Prell from then on. When loading I first pushed a primer and a stick of powder into the back of each hole, to "prime the Prell" so to speak. I then dumped Prell out of the bag into a "loading can." Then by "blowing" it with a compressed air loading hose, I blew Prell up into the holes and inserted "pilgrim hats" (funny, plastic, bottlecap like things) into the end of the holes to keep the Prell from dribbling out of the drill

holes. When ignited, of course, the primer stick touched off the Prell resulting in a powerful explosion.

One day, about a month after almost being blown off the planet, I was standing on the station waiting for a ride up the shaft at the end of the shift. I heard one of the new "hires" complaining to my partner that he'd cut his arm and was afraid of infection. Now old Jerry was a happy-go-lucky sort of a fella and loved to play tricks on guys.

He told the lad to "go over there and put your arm into that sack of Prell, that'll disinfect it."

All of the men standing around the station knew what was going to happen next from their own "burning" experiences, but we didn't say anything. We didn't want to spoil Jerry's joke. The kid walked over to the partially open sack of Prell and smiled as he stuck his arm into it, just as Jerry had suggested. His smile suddenly faded, turning instead into a grotesque mess as he let out an awful scream. The memory of June putting his "cure" on the galled kid over at the Crescent flashed through my mind.

Something else flashing through my mind was terror. Miners are deathly afraid of loud noises, or at least I was, and that terrible shriek sent cold chills down my spine. I don't think it did the kid much good either. After that he had sort of an attitude when it came to Jerry, I think. At least he seemed to be put out whenever Jerry tried to talk to him. Hell, he couldn't take a joke or nuthin'... but I could see why.

I had an interesting experience one day regarding the sand pipe in my stope. Before I tell the story, though, let me explain again how sand pipes work. Sand pipes, of course, bring sand down from the surface to fill mined-out cuts. From the big sand tank on the surface, the sand-pipe system runs down the shaft alongside air and water lines, eventually branching out through the drifts. Thus, it is part of the "pipe work" that hangs on the walls along with the air and water lines and other stuff. From the drifts, sand pipes climb up or down, as the case may be, and enter each of the stopes. On the surface, the sand line is a heavy 6-inch pipe. However, by the time sand lines branch out into the stopes they are a manageable 3 inches in diameter.

One day when hosing down the dust around the top of my raise, I was surprised... no shocked, to hear someone talking, especially since I was the only one there. This was weird. I looked all around thinking that someone must surely be hiding somewhere and was trying to pull a trick on me. I didn't see anybody anywhere, though, and I still heard voices. I was just about to think that I was losing my mind, when I finally traced the sounds down to the top of the 3-inch sand line. Dumbfounded, I sat down and looked into the pipe's opening, listening to the sounds of at least two guys talking.

Then I finally figured it out. I thought, "Hell, that's the crew in the stope below mine."

I began to mentally trace out the route of the pipe, from me to them. "Let's see now… the sand line runs all the way down my raise a distance of about 150 feet, and must still be connected to the main 'trunk' line at the bottom of my man-way [I'd forgotten to disconnect it]. From there it goes on back into the drift a ways and must run down through the top of their raise, eventually winding up down in their stope. That's gotta be at least 300 feet from here to there."

I sat there marveling at the situation and noting how clear their voices sounded. After a while I leaned over, cupped my mouth with my hands, and yelled as loudly as I could down into the pipe, hoping someone would hear me. But it was no good. I now could hear a slusher running, which along with their talking, drowned me out.

I sat there thinking, "Hell, this ain't fair. A situation like this really needs something… it's got great potential. It would be a great place for a practical joke, if I could only figure it out."

Then I caught sight of the water hose which I'd been washing the place with, laying on the floor, not far away.

I smiled, "Why not, this will be wonderful."

Smiling all the while, I stuck the end of the 1 and 1/2 inch water hose down into the pipe and turned it on, waited for about a minute, and then shut it off. Then I put my ear down over the pipe and listened.

I heard a gurgle, gurgle (lots of gurgles) and then a very loud, "Son-of-a-bitch!" That left me smiling for the rest of the day. That night in the dry, I didn't say anything about my trick right away, but instead listened to the two miners talk as they changed clothes.

Finally, one of them said to another fella, "Damn, you know… today, I was slushing away and started hearing gurgling sounds. Crap, I happened to look up at just the last second, and saw water come shootin' out of our sand line. It was right over my head. And I dove out of the way so I wouldn't get drowned just in time too. God, I was scared. I thought the damned sandman was starting to pour sand in our place without having the sand line hooked up. You know, like they did in old Jones's place last week. I talked to the sandman, though, and he said he didn't know anything about it."

His eyes darted around the room, trying to make eye contact with anyone who cared to listen to his story or anyone sympathizing with his ordeal. Then he saw me grinning.

I said, "How'd it feel?"

Everyone looked at me and silence reigned for a second. Then suddenly, as if a light of understanding had lit up the place, laughter roared out in the dry.

He was a good sport, though, and soon laughed too. Then he said, "Damn, Dolph, that was a good one, I'll have to remember that." It was good to laugh a little sometimes, to break up the routine of drilling, blasting, and slushing.

A couple of days later, Jerry and I were sitting out in the main drift talking with a couple of the other Galena hands. We had run out of steel, again, and had been put to work cleaning up the drift while we waited for a new supply. The conversation with the two men got around to the sad state of the Silver Valley's economy and their belief that none of the mines were hiring. They were fearful of how awful it would be to lose their jobs, and almost cowered at the thought of being footloose and fancy-free. What they didn't realize, though, was that they were talking to a born and bred tramp miner. I told the two brainwashed jelly bellies that they were completely wrong; a guy would still have no problem finding a job.

"After all," I reasoned, "what about all the other people on the planet? What do they do, just dry up and blow away?" Their doubts grew stronger, which brought them to near fever pitch as they tried to get me to understand their point of view.

I think the conversation did something to me, because that night after shift, I said goodby to Jerry, told Doug our foreman what he could do with his damned chisel steel, and quit the Galena Mine. ✾

CHAPTER 10

Nervous Tramp

"Workin' Lotsa Silver Valley Mines"

The next morning I drove up Big Creek Canyon to the Sunshine Mine and rustled… again. I was right too, they hired me right on the spot. Of course, there was the little matter of a new physical examination to deal with, but I sailed through that.

It was November 1979 and I hadn't worked for the 'Shine for several years, but everything looked pretty much the same, right down to the time clock hanging on the wall in the shifters office. From my brief encounter with the crew in the dry, though, I concluded that they weren't the same men. It seemed like the fire was gone from their eyes, almost as if they'd become peaceful or something and were just going through the motions. After I'd climbed down the long flight of stairs from the dry to street level, I entered the shifters office building. I punched in a time card that again had my name and employee number on it, and walked up to the counter.

As I stood there looking over the counter, I saw the same hustle and bustle, impatient conversations, and busy moods of the bosses as before. I recognized many of their faces, and as I made occasional eye contact I saw that several others recalled me too. I remembered the apparent change in the crew and thought, well at least these guys haven't changed much… maybe just a little uglier.

Then I met Bob, my new shifter, and he said, "You're going to be working on the Alimak raise climber."

Miner slushing from his raise. The slusher's scraper bucket drags muck in towards the chute. Note the iron bars of the grizzly atop the chute.
ASARCO Inc.

I just stood there looking into his eyes waiting for the punch line to his joke, but finally saw that there was none coming. I thought, "Great, now just what the hell is a raise climber?"

I readily accepted the job with a smile, and pointing toward the wall said, "Say isn't that a new paint job?" I noticed a look of confusion cross his face as I turned and walked toward the door.

Then came the routine journey into the mine and the long trip down the Jewell Shaft to the mine's 3,700 foot level. Talk about luck—I climbed onto the man-train through one of the three small doors and sat down in the last empty seat, where I met Greg, my new partner. He was sitting directly across from me. Greg seemed like he was a bit off to me somehow, or at least that's the impression I got after conversing with him for a few minutes. We talked on as the train rumbled and screeched its way across 3,700 heading toward Ten Shaft. He tried to explain what an Alimak raise climber did.

I'll have to admit it sounded interesting, but I just couldn't quite grasp the idea of, "Starting out upside down, climbing through a little trap door, drilling out the…" I didn't want to show how ignorant I was about what he was talking about, so I occasionally nodded in agreement at what I thought were appropriate times. We finally finished the Amtrak ride across the level, made the trip down Ten Shaft, and arrived on the 5,000 feet level. Everything I saw looked so much like it had before that in no time memories of "my" other mines faded into the past. Then we began hiking more than a mile back to the "bore holes." My new working place, however, was even further back, at the very end of the level.

As we walked along, I remembered what someone once told me. "During the fire in 1972, of the 93 fellas who were caught working underground that day, the only two who survived were working around the bottom of a bore hole at the time. It had something to do with the ventilation."

Bore holes are really neat. Whoever thought up the idea was surely a genius. A really big drilling machine, which is about the size of a pickup truck or larger, drills the holes. First, an 11 and 1/2-inch diameter "pilot hole" is drilled from an upper level, where the machine sits, down about 200 feet or so to a lower level. If you were standing on the lower level at the time and happened to be looking up at the back you would see the 11 and 1/2 inch drill bit break through the rock and come down through it. Once the machine has drilled the pilot hole, then a giant bit—I mean this sucker is a good 8 feet across—is connected onto the end of the drill steel in place of the reamer bit. It then grinds out the rock as it goes, leaving a hole that is 8 feet in diameter.

Greg laughed and told me a story about a crew working the bore hole. "They were drilling with the big bit and pulling muck from the bottom of the bore hole. It was Friday and the end of the shift, so they shut down for the weekend and went home. Sometime after they left, a water hose must have broken up by the machine and water flowed into the bore hole. Since the drillings were still choking off the bottom of the bore hole, all that water couldn't go anywhere. It just started building up in the bottom of the plugged bore hole.

"When they came back after the weekend, they just didn't know that there was about umpteen thousand gallons of water in the hole and dammed back up by muck. One of the miners, standing by his mucker, picked up a rock. He threw it up at the cliff of muck in front of him trying to start it running, so it would fall down and be easier to muck up."

Then Greg said, "Damn… that little bit of rock must have started things moving too because then all hell broke loose. A few seconds later it was as if some giant had flushed his toilet. Those thousands of gallons of water came gushing out all at once, pushing the wall of muck in front of it. It blew the two miners, their motor, mucker, and everything else, right down the drift, too."

He finished his story by chuckling to himself and saying, "As it turned out the guy who threw the rock

lost a finger or two from hanging onto the sharp side of a steel mat that was bolted onto the wall. The water hit him so hard that it pulled his boots right off and slammed him up against the back. His partner was sitting in the motor's cockpit and hung on through it all. It scratched both of them up pretty good, but at least it didn't kill them."

I listened intently to his story but really couldn't find anything in it warranting a laugh. Like I said, Greg seemed like he was a little offbeat to me.

Just as he'd finished his story, we walked by the bore holes. His timing was perfect, almost as if he'd planned his story to match our slogging pace as we trod over the uneven ties and rails. The holes—there were two— were awesome looking. Both had been finished and cleaned up, and I walked over to one of them and stood there facing up. It was like looking into an 8-feet-wide gun barrel.

Then we continued on back toward our work place. About 10 minutes later we finally came to the bottom of our stope, which looked pretty much like all the rest of the stopes I'd ever worked in. But after we'd climbed about 20 feet up a couple of ladders in the man-way, it was a whole different ball game. I couldn't believe that all the equipment up in there had come up the timber-slide, but that's the only way it could have been hauled in, I guessed. I knew that mining engineers were real wizards at finding ways of breaking down equipment and then reassembling it again where needed. I stood there thinking, "They sure did a marvelous job with all this stuff."

By then, our nipper was down below with dynamite that my partner had ordered. We signaled for him to raise the skip up our timber-slide, and we off-loaded our lunches and electric blasting caps. We returned the skip to him and he in turn next sent up two cases of dynamite (we couldn't send up the primers and powder at the same time in the skip because of federal safety regulations). There was a tremendous shaft, for want of a better word, that went up from where we were. Actually, it looked more like an empty raise without the usual supporting timber, chutes, timber-slide, ladders, and the like. It also appeared to be laid over at about the same pitch as the seams in the rock, probably about an 80-degree angle.

On the upper side of the 12 x 12 feet, or whatever it was, hole, a rail had been bolted to the wall. This rail looked sort of like a massive, continuous bicycle chain that ran straight up the hole and disappeared into the

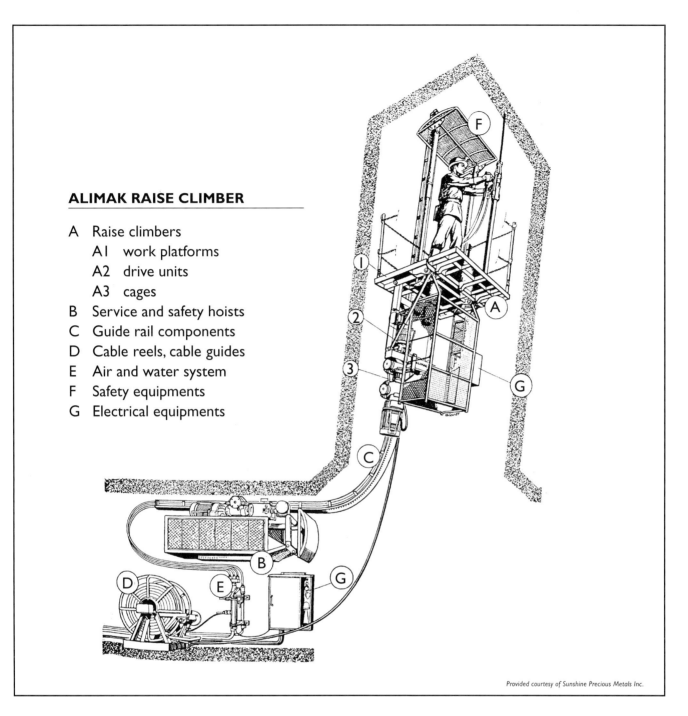

ALIMAK RAISE CLIMBER

A Raise climbers
    A1   work platforms
    A2   drive units
    A3   cages
B Service and safety hoists
C Guide rail components
D Cable reels, cable guides
E Air and water system
F Safety equipments
G Electrical equipments

Provided courtesy of Sunshine Precious Metals Inc.

darkness. The climbing machine was attached to this rail by what looked kinda like large bicycle gears. I stood staring at it in disbelief. A two-man wire cage was bolted onto the drilling machine, as well as a huge spool of 6-inch, or whatever it was, air hose, a smaller water hose, and other machinery. The spool looked sort of like the ones seen in hardware stores that garden hoses are rolled up on. I didn't have much time to gawk at things, because my partner was on a roll. He put our lunch gear, drill bits, and dynamite in a box on the work deck and we both walked around behind it.

That's where things got weird. The cage that was bolted onto the work deck was two bodies wide and laying horizontal. Greg said, "Get in." I did and so did he. We were laying there beside each other in our odd hooked-together baskets, when he started laughing. He was remembering when a new superintendent crawled into the cage for the first time.

He said, "You know that dumb bastard got in head first? Hell if we'd gone up that way, with him in that position, he'd have been upside down when we got there." I was relieved that I hadn't made the same mistake.

About that time Greg pulled on a handle and I heard the sound of escaping air. The contraption began moving forward with a jerking motion, and then began to climb up into the hole. That's when we began standing up instead of laying down… what a relief. We continued on like that, climbing upward for what seemed like a long time. I looked down through the screen and watched the muck below as it gradually disappeared from sight as we got higher and higher. Soon, I was staring down into blackness.

By now we were over a hundred feet up in the raise, and, as we jerked along, my partner pointed up, saying: "That little trap door over our heads is jammed. I never use it, though. Once we get to the face, I just climb up out of this cage and around the outside of the deck to get up on top of it."

As he talked, I looked up at the little trap door over our heads, hoping there'd been something he'd overlooked and that there really was some way of getting it open. When he had told me that I'd have to climb out around the outside of the work deck, I skeptically thought, "Yeah, right."

We'd gone about 190 feet up the raise, and our Alimak was climbing along just fine. I didn't know whether the fella who invented it was named Alimak, or if it was a combination of letters which meant something else altogether. I was deep in thought when the damned thing finally came to an abrupt stop. As promised, Greg pulled himself out from his side of the cage and climbed around the outside of the deck and onto its top. I could hear him walking around up there. Then it was my turn. I didn't want to look like a fool, so I climbed out my side of the cage too. I put a foot on a small rock outcrop on the wall, and was just making my last move up through the 2-feet-wide space between the work deck and the rock wall, when I happened to look straight down into the darkness beneath my feet. I made a mental note: "I sure hope the brake on this damned thing holds."

We set up our buzzies and began to drill straight up into the back (face). I thought idly as I drilled, "The reason the Sunshine hired me this time is probably because they know I'd been back stoping over at the Galena." Back stoping is essentially what this was. We drilled out 35 holes for our round, put a few 6-feet-long bolts through 4-feet-long steel mats to help support the walls, and then put our machines away. Next, we

Mucking out a drift round.
ASARCO Inc.

primed the dynamite with electric primers and loaded the drill holes. Then we began a long, jerking crawl back down the rail toward the bottom of the raise—just the reverse of what we'd done at the beginning of the shift, only this time I was a lot wiser.

After reaching the bottom, we put everything away and climbed down our man-way ladders to the drift. Then we walked down to a "hot shot" blasting box—like the ones you see in the movies where a fella hooks two wires onto two electrical poles. The box, of course, was out toward the shaft, away from the stope. We yelled "fire in the hole" three times, as required by federal law, and then let 'er rip.

In the following days, the procedure remained pretty much the same, the only difference being that we were 6 feet higher up each time when we blasted a round. We'd been able to blast two or three rounds a week when I first started working on the climber, which was a pretty good showing, and the money seemed to be good, too. But then it got harder and harder to make our rounds. We had problems with the fact that the place was so damned far away from the shaft that it proved difficult to haul all of the muck, particularly if there were glitches somewhere in the system. As they say, "The longer it takes, the less you makes."

I stayed with it, though, for a couple of more weeks, hoping things would get better. But our money finally dwindled down to the point where it was hovering just above day's pay, the minimum guaranteed wage. Then one morning as I was preparing to leave home for work, I got to fussing around with my lunch gear, felt a wave of frustration, and said, "Aw… the hell with it. It's time to tramp out again."

My elation that morning was intense. I could never really understand why I got so excited every time I got tramping fever. A lot of people hated moving from job to job, like the two fellas over at the Galena who were afraid of quitting, but I really loved it. I felt like something was amiss, though—it was the same feeling as when I'd hired out at the 'Shine this last time. Maybe the fellas over at the Galena were right after all; the mining industry was evolving somehow and things just didn't seem like they were the same as when I'd tramped out before. I felt like I was changing, or at least, I knew damned well something was.

Then, I thought, "It's time to go see Albi at Bunker Hill, and this time I'll go directly up to the foreman's office."

When I applied there for work, I was accepted with open arms, especially since my Sunshine physical was only about three weeks old and still current. I was ready to go to work immediately. I showed up at the Bunker Hill the next morning with high hopes and looking for a good "home," or stope, but I was told to report to Bill Weeks's labor pool instead. The labor pool consisted of guys and gals who didn't have steady places to work, so they congregated here at the beginning of each shift to receive assignments for the day. When I walked into the big room, I met a wall of discouraged faces. I recognized some of the fellas who were sitting on benches circling the room and walked over and sat down beside one of them. It was Rich; we'd worked together somewhere before, but I couldn't remember just when or where. He was the friend who'd encouraged me to join the Wardner Industrial Union.

Rich had been looking down at the floor. As I approached, he looked up, recognized me, and said, "Oh, hi Jerry… what are you doing here?" I sat down beside him and began telling him about my escapades of the past few weeks.

Finally Rich shook his head in disbelief, saying, "Man it's bad here. They're not startin' any new stopes up at all. Just finishing up the old ones. Most of us here in this room are miners waiting for new homes. But every day we wind up with a muck stick [shovel] diggin' out switches [track repairs], packin' supplies, or whatever else they find for us to do. And most of us can't quit because we've got too much time in. We're stuck."

I'd been looking around the room as he talked and saw at least four other miners that I knew. As we made eye contact, we each smiled, faintly, in recognition. All but one—he looked like he was still comatose from the night before. I thought of the two Galena miners again, who warned me about the same gloom and despair that Rich was talking about. Now I wasn't one for giving up easily, so I excused myself from Rich, got up, and walked into Weeks's office. Bill was busily scribbling something down on a sheet of paper with the stub of a pencil.

I said, "Bill?"

He looked up, and replied, "Yeah?"

Then I introduced myself and said, "I hear that a lot of the guys waiting in here are looking for new homes… how long would a new fella like me have to wait for one?"

Bill laughed, dropped his pencil on the table, and leaned back on his wooden chair so that its front two legs came off the floor and his back rested against the wall. He said, "Well Dolph, how old are you?"

I saw what he was leading up to and interrupted by saying, "Well, if it's all the same to you, how 'bout I get ahold of the Crescent and find out if I can work over there?"

He quickly replied, "Great," and mumbled, "that'll be one less that I have to worry about where to put to work."

Then without saying another word, he leaned forward and the front two legs of his chair dropped to the floor. He picked up his gnarled, chewed-on stub of a pencil and resumed marking his papers.

I said, "Can I use your phone?" He just pointed to it and didn't look up from his work.

I called the Crescent and they agreed to put me on the following day. I thanked Bill as I left. I worked with Rich for the rest of the day, cleaning up a tail drift on 9 level.

The next day, as I drove up Big Creek canyon toward the Crescent Mine, I passed by the corner of the Sunshine's parking lot, which was located just across the valley from the Crescent. Things looked the same to me, and yet somehow different. After I'd parked my rig and walked into the dry, the first guy I saw was the jerk who'd given me the warning slip for littering the mine with sunflower seeds when I was at the Crescent before. I thought, "That's sort of a rotten way to get started."

I got my gear and dressed down, then went underground with the crew on the man-train. It'd been three or four years since I'd been down there. But somehow, I remembered everything that I saw, right down to the scars in the rock that the miners left with their drill steel when they drove the main drift, so many years before.

Later on that day, the shifter came by and I took the opportunity to ask him the same question that I'd asked Bill Weeks the day before. At least my "new" shifter didn't laugh, but his answer was pretty much the same. "We've only got three stopes going right now, and we have to give all these guys who've been with us for a long time a chance to go mining. Once you have as much seniority as they do then it'll be your turn." Again, doom and gloom.

I finished out the day at the Crescent, but that night after work I called the Galena Mine. I told them that the physical I'd taken for the Sunshine was still current (there was a 30-day expiration time on physical examinations). Consequently, the next morning I showed up for work at the Galena, ready to give it another try. The fella in the timekeeper's office made a statement that's stuck with me ever since; he said, "Lookie here, now you have to start all over again."

Fortunately, my old foreman, Doug, didn't seem mad about the crack I'd made when quitting not long before—you know, the recommendation I'd made about

"Pay-Day" sketch by miner Buck O'Donnell, 1965.

where he could put my chisel steel. Or at least if he did, he didn't show it. I was a little worried about that one.

The Galena had some young shifters who were right out of engineering schools somewhere, and I got me one. Then, I was given a partner with a stiff neck and a stope down on the mine's 4,900 feet level. The stope was in a "300-foot lift"—that is to say, the levels were 300 feet above one another, thus my new stope's raise was 300 feet high. Most levels were only 200 feet, or so, above one another, but someone in all his wisdom had decided to make those levels an extra hundred feet apart.

My new partner's name was Don, and he and I were both new to this work place. That first climb up the man-way ladders to the stope was a real adventure for both of us. The stope was located 250 feet above 4,900 level, and its man-way was about five rest-stop periods high for me. I felt like someone had kicked the wind right out of me by the time I finally crawled out onto the floor of the stope itself. Don wasn't in much better shape either.

We sat there talking for a while trying to get our breath back and he explained why his neck was stiff. He said, "I worked here a long time ago and was told to take a plugged sand line down. They gave me this damned drunk for a partner that day, but I didn't know it at the time. I was standing beside the tracks straddling the piss ditch with my back to him, and I told him to catch the pipe if it fell. Then I went to work with a socket wrench undoing the bolts and when I finally got the vic clamp off, the damned pipe dropped right on my head. The pipe was really heavy too because it was full of sand. When it hit me, it knocked me cold.

"I fell face forward into the piss ditch and would have drowned if it hadn't been for a couple of electricians who just happened to see me lying there. The damned drunk had whiskey in his thermos and was nippin' on it when I got hurt, I guess. Well anyway... the way it turned out was, he got fired, and I got a permanent stiff neck. That was a pretty good deal, huh?" Don couldn't turn his head around to see behind him on one side at all. He had to pivot his whole body. He was a good worker, though.

Now we were ready to go to work in our brand new (to us) 50-year-old, or whatever it was, breast-down stope. Our young shifter said he wanted to finish up the floor that was being mined out, and then I could try a back stope cut (i.e., mine out the next floor with buzzies). He thought the ground was good enough to hold up. A back stope could be mined out much faster and cheaper than a breast-down place, since the miners drilled straight up into the back all the way from the rear end of the cut out to the raise. Then they could load all of the drill holes with dynamite and blast down the whole cut with one shot. That left the back eight feet—or whatever the bosses decided the depth of the holes should be—higher up. In a breast-down cut, on the other hand, the miners could blast only a six- or eight-feet advance each shift.

One thing I really liked about the Galena's way of mining was that both partners worked on one face. That is to say, in most (or maybe all) of the other mines in the Valley, each miner had an individual heading and was expected to blast rounds on his own side of the raise. Something that our young shifter neglected to tell us, though, was that there had been a fatality in our work place a few months before. Some young fella didn't bar down well enough, and a large chunk of high-grade ore fell out of the back and flattened him right out.

We'd been working the place for about a month, when one day near the end of a shift we were sitting back in the stope a ways, up on the foot wall, waiting for the time to climb down the man-way. The foot wall laid over so much that it reminded me a lot of the stope I'd had at the lower Bunker Mine, but this place was a little steeper than that.

As Don and I talked, I sat up near the top of the wall near the back, because the air was better up there. I was idly pulling rocks out of the wall and chucking them down onto the floor. I picked loose one especially "stuck-in" piece of rock, and after I'd thrown it I noticed air coming from the hole that it left. Now I'd never heard of air coming out of solid rock before. It just wasn't possible, but there it was... a breeze.

I told Don about it, and he climbed over to where I was and we both began to investigate. After removing a few more chunks of rock, I saw a small hole in the slick wall instead of just the cracks that were there before. Then I put my face down against the wall, and peered down through the hole.

"Hell," I said to Don, "there's an old raise down in there. I can see timbers, cable, ladders... there's a whole set-up down in there. And it's so deep that I can't see the bottom. Something else, too, the crust of rock we're sitting on looks like it's only a few inches thick."

We both quickly backed off. When I barred out another piece of rock to get a better look, a lot of the wall gave way and fell into the hole, leaving a small chasm about 3 feet across. The way it turned out, the engineers had no record of the old raise and no idea it was even there.

Our baby-faced shifter was sort of a likable fella, but new to the job, and afraid of not doing it good enough too, I guess. When he came through our place I pointed out the wall to him and casually mentioned that it might be a good idea for me to put a "stull" in there. He nodded and grunted in absentminded agreement. To tell you the truth, I don't even think he hardly knew what a stull was. Well, anyhow, I got busy after he left and completely forgot about putting in the stull. But the next day when he came through the stope again he saw that I hadn't installed the stull that "he'd" told me to put in.

So he said, "You'll get a warning slip for this. You must obey orders."

Damn that made me mad, but I just smiled and said, "You want stulls, huh?"

He replied, "Yes, we have to have stulls to support that wall."

This really got to me, so after he left I spent the rest of the day putting in stulls. I put in big ones, little ones, and crooked ones. In fact, by the time the shift ended I had put in so many stulls that it looked like a forest back in there. It no longer was possible to even walk back into the stope, let alone work in there.

When I went out that night, I found him on the surface and said, "I put in those stulls that you were talking about. And I think I have enough of them too."

You know what that jerk said as he handed me the warning slip that he'd already made out? "Well, it's about time."

As soon as he said that, I crushed the slip of paper in my hand and threw it into the trash bucket. Then I walked over to Doug's office and turned in my time... again. This was the last thing I would've thought would happen when I went to work that morning, but it was the only thing on my mind as I left the mine that night.

I pondered about what I'd just done on the way home, and finally figured out the answer to the lingering problem that I'd sensed and which had bothered me so much for the past month or so. The people around me were changing, or so I thought. Their fire was gone. They had turned into "yes" men. I really missed the old free-spirited souls who got all drunked up, fought in the bars all night, and battled with the ground all day, and wondered where they'd all gone. ✿

CHAPTER 11

Boatswain's Chair

Lucky Friday Mine… Again

The next morning I drove over to the Hecla Mining Company's hiring office, which at the time was in Wallace, the Shoshone County seat. (The office has since been moved to Coeur d'Alene, about 50 miles away, much to the chagrin of many Silver Valley residents.) It was really refreshing to look for work on the eastern end of the Valley again for a change, instead of bouncing back and forth from mine to mine at its west end. It'd been many years since I'd worked in Hecla's Lucky Friday Mine, and that had been for only a short period of time in 1972. I figured that with any luck, I'd be able to get back on again. I was running out of mines to look for work in.

I waited in a long line before it was my turn to see the hiring man. We talked for about half an hour and he set me up for a physical examination, since the one I'd taken at the Sunshine had finally expired. I'd been going in and out of the doctor's office so often that I was on a first-name basis with most of the nursing staff. I passed the physical with no problems, as usual. Sometimes I almost wished that I'd fail the damn thing to break up the monotony.

It was January 1980. On the first day that I walked into the Lucky Friday's dry, carrying a pillowcase full of diggers, that feeling I'd had about something being wrong in the mines somehow vanished. I thought, "This is really neat. It's been a lot of years since I was

here last, but I think I'm going to like this place just fine."

After bouncing around the mining district as much as I had, I noticed it was becoming nearly impossible to hire out at a new mine without knowing at least a couple of the miners already working there; a lot of us had become Shoshone County tramps. When I walked into the Lucky Friday's dry, I saw three guys right off that I'd worked with somewhere in the Valley at one time or other.

Back stoping was something the Lucky Friday attempted occasionally, and since I'd done a bit of it at the Galena, I was put to work in one of the mine's two active back stopes. Another reason that I was put to work in the back stope was that all of the rest of the work places were full at the time. I was the stope's third man on the mine's 4,050-feet level (normally, of course, there were two guys in each stope). In most places, Mr. Air Blast canceled out any hopes that the mine might have had for developing back stopes, but the ground around these two places was holding up good.

Except for being really crooked on one end, it looked like a typical stope—8 feet wide, 150 feet long, and with an 8- to 10-feet high back. As I stood at the end with George Lee, one of my new partners, I asked him, "Why is this end so crooked back in here?"

He replied, pointing with an outstretched finger, "The vein takes a big jog back in there and really gets rich. Maybe a couple of thousand ounces of silver to the ton."

Then I asked, "Where's the end of the stope in relation to stuff up on the surface like the Interstate 90 freeway?

Modern rubber-tire vehicles known as LHD's (load-haul-dump) have made underground ore handling more efficient on the lower levels of the Lucky Friday Mine.
Hecla Mining Company/Van Gundy Photography, Spokane WA

He said, "We're right about under the highway right here. In fact, the geologists tell me that we're mining right into the end of another mining company's property back in here. And that Hecla's paying the other company part of the proceeds from what they get."

As he spoke, I was looking down at the heaps of rich, shiny-looking ore while thinking about the price of silver being up around $30 an ounce. I realized that some waste rock had to be taken out along with the silver ore in the face, because the vein itself was only about 6 inches wide. The slusher's bucket was about 3 feet wide, consequently the high-grade ore in the vein was going to be diluted quite a bit by that wide of a cut, but still... I said to George, "Man we're standing on a damned fortune here then, aren't we?"

He just smiled and said, "Yeah, I guess you could say that. The standing joke among the miners here is to come in after a fresh blast, wash off the face with a water hose, and see 'E Pluribus Unum' printed on the rock. Like what's stamped on the face of a silver dollar."

None of the other miners in the back stopes were using what was called a "Vee" cut (i.e., holes drilled up into the back at an angle, like an upside-down letter "V"). I usually drilled a Vee cut in a back stope round. This was why: if the holes were laying over slightly when they were filled with high explosives, then the blast was more effective in "hammering" out the ground. Otherwise, if one of the holes "booted," or accidentally didn't go off, and the holes had been drilled straight up, then the next hole behind it wouldn't "pull," or break out the ground all the way. And, from there on, each hole would pull progressively shorter the further back from the booted hole, until finally the round wouldn't pull at all.

I blasted my first 150-feet-long round out with standard fuse primers and really made a mess of things. I couldn't drill in my Vee cut very well because someone had left the back too low and I couldn't get under it to drill the holes. Thus, my drill holes were spaced too far apart to break the ground out.

I'd never used Nonel blasting primers before, but now I got my first chance to try them out here. Nonel primers are factory-sealed, thin plastic tubes. The ones I used were 12 feet long. I didn't really even know what their name meant—maybe Nonel(ectric)? George helped me load my Vee cut with the primers. We pushed the caps into sticks of powder and shoved them up into eight drill holes. After we'd loaded the primers and dynamite, I stood back and looked at our work. The

Down pressure has crushed this cap.
Bruce Baraby, Wallace ID

ends of the Nonel tubes were dangling out of the holes. Then we filled the rest of the holes with more dynamite.

When my Nonel primers ignited at exactly the right sequence, it blasted out a chunk of rock that had to weigh at least 10 tons. Yeah... it blew out that one huge pie-shaped piece, for everybody—partners, shifter, just everybody—to see. And I felt like a fool too. Here I was a big-time back stoper who'd worked in mines all over the Valley, but "live and learn," I always say.

A lot of the miners in the Lucky Friday, and the rest of the Silver Valley mines as far as that goes, were from families who'd lived in the area for many years. A lot of people were related to each other in one way or another, had intermarried over the years, and had gone to school together. Sometimes it almost seemed like we were holding a high school class reunion down in the mine. I always felt a little out of place when some of them got to talking about how someone's "uncle had married a sister of"... etc., etc.

Examples of these long-term residents of the Valley working in the mines are everywhere. For instance, my shifter Ivan Zeller, nicknamed Shorty, was an old-time area miner. Shorty's brother Mel Zeller likewise was a shifter in the Lucky Friday, and both also had worked for many years in the Star Mine, which is up Burke Canyon not far from Wallace. Shorty also had at one time or another been partners with Tom Barton, my old shifter in the Sunshine Mine—you know, the blue rooster comb guy? Well... when I was over at the Sunshine and Tom was my shifter, he once told me about a partner he'd had over in the Star Mine. "His nickname is Shorty," Tom said, "and he's so short that he had to stand on a block of wood to be able to drill with a jack-leg. The little fella was one hell of a miner though."

Did I say I'd tramped around from mine to mine a lot? It sounded to me like these guys made a career out of it. Shorty's brother Mel, however, was eventually fired from the Lucky Friday because, as the story reportedly went, he saw how unfairly the bosses were treating the miners. He put up a fuss and was let go.

After a month of the old slush, drill, and blast routine, my big chance came for an opening in another stope. It was up on 3,850, which was 200 feet higher in the mine than the back stope I was working in at the time. Now, is that moving up in a job, or what? And it was one hell of a place too, from what I heard. The stope was nearing the end of its working life after about five years and was in the process of "pulling sill." This meant that the mining crews—many different ones too, over the years, I'm sure—had mined all the way up from 4,050 to the 3,850 foot level, and were just finishing the place up. In other words, pulling sill is the final stage of mining a stope that is just breaking into the level above.

My new partner, Rick, was a hot-shot young fella who was out to burn up the world with his mining expertise, or so it seemed. He was from Arizona, born and bred. The guy that I replaced had been Rick's partner in a mine somewhere down around Casa Grande, Ari-

zona. The stope was all timbered, a standard procedure when pulling sill, and we were working about 20 feet down from the floor of the main 3,850 drift. We had an opposite shift in the place too.

It seemed like all that Rick and I did was put in timber… and put in timber. Man that place was big. He and I worked right along, though, and then one night we were visited by Mr. Air Blast, but luckily in between shifts. He hit us so hard that he ripped the stope's back out, and everything just sat right down on top of our timber. You just couldn't imagine what we saw the next morning. Picture this: the place was 46 feet wide, and perhaps wider in places, and it all had been bolted and timbered up really well. When I say timbered, I mean caps the size of trees—a couple of feet thick, and 16 feet or whatever long. They were butted together end to end because the stope was so wide and then covered with wooden bulkheads and semitrailer loads of lagging. Eight-feet-long wooden posts that were at least 8 to 10 inches thick, stood under the ends of the caps. All the wood used underground, by the way, was good, hard tamarack, which lasts a long time without rotting. It has often been said that there is more wood underground in the Silver Valley mines than there is standing in the Coeur d'Alene National Forest. I'll be the first to agree with that estimation too.

Like I said, when the blast hit, the whole back just sat down right on top of our pitiful timber, and crushed

At one of the Lucky Friday's shaft stations, miner "Bo Hunk" looks down into the pocket where ore is dumped.
Bruce Baraby, Wallace ID

and broke all of it. I just couldn't imagine how much weight it took to break that much wood, or should I have said, "Crush and bury that much wood." As Rick and I walked to the end of our crosscut on the morning after, and stood looking down into our workplace in amazement, another boomer hit. We scrambled back down to the drift trying to dodge falling rock and belching clouds of dust. Talk about scared; I heard the awesome sounds of timber groaning and breaking behind me as I ran. The only thing we really saw in those brief few seconds as the blast hit was the top of an enormous smooth slab of rock that fell right on our timber. It looked like the back had all come down in an 8-feet-thick piece. I think I almost wet myself in all the excitement.

After we'd finally gotten far enough away from the stope to emerge from the thick cloud of dust, Rick looked over at me and said, "Damn I hate this place." He was covered with dust and sort of fuzzy appearing, and looked like an angry ghost. That night he quit and went back to Arizona. "Where there ain't any air blasts," he said.

George Lander, the mine's foreman, called me into his office the next morning and explained the situation to me. "I've decided to pull you out and let the stope sit idle for a while. We're going to keep it shut down while it's trying to settle down in there."

Just as he said, "it's trying to settle down in there," I suddenly flashbacked to my brother Gary's stope over in the Crescent Mine. I wondered if this one would ever settle down enough to be safe to work in again. I don't think Gary's ever really did. Incidentally, when "pulling sill" the ground pressures normally are tremendous because the stope comes up right beneath the level above it and those old rotten workings usually have been sitting there long enough to really get chunky and loose.

As I said, Rick and I had been working opposite of two other guys on another shift—their names were Bobby Burton and Ken something or the other. With Rick gone, of course, the three of us were "farmed out" into other work places as our stope settled down. After a few weeks, however, George finally decided that the place was just too dangerous to mine using two crews a day. His logic was, "The faster the ground is being blasted and moved the more common the air blast activity becomes."

As he was telling me this, I thought, "Damn, that's going to leave me without a steady work place again."

View down the stairway to the parking lot at the Lucky Friday. "This sure looked good after a hard day underground."
Hecla Mining Company

Then he continued, "... but your opposite partners Bob and Ken have assured me that there is enough work in the stope to keep three miners busy even if they are all on one shift. So I've decided to move you over to their shift and you can all three work together in there, but be careful."

The stope popped, snapped, and boomed for several more weeks before we were finally able to go back in and start working again... together. I had been working the shift opposite of Bobby and Ken for about six months, but I'd never actually seen them. We seemed to just pass each other in the night, if you will.

Finally, the big day to move back into the stope came. George was satisfied that the place had settled down as much as it was going to, and I'd been told to switch shifts. I was really anticipating meeting my elusive opposite crew, and I'd heard a lot of good things about Bobby, the lead man, too. From all that I'd been told, I'd built up a vision in my mind of him being a "mighty miner"—complete with muscles bulging, back arching, and brain straining. For at least six months, a fella who had a basket next to mine in the dry had been filling my head full of tales about this really massive miner, Bobby, "Who would put all of us to shame."

That morning, in the dry, I finally met Bobby for the first time, but instead of a "mighty miner," what did I see in front of me but a stooped, aging miner in his late 50s with one glass eye. As luck would have it, the storyteller just happened to be right there next to me when I met Bobby. His gleeful, mischievous grin explained it all—this was a really good one, I'll have to admit. I told him so later too.

Bobby, Ken, and I hit it off right away, though, and I felt a little exuberant as we headed on down toward "our" stope that first morning. I thought, "This is going to be a great experience for me, having partners who really know what they're doing." My old partner Rick was a pretty good miner I guess, but he had a real attitude, or at least it sure seemed like it to me. He constantly complained of how we were being "screwed" by the management. The way he came across, everybody was screwing each other. The ladies of the night, who'd established some of the oldest and most lucrative businesses in Wallace, were being screwed by the miners. The miners in turn were being screwed by the mining companies, and the mining companies themselves were being screwed by the foreign metals markets. I really got tired of listening to his kind of thinking all of the time and was looking forward to a change.

I wasn't disappointed either. With Bobby's brain, and Ken and I as the muscle, collectively we did indeed make up the massive miner that I'd envisioned. After about two months we were finally getting the place pretty well back into shape again. I began getting these really inspirational thoughts like, "See there Mr. Air Blast. You can knock us down but we'll just get right back up again."

Then one day at the end of the shift we were on the station waiting for the skip to come down. I was overhearing the conversation of the young summer help guys, who talked about everything from how cute she looked in those "skimpy little things," to remembering when someone fell through the ice last winter. All of a sudden someone yelled, "There's fire in the shaft."

Now that was a statement to end all conversations, for sure. I looked quickly over at the shaft hoping that whoever made that statement was just trying to pull some sort of sick joke. But sure enough, I saw sparks falling down the shaft and an occasional whiff of smoke followed. About that time Ken, who was one freaked-out dude most of the time anyway, came running up to me. His pale face was contorted into a distraught, desperate, anguished look, and in a fever pitched voice he screamed out, "We're all gonna die." I looked past him at the youngsters, and saw the same look of desperation forming on their faces too, and thought, "Damn that's all we need down here. A bunch of idiots running around beating each other up."

Even though I was getting nervous about the sparks too, I slowly brought a smile to my face and laughed. Instantly, the desperate expressions faded, replaced by a look of confusion on the faces of about 15 people standing in front of me. I said, "Sure, we are… if you believe that, I've got some beautiful lakefront property in Florida that I'll sell ya."

I always figured that a smile and laugh will settle a lot of problems, and it sure worked here. Relief spread through the youngsters, unwarranted though as it might have been. But old Ken was still in my face. He quickly sat down beside me and loudly said, "If we get out of this, the first thing that I'm going to do is go right down to the whorehouse and kiss my wife."

With this statement I thought I felt a deep collective "What?" from the rest of the guys, because they stopped their excited jabbering and again fell silent. During all of this, Bobby sensed the crowd's desperation too, because he'd gotten up and walked over to the telephone hanging on a post near the shaft gates. He'd called the hoistman to report the sparks in the shaft. At about the same time Ken had finished his statement about kissing his "wife" and the kids again were appearing bewildered, Bobby shouted out, "The hoistman says that one of the mechanics has been welding on the station near the top of the shaft, and started a little fire behind a wall plate down in the shaft somewhere. They're trying to find it right now."

Wall plates are wooden panels in between the shaft's corner posts. I knew the shaft had a sprinkler system for just such emergencies, but I looked and didn't see anything more than the usual "light rain" coming down. I was surprised that a fire could even get started in the shaft because of all the moisture there normally was in it.

Considerable time had now passed by, and the simmering mood of desperation began turning to anger. I heard someone yell out, "Why the hell don't they lower a skip down to us and get us out of this damned place?" This was followed in the next hour by lots of disheartened grumbling and uncertainty.

Finally the smoke and intermittent sparks stopped falling down the shaft and, eventually, we heard the rumble of the skip coming down the shaft. We loaded onto it and were on our way up. In the meantime, Ken must have regained his bearings a bit and I think he felt a little embarrassed about his declaration in front of the whole crew about kissing his old lady in the whorehouse. He told me that she worked as a secretary/janitor, "over there." Incidentally, I noticed that all the other guys on the skip were listening intently to his explanation too. There were quite a few houses of ill repute in Wallace, or so I'd heard, but my ol' lady refused to let me go and find out how many there actually were.

The fire behind the wall plate in the shaft wasn't the only thing that was smoldering that day. You talk about some angry troopers—it was like a mad beehive in there. On the way up the shaft they worked themselves into a frenzy before spilling out onto the top station. Their anger persisted for weeks after that, too, and finally was abated only when Marvin Graham, one of the mine's foremen, was transferred to another Hecla facility. From what I'd heard, Marvin was the one who had decided to leave us underground while the fire was being "worked out." Personally, I didn't think he had a choice in the matter, since the skip would have had to pass right through the trouble spot. If indeed a full blown fire had developed, the flames would have been right in the path of the skip.

I remembered a story a friend had heard about a tragic fire in a mine that I think was in Mexico. The fire actually wasn't in the mine, but on top at the surface. As his story went, oil drums stored near the shaft had somehow burst into flames, causing a really stubborn fire. The "top landers," or surface workers, persisted in their efforts and finally were able to contain the "barrel melting" fire. When they called down into the mine to reassure the crew that the fire was out and that there was no further need to worry, no answer came back. The entire crew of a hundred or so fellas had died from smoke inhalation or suffocated.

Things settled down after the shaft fire, and the days ahead were routine. We'd finally gotten our stope into a mining mode and were breaking rock again. I was talking to Bobby one day and the conversation got around to his glass eye. I didn't really want to mention his missing eye because, of course, I didn't know if he was sensitive about it, but I was really curious about what had happened.

Bill Kierig resting on a screen over his timber-slide at the Lucky Friday. All materials and equipment are brought up into the stope through the timber-slide.
Steve Thomas, Coeur d'Alene ID

He volunteered to talk about it, and said, "I drilled into a missed hole once and got this eye blasted out." He gestured up at the staring glass orb protruding from his face. He continued, "When the dynamite that was still in the hole went off, I almost died. When it exploded it blasted rocks into my face, chest, and punctured one lung too." With that he grabbed the right side of his chest.

Then he sort of chuckled, and said, "I can't see very good at all when I'm hunting deer and elk. And I have this old white Scout that I use when I go out. Well," he went on, "at least it use to be white. I went hunting last winter and while I was out walking in the woods it started snowing. After I got back down to the road again I looked but just couldn't find the damned truck to save my life. I was standing on the road about where I parked it too, but looked and looked and still couldn't see it. Then I began to worry, because it was really gettin' cold and I needed to get home. The snow finally let up a bit and then I saw it. I'd been standing not 50 feet from the damned thing all the time. I was so mad that after I got home that night, I got me out a can of red spray paint and just sprayed the hell right out of it too. Now it's sorta red. Don't look like much but at least I can find it now."

As we mined the stope we still had some repairs to make, including rebolting the walls of the main drift. Thus, we had to cut out the old iron rock bolts and the metal mats that had been wrapped over the walls be-

Stope ready for sand-fill. Burlap wrapped around the chute
allows water (only) to drain
through.
Steve Thomas, Coeur d'Alene ID

tween the bolts. One day as Bobby and I busily cut out a mess of the bent-up crap with a cutting torch, I happened to look back down the drift toward the station. I saw a cloud of gray smoke and, at about that same time, the cap lights of four guys coming through it. We shut off our torch and waited. Talk about feeling stupid… as they approached, I looked down on the floor and saw an old discarded glove that had caught on fire from the sparks of our torch. It was smoldering rather heavily, too. Our unexpected visitors included Shorty and several hastily gathered mine rescue people. I was really relieved that our blunder didn't cause more trouble than it did. Our visitors were relieved too once they found out where the smoke came from.

Shorty said, "We very nearly evacuated the mine, because of this. Be a little more observant, next time."

All of the deep, modern underground mines that I knew of used a "stench warning system." When a situation warranted it, a specified person like a hoistman or a boss opened a bottle of really rotten smelling chemicals into the air system. The idea was that miners, however remote their location in the mine might be, would smell the rotten egg odor. This indicated to the workers that there was an emergency and that they must evacuate the mine. The primary escape route in the Lucky Friday, by the way, was through the main, and only, shaft.

One time, Bobby and I did something really embarrassing. We'd finished drilling and loading out our round with dynamite, and we thought it was near quitting time. Bobby looked down at his watch, and said, "Light 'er up, it's time to go." I didn't carry a watch at the time and relied solely on his to tell the time. So I struck a match, lit the end of the fuse primer, and we climbed up to the level and walked on out to the shaft. Bill Greenland, our shifter then, happened to be there and asked what we were doing out at the shaft so early. I asked him what time it was. He said, "One o'clock." My heart sank. Blasting time was supposed to be at Two o'clock.

I suddenly had the idea of climbing back down into the stope and somehow extinguishing the fuses before the round went off. But I knew that instead of getting three days off without pay (the standard penalty for blasting early), I would either be killed because I wouldn't be fast enough, or fired because I wasn't smart enough. About then, we heard the dull thuds of the exploding dynamite going off in the drill holes. We had, indeed, blasted a full hour too early. I spent the next three days cooling my heels and looking for my very own pocket watch. I'm sure Bobby felt bad too, because he'd misread his watch with his one eye, putting us and everybody else in the mine in a dangerous situation.

One of the most serious sins underground is to not guard your blast against someone accidentally walking into it. Over the years, there have been a lot of widows and orphans because of that little mistake. Another major worry is that an exploding round will trigger a visit from Mr. Air Blast, a very unwelcome fellow.

The slusher path in our stope was very narrow in one place because of the busted-up ground and timber. That made it necessary to hang the electric slusher's power supply cord, the water, and air hoses all together on nails, which we hammered into the posts just beneath the caps. The posts stood vertically on either side of the slusher path.

It was a Friday and I'd blasted the last round of the week before going off shift. (The mine's crews rotated the start of shifts; i.e., two weeks starting in the mornings alternating with two weeks starting in the afternoons). We'd just finished our afternoon stints, so the following Monday we were back on the day, or morning, shift. When we came into the stope on Monday, I found that some of the "fly rock" from Friday's round had knocked the power cable down and cut the water hose in half, leaving the slusher path knee-deep in water. We needed to straighten things up.

I asked Bobby to go out to the electric panel and shut off the 440-volt "juice" that was running through the "hanging down" electric wire. We both were about half-scared to death of electricity, I guess. After he'd left, I looked over all of the hanging stuff, and thought, "Hell, this shouldn't be a problem. All I have to do is lift the wire back up and hang it on the nail again." It was only hanging down a few inches lower than it should have been.

I knew that if a fella grabbed hold of a "live" wire his muscles would contract and he wouldn't be able to let go of it. I wasn't going to grab the wire with an open hand, of course, so I thought I'd hold the back of my glove up beneath the wire, picking it up only about a foot from where it was broken. Something I'd forgotten about, though, was that I was standing knee-high in water, and the electric wire was dripping wet too. I began lifting my hand, and just as I barely touched the wire with the back of the glove, electricity slammed into me. I heard myself screaming and I blacked out. The current was running from a break in the cable, up

Sand being pumped into a stope from a sand tank on the surface. The stope area beyond the wall already has been filled.
Steve Thomas, Coeur d'Alene ID

through the water along the wire, and down through me and into the water hole I was standing in. Bobby must have shut off the juice right about then. It was a miracle I wasn't killed by stupidity, and Bobby didn't have to find his partner all cooked up when he got back.

A lot of our time in the stope was spent much like I'd imagine a garbageman in downtown USA would have spent his day on the job. The ground was badly air slacked, and we had to constantly take out and replace rotten wood. We filled one whole mined-out end of the stope with broken, rotted timber and other trash, and then built a wall in front and covered it all up with sand.

We'd finally gotten to the other end of the stope— the really big 46-feet-wide end. We were waiting only for the ore in the chute to be pulled by our motorman, and then we would be ready to sand-fill the mined-out cut. We'd told Bill that we were ready to pour, but that the chute needed to be pulled first. Well… there was a breakdown in communication, I guess, because when Bobby and I came into work the next day, our stope was filling up with sand. (Ken had been moved to another stope, temporarily.) That is to say, "The sandman had visited us during the night." I was elated, because stopes usually had to take turns getting sand in order of their importance; for example, some stopes that were air blasting badly had to be filled first. The less time I had to worry about screwing around in different work places

all over the mine waiting for our place to be filled, the better I liked it. I knew that Bobby wouldn't have any problem in finding a place to make money while we were waiting, though. Hell, he had about 15 years more seniority than anybody else on earth, and that was another reason why I liked having him as a partner. That let me "team bid" with him, whereas if I'd been on my own I would have been on the bottom of the new stope bidding list. The bosses, of course, let the miners with the most seniority have the first choices of where to work.

And there it was… sand. I told Bill, "That's great, we should be full of sand by tonight [it took three shifts to complete the pour]. Then we'll probably be able to get back into the stope and start mining again by tomorrow." This would allow the excess water to drain out of the stope down into the chute during the graveyard shift.

Then I asked Bill, "How many cars did they get out of the chute before starting to pour the sand?"

He didn't know, but said he'd find out.

Bobby and I went on down into the mine and baby-sat the day-shift sandman. Later on, Bill came around on his rounds, and said, "They didn't pull any muck out of your chute… was there some in it?"

My heart sank. I said, "Hell, it's full. There's 180 feet of high-grade ore in that damn chute just like I told you yesterday."

He said, "Well yeah, I wrote it down in my book too, and they should have pulled it before starting to pour the sand."

There it was, 180 feet of high-grade ore probably worth a king's ransom, stuck up in the chute. It was too late to pull the chute, too. When sand is poured into a stope, some of it inevitably runs through the burlap covering over the top of the chutes and through cracks in the metal crib's joints. Consequently, some sand flows down inside the chutes and comes out on the drift below. Because of this, a two- or three-board high dam is built in the drift down below. This dam is always situated "downstream" a ways from the chute opening, thus preventing the sand coming out of the chute from running all the way out to the station. It makes mucking up after the sand-fill easier, too. But this dam and its sand also cuts off access to the ore chute during the pour.

Furthermore, problems develop if ore is left in a chute during a sand-fill, especially a crib chute as old and bent up as ours was. The sand that works its way into the chute tends to "set up" if muck still happens to be in the chute, as in our case. It then becomes very difficult to get the trapped high-grade muck out of the sand-clogged chute.

Thus began our big project—"the cleaning-out of the chute." We started on the next shift after the pour was finished. First we had to tear down the little sand wall on the level down below and muck up all of the sand that had spilled. Then we brought in an empty muck train to pull what ore there was left from out of the bottom of the chute. But we were only able to get about 20 cars, or so… and that was it. There should have been closer to 50 cars of ore in there. The stuff we'd pulled was really beautiful, though. It was rich, black, shiny tetrahedrite (silver) ore. However, probably a hundred feet, or several hundred tons, of high-grade silver ore was still stuck up in there.

George called Bobby and I into his office just before shift the next day. I noticed that he held Bill's report in hand. I think he was very determined to recover the hundreds of thousand of dollars worth of high-grade ore that was still trapped in the chute, because he said, "We've got to get it down so do what it takes. I'll pay you $200 a day apiece to do it."

That was our cue… money! After we left the office, I talked with Bobby, and then ordered a boatswain's chair, cutting torch, and a bunch of other junk like that from Bill. Our idea was to rig up a sheave block, or pul-

ley, right above our 4-feet-diameter, 180-feet-deep timber-slide, which ran parallel to the hung chute all the way down to the level below. We would take turns lowering each other into the tube on the end of a 3/8th inch cable. Then, suspended in the timber-slide with a cutting torch in hand, we'd try to cut an access hole through its metal side and tunnel through the sand into the clogged chute, hopefully finding the hang-up. That way, maybe we could find what was keeping the ore stuck in there and possibly break it loose.

Everything went smoothly to begin with… the equipment was set up and we were ready to go. Then came the big question, "Who was going down the tube first?" I decided that I should give it a try. "After all," I reasoned, "Bobby's already got enough trouble, what with his one glass eye and all."

I climbed into the chair, which sort of looked like a seat on a playground swing set, but it was connected to just one strand of cable. While rigging it up to the sheave block and a small air tugger, I also connected a safety rope to the "D" ring on the back of my safety belt just in case.

Then came the big moment. I told Bobby to tighten the cable up a bit, which he did and I felt my feet lift up off the floor. My body swung out, and I hung in mid-air over the center of the 180-feet-deep hole. As I dangled there, I suddenly had a flashback to the time I'd put a safety harness on upside down over at the Galena Mine (that was a little different, though… it was a harness, instead of a wooden seat). I felt warm air rushing up out of the darkness beneath me, and wondered how it was all going to turn out. I looked Bobby squarely in his one eye, swallowed, and said, "Lower away pard."

He nodded and pushed forward slowly on the handle of the tugger and I experienced "that old sinking feeling" again. As I slowly dropped below the top of the metal crib, I lost sight of him and suddenly shuddered with dread. I remembered the stories I'd heard about welding crews being burned alive in metal pipes when they were working. But I reassured myself and thought, "That was because they had a build-up of acetylene gas in an enclosed space. Look here, I have all this air whooshing by, to carry away the fumes."

We'd already planned that Bobby would let out about 100 feet of cable, then he'd stop the tugger, and that was where we'd put in our hole. I waited and waited for him to stop, but he kept right on slowly lowering me down deeper into the hole. Man, it was a long ways down in there. I looked up and could clearly see the

The top of the sand-fill becomes the floor for further operations.
Bruce Baraby, Wallace ID

joints of the metal crib right above me. The cribbing was stacked like bricks, with joints not matching. Looking further up... the crib tapered away in the light of my cap light, until disappearing completely into darkness above that.

Bobby was letting the cable out so slowly that I had time to look through the crib joints on the side next to the chute. "Hell," I thought, "its empty back in there." I could see an open space of about 6 or 8 feet with my light, to what looked like a wall. I took my pipe wrench out of its holder and hit the crib, while listening intently, for a hollow, empty sound.

Suddenly the chair stopped, and Bobby's muffled voice yelled down from above, "You all right Jerry?" I was surprised that he'd heard me hit the crib and stopped the tugger. I was reassured by the sound of his voice because then I knew that I wasn't the only human left on the earth. The trip was doing strange things to my mind.

I shouted back, "Yeah, this crib is just sittin' here. It doesn't even look like there is any sand around it at all. Not where I'm looking, at least."

He yelled down again and said, "What's it look like below you?"

I directed my beam of light between my legs into the darkness and, after my eyes focused, I replied, "Mashed ... good thing you stopped. Looks like the crib damn near pinches off about 10 feet below me. Sure's hell isn't room for me to go through it sittin' on this chair, that's for sure."

Then he responded, "We'll stop there then, you're about a hundred feet down, near as I can figure."

About that time I heard a rock, must have been about the size of a golf ball from the way it sounded, falling down the timber-slide above me. It banged back and forth off the metal sides of the crib, somewhere up there. I drew my shoulders in and tried to get as small as possible, knowing that my body nearly filled the timber-slide, what with me sitting on the "swing seat" like that. I waited in sort of a half standing-up position. It was getting louder the closer it got, rattling and banging off the sides of the crib… still coming. Then I saw something flash by my light and, luckily, it flew right between my knees and on down the chute. I could hear it banging loudly off the crib below for what seemed like a long time.

I yelled at Bobby, "Be careful up there."

He shouted back, sheepishly, "Sorry about that."

I didn't really know for sure what was left or right, and for that matter up and down were a bit vague too. There were no landmarks to follow, only that round tube.

"Everything is round in this damned place," I thought, and laughed aloud at my own joke. The sound of my voice was gratifying; it interrupted the deathly calm.

The only other sound I heard was the whoosh of the hot air as it made its way past me up the chute. I hung there, feeling the warm, dead air rushing by. I was grateful Bobby hadn't blasted a hole right through me with that zillion mile an hour missile he'd sent down.

Wanting to keep in voice contact with Bobby, I said loudly, "Where should I start to cut this damn hole?" Bobby didn't answer my rhetorical question, and I felt sorta stupid right about then too, for even asking it. After all, how could he have known? But I shrugged it off.

Finally I remembered the angle of the chute, and figured, "If the timber-slide is leaning over at the top, and the hung chute is 'off to the left' up there, then it should still be off to the left down here as well."

I looked up and yelled, "Here we go, turn on the gas." I had kept the hoses empty when coming down, just in case they would somehow leak gas. A few minutes later, I heard the hiss of gas, and I grabbed the striker, which I'd wired to the boatswain's cable at its joining "Y" just above me. I didn't want to accidentally drop and lose the striker down the hole. After a few flashing tries, I had a neat little flame coming out of the torch head.

Then I was almost… well, "happy," I guess that would be the word I'd use. I finally was able to begin cutting through the metal crib. But I wasn't happy a little while later when the metal crib began "cutting" me up as well. Sparks and bits of molten iron snapped and popped off the sides of the crib like grease off a hot skillet, and peppered my legs.

"Pain… I'm on fire," I thought. Spitting, snapping sparks and smoke obscured my vision. My eyes were safe, of course, because of the industrial strength sunglasses I was wearing. I was glad about that, for sure. But there was nothing to protect my legs, and I howled with pain as the burning metal seared through my rubber slicker pants in a dozen places and into the meat of my legs. I brushed frantically at the "pain spots" and soon had them under control.

Bobby must have heard me because then came a muffled barrage of questions, "Are you all right? What's happening down there? Do you want me to pull you up?"

I thought, "Now there's an idea." I shouted back, "Yeah… its your turn."

I was soon at the top again, and lying on the sand floor. I pulled off my britches and saw that my legs were peppered with little red blisters. I was still in pain, too. We talked for awhile, and I warned him about the sparks and flames. Then he climbed into the seat with all the gear that I'd had on, but he was taking his rain coat down with him, too, to cover his legs. Soon he was down at the spot where I'd cut out "my little bit" of crib. Actually, all I'd been able to cut out before I "wimped out" was a line about 10 inches long. I felt sorta guilty about it, too.

I was getting really proud of Bobby, though, after he'd spent about an hour down in the hole. Then suddenly, I heard him yelling too. I jumped to the edge of the hole and yelled down, "What happened? Are you all right?"

A few seconds of silence went by and then he very calmly shouted back, "When I finished cutting this piece of crib in half, all the pressure against the outside of the timber-slide made the crib jump in toward me. It just scared me, that's all." As I stood there listening to his muffled reply, I could imagine his surprise when that happened. Especially considering he could only see out of one eye.

We traded places again, and it was the same for the rest of the shift. The next day came along, and then the next, as we jockeyed positions back and forth in the timber-slide all the while. The days stretched into weeks. We'd gone through the side of the crib and were slowly chipping away at the hard sand with shortened Fin hoes, burrowing like a couple of moles and happily thinking about our $200 a day.

Then one morning as I was about to head off to work, Bobby called me on the telephone. He said, "Our union contract ran out and we're out on strike now."

I knew that negotiations between the company and our union were going on, and had been for some time, but I'd hoped that some last-minute deal could be worked out. We talked for a while. I thanked him, and hung up.

Then I sat down at the kitchen table with a cup of coffee and thought, "Union strikes have chased me all over this damned Valley over the years. And now finally, all the way over to the Valley's easternmost mine, the Lucky Friday. I don't dare quit and try to go into one of the other mines again either. Those days are over, for all practical purposes."

Here I was, sounding like the two fellas over in the Galena who'd warned me about tramping out. One thing I was glad about, though, was the timing. It was just before our contract pay period, and tomorrow Bobby and I would receive our big gypo checks for our two weeks of climbing up and down our timber-slide looking for that damn hang-up in the chute.

The next day I went up to the mine to collect my check and took my place at the end of a long pay line. The window hadn't opened yet, and the fellas were talking and laughing about what they planned to do on their unplanned vacations. I thought, "Well, hell, I can take off now… legally. After all," I thought, "with the check I'm getting this week, I'll be able to afford it." I was beginning to get excited—the same excitement I felt whenever I tramped out.

The window slid open and we began moving forward. Upon reaching the lady behind the window, each person called out his employee number and received a check. Then it was my turn. I reached out, eagerly grabbing my check.

As I turned to walk off, I looked at it… "Son-of-a-bitch," I exclaimed loudly. When I looked up, I noticed many sly gleeful grins from the people in line. It was as if they were saying, "Oh, you got screwed, huh?"

I turned and walked straight into George's office. As I entered, he looked up from his desk. When I saw that I had his attention, I asked, "What happened to the $200 a day that you promised us for working on the chute? This check is only for day's pay."

He replied with something like, "The money just wasn't there for the project yet. It's too early. Maybe after a couple more weeks we can put it into force… and besides that, we didn't have anything written down either."

I talked to George for a while longer, but just couldn't get him to change his mind. One of his foreman was standing right behind him during our conversation, and the entire day too I'll bet… for protection, probably. It was like talking to a stone wall, though, and I finally gave up. I turned and as I walked out of the office, I noticed a line had formed outside George's door. Some of the people with the sly grins that I'd seen before were in the line, but their expressions had since turned grim, stone-faced, and angry. Then it was my turn. I gave them my best, "Oh, you got screwed too, huh?" look as I passed by.

As I walked out of the building, I thought, "A fella can't help but like old George, though. He sure is a silver-tongued devil. He could screw a guy to death and still make him like it." ❦

CHAPTER 12

Legal Tramp

Hack Canyon Mine, Fredonia, Arizona;
and 16 to 1 Mine, Silver Peak, Nevada

I went home and showed Jo Ann the small paycheck. She was disappointed too I think, but didn't let on about it very much. During the conversation she said, "I've got an Uncle Claude in Arizona who works in the uranium mines down there. My relatives don't hear from him very much, up here, but… maybe you could get a job there for a few weeks. Until the strike is over anyhow."

Jo Ann's suggestion sounded great to me. I felt a wave of excitement surge within me at the possibility of taking another road trip. I started making phone calls, first to her Aunt Rose; I was sorry to find out that Uncle Claude had died of cancer a year before. I didn't like to hear that little bit of trivia for another reason too: I'd heard that uranium mining was a real known killer, as far as cancer went.

But, I needed a job, and Aunt Rose said, "Roger Smith is my next door neighbor. He's a good friend and works for a uranium mine." She gave me his telephone number.

I called Roger up. After introducing myself, I told him that Rose said I should call. I said that I'd been working in the deep mines of North Idaho, but was out on strike and needed a job for awhile.

He finally said, "Come on down, if you want to. We'll probably be able to find something for you to do."

Thus, this part of what would be my "legal tramp" was taken care of. By the way, the reason I call it a "legal tramp" is because I had a real need to find tempo-

rary employment. Anybody could see that I had a job pretty much lined up and a legitimate reason for hitting the road… I wasn't just "tramping" because of wanderlust. But I'll admit, when anyone gave me an excuse to travel he'd better not have been standing in front of my old pickup truck because he'd get his toes run over for sure.

Then I asked myself the question, "Do I want to head out alone?" The answer I kept coming up with was, "No." I needed someone with me who would share the driving, expenses, and such. Jo Ann couldn't go because of Jason, who was a fourth grader. I began calling other guys from the Lucky Friday who, of course, were out on strike too. Finally, after several calls, I spoke with Clayton Grubham, whose nickname was "lug nut." He agreed to tramp out with me.

When I'd first heard his nickname several years before I thought he must be one hell of a good roadside mechanic. But this is how he got the name… as the story goes, he and a friend were drinking heavily while on a road trip over in Montana someplace. They passed by another driver who'd pulled his car off to the side of the road and was changing a flat tire. Well, they stopped, backed up, and Clayton stepped out and approached the man, who was down on one knee changing the tire.

Clayton asked, "Can I help you with that tire?"

The guy replied, "Yes, if you want to."

Whereupon Clayton reached down, grabbed a loose lug nut out of an upside-down hubcap, and swallowed it! Then he and his partying friend jumped back into their car and drove off, leaving the completely bewildered man on the roadside staring after them as they

After hauling in a cap on a timber-truck, a nipper prepares to raise it up the timber slide to waiting miners. Note the timber slide's skip (can).
Hecla Mining Company

Legal Tramp 147

drove away. Thus was the origin of the nickname "lug nut." I figured that anyone with a mind like that would be sort of fun to tramp around with, or, at least, he probably wouldn't be boring.

I spent the rest of the day outfitting my old Chevy pickup and its 8-feet-long camper. My excitement was becoming almost unbearable by then. The next morning at 8 o'clock, as Clayton and I had agreed, he came over to my house, parked in front, and we drove off down the road on our new adventure. We'd decided to head through eastern Washington, and down into eastern Oregon and Nevada. We reasoned, "If we can get on somewhere in between here and Arizona, so much the better. We'll be closer to home that way."

At the end of the first day we reached Burns, Oregon, and stayed overnight in a grocery-store parking lot. The second day we rolled into Winnemucca, Nevada. I had a list of telephone contacts with me, and one of them was John Metcalfe, a former manager of the Lower Bunker Hill, who'd hired me a couple of times before. I'd heard through the grapevine that he was managing a tungsten mine in Winnemucca and was hiring.

I gave him a call, but he said, "I just hired a couple of miners today and won't need anyone else for at least two months, but you might try Battle Mountain. I've heard they're doing some hiring over there."

I thanked him, saying, "Maybe we'll be by again in a couple of months and check with you then." I was never one to burn my bridges. We left Winnemucca on his advice, and after driving another 50 or 60 miles further east reached Battle Mountain. It was getting late, so I pulled into a parking lot in front of what looked like the town's only casino and we spent the night.

The next morning, Clayton and I walked over to the coffee shop on one end of the casino for breakfast. There, we met four guys whom we knew as past workers at the Lucky Friday. They were working in a local silver mine located a few miles south of town.

One of the miners, named Fred, said, "You ought to try our mine, maybe you can get on. It'd be nice to have someone else from up home way working down here too."

When Fred had worked in the Lucky Friday, I use to always see him looking up at the back, or ceiling. And at first it was really unnerving and I felt like I should be looking up there too or I might miss out on something. I asked someone why he did that and was told he had poor eyesight. He could see much better by squinting, and tilting his head back. That's what made it seem like

Clayton Grubham
Bruce Baraby, Wallace ID

he was looking up all the time. When Clayton and I first walked into the restaurant, I knew instantly it was Fred. I hadn't before, or since, seen any other "ceiling watchers," or at least any who were as good at it as he was, that's for sure.

We thanked them and after finishing breakfast set out across the desert following their directions to the silver mine. The desert, though barren, seemed to have a "glow" that morning, and we were excited about the possibility of landing a job not too awfully far from Idaho.

After driving by many treeless bluffs and brush-filled draws, I entered what I thought was the right road. It turned out to be the wrong place and we wound up on top of a barren mountain. There we sat in the truck, looking up at a 10-feet-high chain link fence and a guard shack off to the side. There was a nasty looking fellow looking back at us from the shack's window, too. A sign on the guard shack said something like, "No visitors, no samples, no entry…" and a bunch of other "no's" I can't remember. It looked like the entrance to an open pit gold mine.

We backtracked and eventually found "our" mine out behind and at the base of the same mountain. It all appeared to be pretty valuable real estate, I'd say. As we drove onto the property, a fella stepped out of a small old 10 x 45-feet trailer house, which sat near the mine's entrance. I pulled up beside him and explained that we were looking for work. He waved us into the trailer.

As we entered the office, I glanced over at the mine's portal, which wasn't far away. I could see the top of a decline-type drift and a couple of impressive-looking diesel trucks parked off to one side. We sat there in the trailer talking for a while and I happened to be facing out a window. The scenery would be best described as flat, sun drenched, and hot; and, about a million miles away, there was a thin line of treeless mountains. I was trying to imagine what coming to work there every day would be like as the man talked.

He said, "It will be a few days, but I can use you because of your mining experience, but not your partner here because of his lack of it. Come around on Wednesday if you want the job." It was Monday then.

We thanked him, returned to the truck, and drove back toward Battle Mountain. Clayton was quiet on the way, and I knew that he was really disappointed. Just before we reached town, I noticed three motor homes parked a couple of hundred feet off the main road out in the desert. We set up camp again in the casino's parking lot, and later that day I asked one of the locals about the motor homes I'd seen.

He said, "Battle Mountain isn't set up for tourists yet because of its old sewer system, so tourists have to park outside of the city limits. Someone's going to put in a trailer park, though, for all of the miners that are coming in... someday."

Clayton and I were getting a little ripe by then, which is one of the drawbacks of tramping in a pickup camper, especially without air-conditioning. We decided to sneak into a small hotel located nearby and grab a shower. Well, things started out great. There were two shower rooms on the second floor and we were putting them to good use. I was standing there in the shower thinking about the day's events when suddenly I heard muffled sounds of someone shouting.

I hurried and finished up. When I opened the door into the hallway, there was a little old guy standing there holding a broom... bristles up. (I found out later that he'd actually just finished chasing 220-pound Clayton out of the hotel with his flailing broom.) I acted nonchalant and he only gave me a few sharp words as I passed by him. Later, we found out that we could have taken showers there for two bucks each, without suffering from the wrath of the little fella and his broom.

When I woke up in the camper the next morning, Clayton wasn't there. I didn't find him in the Wild West atmosphere of the casino's restaurant either. So I started the pickup's engine, and drove around looking for him.

I was thinking, "He couldn't have gone far, not in a town this small." Finally I saw him up ahead, walking down the road kicking rocks. He had his head down, deep in thought.

I thought, "I'm going to have some fun here." With the truck still moving, I shut off the engine and coasted silently up behind him. When I came alongside, I think it scared him, because he heard the crunch of the truck's tires on the gravel and he looked up with a wild look in his eyes.

I said, "What are you doing?"

Seeing it was me, he calmed down, saying, "Nuthin'."

Then I said, "Good, get in then... let's go to Arizona."

His face lit up like someone had just given him a birthday present. He said, "But I thought you were going to work at the silver mine."

I responded, "We came down here to work together pard and that's the way its going to be."

We parked that night by a truck stop near Salt Lake City, Utah. The next morning, after downing many cups of good, hot black coffee, we took off down the road again, and that afternoon reached southern Utah. After pulling off the road to get our bearings on our map, I noticed a shortcut heading east toward Kanab, more or less our destination. We took it, and in the beginning the road was much the same as the ones we'd been driving on. But it soon began getting steeper and steeper, and eventually we were winding around sheer cliffs, first this way and then that. It started to get colder, and I was in awe of the patches of snow that appeared alongside the road.

My old pickup sounded like it was on its last legs too. It just creeped along, as I kept the gas peddle firmly planted to the floorboard. The engine clattered and the tail pipe smoked badly, but the old girl finally made it to the top, where we saw snowbanks four feet deep and people skiing past us. Slowly gaining speed again, we drove by a ski lodge and a sign that said the summit of this pass was somewhere around cloud level.

Later that day we finally made it down to Kanab, which is just on the southern border of Utah, and seven miles further south we came into Fredonia, Arizona. Then, after a little help from "Ma Bell," we found the office for Energy Fuels Nuclear, Inc., Roger Smith's uranium mining company. We spent the night in the camper parked on a gravel side street.

The next morning, Clayton and I entered the company's portable metal office building (I think it was a double-wide trailer). I told the good looking little miner behind the front desk that I'd talked to Roger Smith over the phone a few days earlier and we were looking for work. Actually, I was a little concerned here because I hadn't told Roger I'd be bringing a partner along. Then a voice from a guy in another room who must have overheard me talking said, "Have them fill out work applications."

When we completed the forms, we were directed into the back office where the voice had come from. Pete Canfield, the mine's superintendent, rose up from behind a desk. Clayton and I introduced ourselves and we shook hands.

Pete then asked to see the applications. As he read the forms, I began our sales pitch "Yeah… I spoke with Roger Smith over the telephone a few days ago. He said to come on down and that you'd probably be able to find something for us to do. We've been working in the Lucky Friday Mine up there, but it's out on strike now so my partner here and I are out looking for work."

I went on talking and, after I'd finished telling Pete about all the wonderful things we knew about mining, he finally replied, "I'll probably be able to put you fellas on."

I congratulated myself, thinking, "By God, the old sales pitch worked. I should be selling used cars."

"But," he continued, "first I'd like for you to take a ride out to the mine and look us over. I ask all of our potential new employees to drive out there and check things out first… instead of our going to all of the trouble of completing physical examinations and paperwork, only to find out later that the guy decides he doesn't want to work in the mine." Pete finished by saying, "I just sent two other fellas out there too. You might see them on the way."

We thanked him and picked up a map from the little lady at the front desk. Then we headed out toward the mine. We drove a few miles west on pavement and then turned off southwest onto a gravel road. We continued on through miles and miles of bone-dry prairie and ravines. Eventually, we saw another pickup coming our way.

Clayton exclaimed, "I wonder if these aren't the guys that Pete said we might see out here? They look like they could be returning from the mine."

As we approached each other, I slowed down and so did the other pickup. As I came to a stop, a thought suddenly flashed through my mind, "Hell, this is like being in a western movie." I half expected the Duke to come riding over the hill right about then.

The two fellas in the pickup stopped too. They told us they were Colorado miners who, a few days before, had decided, "There must be better places to work in than this," and quit their mine. That, incidentally, is the "Hail Mary" of the tramp miner.

As the driver talked, I glanced into the open back of his pickup truck, and saw a car jack, two sleeping bags, and a cardboard box, all covered with about two inches of red dust. I asked them if they were going to "hire out" here at the Hack Canyon Mine, and they both simultaneously and loudly declared, "No."

Then the driver said, "We're on our way over to Bishop, California, to rustle another mine over there."

After our conversation ended, we continued on. After driving for about 20 more miles, we finally found the mine, situated in sort of a canyon in between two enormous table-topped mesas. Located there was a large metal-sided mechanic shop, electrical transformers, a double-wide trailer that looked like it was the dry, diesel trucks, muckers, and a lot of other equipment scattered around, and a 14 x 70 feet trailer house, which I guessed was the office. The layout looked like a well organized and financed operation.

As I sat there in the pickup, my gaze wandered up to the enormous cliffs. I happened to notice a solitary bird soaring in the morning air, about 200 feet above us next to the sheer cliff. We got out and took some time to "look the mine over," and then drove back into town.

We passed several more high mesas on the way. Suddenly, Clayton exclaimed, "I'd sure like to jump off one of them." I'll admit, I was taken back by his statement. Then he went on to explain that he'd just bought a hang glider for $2,000 from someone back up in Idaho and he was just itching to try it out.

Our conversation got around to how much we disliked all the dust on the way. But Clay and I both agreed that it probably just was the way things were down here in this part of the country. We also talked about how our "poke" was shrinking and how we needed a grubstake.

We returned to the mine's office in Fredonia and told Pete we wanted the jobs. Then, we began the hectic hiring-out process. During one of my many trips in and out of the office, I happened to glance out back and saw a helicopter parked beside a large metal-sided building. I walked over to the helicopter, impressed with how new and clean it looked. A fella noticed me there and came over to talk. I told him we were from Idaho and just hiring out, and how I liked his helicopter.

He said, "The company has three of them flying out of here. Energy Fuels owns a lot of mining properties and we're doing a lot of exploration work. So the helicopters are busy most of the time."

I mentioned that I'd never hired out in a uranium mine before, and that I'd been working thousands of feet down in North Idaho's silver mines.

He asked about the ore "up there."

I replied, "just a minute, I'll be right back," and I walked to the camper and picked up a baseball-sized chunk of high-grade silver ore that I'd brought with me.

He thought the heavy ore sample was interesting and wondered how much background radiation there was in it. He walked over to a shelf inside the building and brought out a Geiger counter, while exclaiming, "All rock has some background radiation in it." But when he tested the silver ore, he was amazed to find that it didn't have any. The Geiger counter's clicking stopped when the sensitive instrument was placed against the ore.

The next day or so went by quickly. Clayton and I took up camping in an RV park on the southern edge of Fredonia. We took physical examinations, finished hiring out, and almost before we knew it were sitting in a new Ford 4 x 4 van in front of an abandoned gas station on the southern outskirts of Fredonia. There were eight other employees in the company van too, and behind us was a second van filled with the rest of the mine's crew. We began the 37-mile trip out to the mine.

I took in the scenery during the drive. Someone said the mine was only about 13 miles north of the Grand Canyon. The views truly were beautiful; I noticed big-as-hell reddish looking skylines, building-sized boulders, far off rimrock and flat-topped mesas, and hills everywhere. Something else I took in was about half of the dirt in Arizona. It seeped in through the tiny joints in the new van, hanging like a pall in the air. The dust got so bad that I felt I was suffocating and opened a side window. Hot desert air gushed in and so did more very fine, throat-choking dust.

As I looked around the lurching van into the grimacing, coughing faces of the occupants, I remembered the two sleeping miners I'd shared a compartment with in the Sunshine's man-train, which now seemed like a

million years ago. I remembered how they slept; their heads bouncing and rolling in unison as the car's wheels screeched around the corners. These miners were asleep too, but God only knows how.

The fella sitting beside me noted my discomfort and said, "The big trick is to ride in the rig that's up in front. There's no guarantee which rig is going to take off first, though."

I looked back through our dirt-caked rear window and saw the other van rocking and rolling right along behind us. Their plight must have been worse than ours because all I could see of their vehicle through our billowing cloud of dust was an occasional fender, door, or the dust-covered windshield.

We made the trip to the mine in bang-up time really, and soon were climbing up a staircase and entering the double-wide trailer that served as the "dry." Then in no time at all we were outfitted with diggers, lamps, and caps, as well as the normal "glazed looks" on our faces which seem to be typical for miners everywhere. We climbed into the back of one of two diesel trucks waiting for us. As the truck engines roared to life and sat there "warming up," I leaned back and listened to the engines' echoes drifting off the canyon walls. The metal felt cool against my neck and the vibration of the truck's diesel engine was almost soothing. I looked up at the partially shaded cliff wall and again saw a bird soaring high above. I wondered if it was the same bird I'd seen a couple of days before.

The miner who'd been sitting beside me in the van was also in the truck. He knew Clayton and I were greenhorns and he offered a little information about the place: "Someone back in the old days discovered copper ore here and this place was originally a copper mine. But there wasn't much ore in it and later it was shut down. I heard that it sat idle for many years after that. Then someone else came along and found high-grade uranium ore and now it's a uranium mine. The uranium ore here is really rich too. Someone once told me that the ore in this mine is nine times 'hotter' than anywhere else in the United States."

I thought again about the dangers of uranium mining, and finally vowed right then and there to stay around only long enough to get "trampin' out money." About then our truck lurched forward and followed the other truck, which also was full of sleepy miners, toward the portal and the down ramp. The mine's portal was a hole that had been shot into the base of an enormous mesa. I sat up and turned on my cap lamp. The steep

Pouring silver bars at the 16 to 1 Mine.
Sunshine Precious Metals Inc.

decline extended down at an angle for about 1,600 feet, and at the bottom the road bed leveled out and came to a crossing. From there, it was a hundred feet or so in each direction to both ends of the mine. The whole affair was shaped like a huge distorted letter "T."

We'd talked to Larry Shumway, the mine's foreman, earlier that morning. He'd told us where to go and said he'd talk to us again when we got down in the mine. Clayton and I would be working on the left side of the "T."

Clayton and I got out of the truck and walked over to our assigned place where we saw the bottom of a bore hole. It was divided into two compartments—one compartment was a muck chute, and the other was the manway outfitted with floors, ladders, and air, water, and electrical lines. As we stood there looking things over, I recalled the bore holes in Idaho's Sunshine Mine.

"The way this one must have been drilled," I reasoned, "was for a drilling rig, probably a truck, to have parked up on the surface on top of the mountain over the mine. Then its crew drilled straight down using an 11 and 1/2 inch reamer bit. Once the reamer completed a pilot hole by breaking into the drift here, then an 8-foot bit was attached to the drill steel and dragged, spinning all the while, back up toward the surface following the pilot hole. The bit cut out the rock as it went, leaving an 8-feet diameter hole in its wake."

About then Larry arrived driving his own little tractor. He explained to us, "Two of these bore holes—over 800 feet high and 8 feet in diameter—have been driven

almost all of the way up to the surface at each end of the mine. From the top of the bore hole, the pilot hole extends about 50 feet on up to the surface. We're putting in another bore hole later that will be used for ventilation. Then all three of them will be in a triangular configuration."

He gestured up into the bore hole, "This bore hole is fully timbered all the way to its top. Your job will be to go about 30 feet up and blast out a slusher station into the wall. Once you've finished, we're going to pour a concrete slab at the station and bring down a 40 horsepower electric slusher." I'd seen the slusher he was talking about out in the yard and it was enormous. It looked like it could have weighed a ton.

Larry continued, "We'll anchor the slusher down on the concrete slab and you'll mine straight out from here toward the other bore hole, which is about 200 feet away. You'll be mucking down this compartment in the bore hole right here. A big front end loader will load the rock into the trucks, which then will haul it up the ramp to the surface. There, it will be transferred to larger trucks and sent to the mill."

He further explained that the drill crews had just finished the other bore hole, and the men who had timbered our bore hole had moved over there to timber it too. About then, a front end loader came around the corner and dumped off a tugger, a bundle of nylon rope, two sheave blocks, a couple of small chains, and a spool of cable. Larry left, and Clayton and I got busy stulling down the tugger. Then it was time to put in its cable way up in the bore hole. I grabbed the coil of nylon rope and started up the man-way ladders. Two hundred feet up, I tied off the end of the rope to a post and, yelling "look out below," dropped the coil. It looked weird disappearing down into the darkness, leaving a shaking single strand of rope behind. A while later, Clayton came huffing and puffing up, carrying the heavy sheave blocks and their chains with him. We then used the nylon rope to pull up the tugger cable and tied it off.

We spent the next few hours repeating this laborious procedure. On passing the 800-foot mark, we didn't have much farther to go before reaching the point where we would install the sheave blocks and tugger cable. We could see hundreds of ladder rungs receding from us down below in the man-way as we climbed, and the bore hole's sandstone walls were as smooth as a gun barrel. I began to think things like, "This must be what Hell is like, climbing and climbing endlessly."

Finally, around lunchtime, Clayton and I had the cable, blocks, and chains in place ready for installation in the top set of timber. Though exhausted and shaking from exertion, I looked up and became fascinated by daylight coming down through the 11 and 1/2 inch pilot hole in the very center of the bore hole above us. When I scooted around to get a better look up the pilot hole and see how far it was to the surface, I brushed against a sheave chain. It instantly, and silently, dropped into the bore hole's dark empty chasm and disappeared from sight. This was an essential piece of equipment, needed to anchor one of the sheaves to the timber. I looked at Clayton; anger flashed across his face. Someone was going to have to make a long, long descent down to retrieve it at the bottom of the hole and then make the long, hard climb back up.

I simply said, "Damn it pard, sorry about that. I'll go back down and get another chain somewhere and I'll be back up later."

With a wry smile, he replied, "Okay."

With that, I started climbing down the man-way, but to this day I can't believe what happened next. After descending to only the second ladder, I glancing over and saw another chain laying on that floor up against the wall. I let out a yelp; and Clayton immediately shouted, "Is everything all right?" I grabbed the chain and crawled back up. We then busied ourselves hooking everything up and climbed back down. When descending, I didn't see any other chain or equipment that had been left in the man-way by earlier crews—that chain I'd found had been the only thing left behind.

When we finally reached the bottom, Clayton found the chain I'd dropped laying on the floor of the timberslide.

The next day, with the tugger in place, we began drilling and shooting short rounds, so that the explosions wouldn't damage the timber. It was tight quarters 30 feet up in the bore hole, but everything went well. The next couple of days went just about the same... except Clayton and I were getting hungrier and hungrier. We'd completely run out of food... and money. In fact, about the sixth day I guess, I was digging around in the cupboard trying to find something to eat when I came across an old package of soda crackers that probably were left over from the guy who owned the camper before I did. Can you believe it? I actually hid that plastic wrapper and its five crackers from my voracious friend. Eventually I received some money in the mail from home, so we were all right for awhile.

But I had other things on my mind too. As the days wore on, I'd begun to worry again about radiation and the claim that the mine was nine times "hotter" than any other in the United States. My other problem was that I knew I'd feel real bad if we pulled up stakes and moved on. After all, the mine had given each of us a job when we really needed it.

That night—Wednesday of our second week there—I told Clayton I was quitting on Friday and the reason why. Damn, he got belligerent then, as if I'd called him a dirty name or something. I reminded him of the tenacious yellow stains at the base of the mine's walls. "Yellow cake," from what I understood, is nearly the purest form of uranium. I'd heard cancer rates can be high for people who work around it.

I kept trying to explain my decision further, saying, "I know the mine has radiation monitoring equipment and they keep a close watch on things, but I just don't want to hang around anymore." I even told Clayton how I'd been a dental technician in the Air Force and wore a dosimeter to keep track of the radiation my body absorbed from the dental X-ray machine. It was to no avail; he was still mad.

Finally I gave up and simply said, "Well buddy, it's a free country... stay here." He didn't talk to me for the rest of the day, but the following Friday after work when I pulled my time, so did he.

We unplugged the camper from the power pole and drove out of the RV park, beginning another leg of our tramp. I drove over to the hospital and asked for copies of our physical examinations. I knew that having these

A typical storage magazine for primers.
Bruce Baraby, Wallace ID

Stacked dynamite ready for use.
Bruce Baraby, Wallace ID

records in hand would make it easier for us to find another job. I was really surprised too when the pretty little nurse said, "Okay you can have them."

We drove over to Page, Arizona, a small Indian town by beautiful Lake Powell, and stocked the cupboards of the camper "full up" with groceries. That night we drove back to Lake Powell and parked on its sandy shoreline. When I woke up the next morning, stretched, and opened up the camper door, I saw Clayton walking on the beach. It was a fine sunny day. I really felt great, being free and relaxed again and knowing that I didn't have to worry about radiation anymore. I remembered the big stash of food we'd bought the night before and began looking around for the box of cereal. I looked everywhere, but couldn't find it. I opened the camper door again and yelled out to Clayton, "Where is the box of cereal?" I thought I must have left it in the shopping cart.

He yelled back, "I ate it."

I was astonished and didn't really know what to think, but laughed thinking he was only joking. I played along and yelled back, "You ate the whole thing?"

He responded in an incredulous tone, "Well, it was only one box." I then knew why he'd come with me instead of staying at the mine: he probably couldn't have earned enough money to feed himself.

We left Lake Powell and drove on through Flagstaff and Phoenix, heading for Superior, Arizona. I'd heard that the copper mine at Superior was doing some hiring, and after consuming about 50 pounds of groceries and God only knows how many Pop Tarts, we drove

into the town. The next morning we put in applications for work at the mine's employment office. A question on the form asked, "Are you presently employed anywhere else?" we penciled in yes, because technically we still were employees of the Lucky Friday, and I knew they'd check anyhow. After we'd turned in our papers, the hiring man said, "I'll check on your references. Call me back tomorrow and I'll let you know whether or not I can hire you."

I'd heard rumors from my fellow strikers in Idaho about how some mines would put out the word to other companies about their striking miners. That way, strikers couldn't find work elsewhere and were forced to settle strikes earlier or under less favorable terms. I hadn't really subscribed to this line of thinking, though. The next day, however, when the hiring man said, "You can go to work here, but you'll have to quit up there first," my faith in the system was shaken.

I thought back to when I'd temporarily worked for the Homestake in 1977 while on strike from Bunker Hill. I'd told the Homestake's hiring office about the strike, but they hired Gary and me anyway. Energy Fuels Nuclear, of course, also had just hired Clayton and I knowing we were out on strike. So I knew it wasn't an industry-wide practice and could only conclude that it just was the Superior company's policy.

We thanked him for the offer, but declined. I knew that Jo Ann wouldn't leave Idaho to live in the desert; I'd been calling her about every other day telling her about my less-than-desirable living conditions and experiences. I must have been a little homesick right about then, too—it was a ridiculously hot 110 degrees in Superior that day, while snow probably was still falling up in potato land.

We drove out of Superior, knowing full well that it wouldn't be long before the cupboard would be bare again. Feeling a sense of urgency about finding another paying job soon, we decided to go on down to Casa Grande, Arizona, to look for work on the Lake Shore Project, located some 60 miles from the Mexican border. Hecla had owned the mine at one time, but I'd heard that ASARCO had taken it over. I thought, "Maybe we'll have better luck with them."

We didn't though. We encountered the same situation as in Superior, "Are you presently working anywhere else?" Again I answered yes, and again we heard the response, "You can go to work here, but you'll have to quit up there first."

Then and there I decided that the next time I saw that question on an application I'd pencil in, "No." After all, I thought, the worst that could happen is that I probably wouldn't get hired; but if I wasn't getting hired anyhow, what was the difference? If the mining companies really did have some kind of conspiracy going on, then two could play at this game. As we drove out of the hottest KOA campground on the planet, I felt a slight twinge of hunger for good old Idaho potatoes.

I really had misgivings about finding work at the Lake Shore Project anyway, even before getting there. It was located in what looked like a prehistoric lake bed—very hot and dry, and covered with "stand up" cactus. As we drove on the two-lane paved road headed for the mine, I happened to glance up and see a redheaded vulture winging it right along with the truck—a bad omen indeed.

We headed north through Phoenix to Nevada, and that night pitched camp in the parking lot of Circus Circus, one of Las Vegas's monster casinos. The next day, we drove on again toward the north. I thought, "At least we're getting closer to home, the further up we get."

I kept an eye out for mine dumps and saw a few here and there as we drove through the stifling, super heated desert, but none of them appeared active. A mine "dump," of course, is a pile of "tailings," or waste rock, that's been hauled out from underground and discarded in a heap, usually on a hillside or mountainside near a mine's portal. These telltale scars on the landscape mark the locations of mines, both past and present.

We came up to a crossroads and a sign indicating the direction to "Furnace Creek." Just seeing that name on the sign made us feel hotter somehow. Clayton and I decided to pull into a small cafe/gas station and have a cold beer. I asked the lady who served us the drinks and who really looked like she would rather be anywhere else on earth, "Are there any working mines anywhere around here?"

She said, "Yes," surprisingly enough, and pointing with her finger out through the front window continued, "Go down that road to the edge of the valley (meaning toward Death Valley!) and there's one there."

We thanked her, paid for the beer, and after driving another 20 or 30 miles entered California. Soon we turned onto a gravel road to the mine and in no time were on the edge of what looked like a 200-feet-wide, flat-bottomed crater. The mine's portal had been cut into the crater's wall, and a trailer house had been pulled just inside the portal.

"They're probably just trying to stay cool," Clayton said.

We could just see the front end of a diesel mucker sticking out of the darkness in the drift just beyond the trailer. Sure enough, we found out later that the trailer and equipment were kept underground for protection against the desert sun. We parked, walked into the mine, and knocked on the trailer's door. As we stood there waiting for an answer, I noticed a big temperature difference between out where I'd parked the truck and where we were standing. Suddenly the door opened and I felt cold air rush out. The man and woman inside were glad to see us too; I could only guess because ground lizards couldn't talk and we could. After a few minutes of introductions and such, Clayton said, "We're both on strike and working at the Lucky Friday Mine up in Idaho."

Then the fella, who I guessed to be the mine's foreman, said, "I had a couple of other guys here that I'd hired from the Lucky Friday, but about a week ago they showed up for work drunk and I had to fire them. Yes, you can go to work, but it won't be until Wednesday, and we won't put up with drunks… too dangerous."

We thanked him, walked back to the truck, and soon were driving back toward the crossroads looking for another cold beer. About the time we passed back into Nevada, a wave of truly sweltering heat hit me. I thought about how the Furnace Creek mine looked like it should have been on the surface of the moon. Then, I turned to Clayton and said, "To hell with this place.

This is only Monday and I'm sure not going to sit around here for two days in this heat waiting to go to work in that damned hole. It'd be worse than Casa Grande."

Clayton really got upset again and I sorta expected it. He yelled and accused me of not really wanting to go to work and all kinds of stuff like that. Clayton didn't talk to me for hours; in fact, he rode back in the camper.

We came into Tonopah, Nevada, a very old mining town. The nearby hills were pockmarked with old mine dumps. By this time Clayton had returned to the front seat. I asked a local resident if there were any active mines around, although I had no hopes of that being the case. To my surprise, he said, "There's one over by Silver Peak, and I think it's run by the Sunshine Mining Company."

When I was working at the Sunshine in Idaho, I'd heard about the company's mine in Nevada, named the 16 to 1, but I'd had no idea where it was. We jumped back into the truck, and after driving for what seemed like hours through the desert, we finally found Silver Peak, Nevada. My first impression was, "This town is really old." As we drove past antique looking buildings, I thought, "When it snows back up in Idaho, the accumulation on the roofs flattens really old buildings. I'll bet it's never snowed here at all, because these old structures are still standing."

We asked around and found out where the mine's foreman lived. As we drove along slowly, looking for the correct address, I remembered that this time I'd answer "No" on the work application where it said, "Are you working anywhere else now?" We parked the truck, and as we approached the house I turned to Clayton, saying, "Let me do the talking." He nodded in agreement.

Then I got a real shocker… I recognized the guy who answered the door. I said to myself, "I know this fella, it's Phil Lapp, he was a foreman at Bunker Hill's Wardner Mine."

He recognized me too from when I worked for Bunker Hill, and said, "It's great to see a fellow Idahonian down here in tarantula country."

By golly I really hated to fib to him too, especially after he'd given Clayton and I several beers. When he asked where we were working, I knew that if we admitted to being on strike from the Lucky Friday all we were going to get out of our visit would be the beer.

So, I looked him squarely in the eye, and said, "No, we're not working anywhere right now Phil. We were working over in a uranium mine in Arizona, though,

until I found out that it was nine times hotter than just about any other place on the planet. I got to be afraid of it, so we quit and here we are."

Then I smiled and held up our "still current" physical examination papers that I'd brought in with me. After a little more socializing and a couple of more beers, Phil agreed to, "Give us a try," and told us where the mine's office was located.

The next morning we showed up at the large trailer house that served as the office. We were in our diggers and signed on. Clayton, however, was assigned to a company project in town, whereas I was sent out to the mine. I walked outside and climbed into a 4-wheel drive van for the 9-mile trip out to the 16 to 1. As we drove along looking out through the van's dust-covered windows, I tried to imagine what it must have been like for the miners of a century ago, riding to work on horses and in wagons. We probably ate just as much dust as they did, only we got there faster.

On the way we passed what looked like a tiny 50-feet-wide lake and the fella sitting across from me said, "There are some bikers living in an old house back in town. Last weekend my partner was up here sitting by the pond, taking five, when four bikers pulled up and got off. They had this big old broad with them too. As she hurried past my partner, she said, 'I sure hope you don't mind nudity,' and all five of them stripped and jumped in."

We laughed about this for quite a while. I then asked, "Why is that little lake there? What is it, a natural spring or something? I mean it looks like it's dry everywhere else around here."

He replied, probably as a joke I think, "No, that's Silver Peak's drinking water supply." I thought, "Oh no, I just drank some of it too when we were back in the trailer house."

Soon, the 16 to 1 Mine's portal came into view, and I also saw a large, yellow, rubber-tired mucker. I noted that my prediction about this being another "quick in and out" mine was right; they utilized a down-ramp system for large wheeled vehicles. I'd concluded that mining companies didn't want to invest money in building shafts if they could avoid it, because shafts were extremely expensive to construct and maintain. The mine's portal was a large drift located at the base of a cliff that looked about 150 feet high. Rock bolts had been installed above the portal on the cliff's face; they supported iron and wire mesh mats to hold the loose rock in place. Shops and maintenance buildings and the dry stood near the portal.

We stepped out of our dust-covered van and went into the dry, where I checked out my mine lamp, web belt, and such. As we walked into the portal, I noted that the drift looked like it was about 12 feet high and 20 feet wide, and was a flat, straight shot directly into the mountain.

Jeff, who was my partner for the day, said, "This once was a copper mine… see there?" and he pointed at the floor.

I looked down and could just barely see the tops of two narrow-gauge rails. The rusty tracks looked like they'd been there for a long time. Recently, the company had been in the process of enlarging the old drift to accommodate the newer mining equipment and methods. The main drift went straight back about 250 feet, then made a 90 degree right turn and continued another 150 feet or so to where crews were just beginning to blast a down ramp for the vehicles.

I suppose the 16 to 1 might be classified as a "hardrock" mine, but it was cut into sandstone. Jeff and I spent the day bolting up the sandstone walls and back. I felt sort of sorry about Clayton because he wasn't able to work underground. But, as Phil had said, "He's not a miner yet, but we can use him on the new building we are putting up here in town."

When I asked my partner Jeff which mines he'd worked in before, he said, "Oh, this is my first. In fact none of these guys has ever worked in a mine before. Most of us came from Vegas where we were working on construction jobs."

I thought, "Wow that's just great. I sure hope these fellas know what they're doing around dynamite."

Later that day, out of curiosity more than anything, I watched the drift crew as they loaded their round. I couldn't believe it; they rolled up the ends of the 12- or 16-feet long Nonel primers that were dangling out of a hole like you'd roll up a garden hose. Then they taped each individual primer roll neatly with black electrical tape. This was unnecessary.

I asked, "Why are you fellas rolling up the primers and taping them like that?"

One of the hands turned around and said incredulously, "Why that's the way we were told to do it."

I just knew he was thinking, "Boy, you don't know much do ya?"

It was hard for me not to say anything. I just grunted, "Oh," bit my tongue, and walked off. The next day in the mine again, Zack, our shifter, asked me, "Do you think you can drill out a round?"

I assured him that drilling out rounds was something that I'd rather be doing than just about anything else. All he had to do was point me in the right direction. (Besides, I'd been a little nervous lately and was anxious to blow something up.)

One thing the drift crew did know how to do well, though, was to run their gigantic jumbo. In fact, I was envious. It was a hydraulic-electric, rubber-tired drilling machine, nearly as big as the entire drift. A pair of 15-feet-long booms extended from the front of the machine like enormous arms, holding spinning, hammering drill steel. The jumbo's operator sat up in a driver's seat overlooking the arms. To his right and left were powerful searchlights casting a brilliant light over the whole operation. It was a loud sucker too… it fairly roared when it was doing its business.

Zack took Jeff and me back to the end of a side drift, which the jumbo had drilled in about a week before, and pointed to the face. Man, talk about boot-legs! (Boot-legs are holes in which the dynamite had exploded, but hadn't broken the ground out.) It looked like the 10-feet depth of the drill holes had only been half blown out. Furthermore, the drill holes had been placed a good 5 or 6 feet apart, which was too far apart to be effective. In addition, when the round went off, many holes misfired somehow and portions of the live powder charges now were hanging out of the holes. The round's lifters, or bottom holes, had enough power in them, though, that they lifted what there was of a muck pile backwards away from the face. That left the face entirely exposed, except for right at its very bottom.

There we stood, looking at a real mess—dynamite and primers dangling from holes and a really uneven face with 5- and 6-feet deep boot-legs. I knew that the face had to be reworked and reshot, making it flat again.

After we stood there for a while, Zack said, "None of the rest of the miners here wants to tackle it. Do you really think you can do it?"

I turned toward Zack and with a reassuring smile said, "Don't worry buddy. It'll be a cinch."

He looked relieved as he turned and walked away.

I turned to Jeff and said, "Let's clean 'er out."

We started by using a water hose to flush the dynamite and primers out of the holes. After we'd finished this, we hauled in our jack-leg, air hose, drill steel, and all the rest of the stuff that made us look like we really knew what we were doing. Then I worked my Idaho stope-miner's magic by five-spotting the holes (i.e., drilling in the new holes in a tighter pattern). Soon we were "tearing down" the equipment and then came the trick of loading out the holes.

I said, "Jeff, it doesn't look like it'll take much to break this sandstone out, so we'll just load the back ends of the holes." I remembered how the rounds I'd drilled in the Hack Canyon Mine had turned out, and this reddish brown sandstone looked like it was going to be much the same.

But Jeff became excited, and declared loudly, "But they told us to load the rounds right up."

I assured him that it would be all right and that I knew what I was doing.

I used Nonel nonelectric delay detonators, which are pencil-width, 3-inch-long, chrome-colored primers that are attached to thin, sealed plastic tubes measuring 8, 12, 16, 20, or 30 feet long. The other ends of the tubes have plastic grips. It was up to the miner, of course, to select the tube lengths that best suited the holes he had drilled and to choose the proper sequence of primers. Nonel primers have built-in delays. That is to say, the idea was to use a "O" (zero delay) primer in the hole that the miner wanted to blast first. That hole went off instantaneously, breaking ground out toward the point of least resistance. Then, perhaps the next hole would be blasted with a "1" primer that went off two-tenths of a second later, followed by a "2" at four-tenths of a second, a "3" at six-tenths of a second, and so on all the way up to a number "15," which detonated after nine and six-tenths seconds.

With a wooden powder pole, I pushed a primed stick of dynamite into the back of each of the holes. Then I finished by loading several more sticks into each of the holes, leaving the long tails of the primer ends dangling out of the holes.

When Jeff saw how I was "timing the round," I thought he would have a stroke. I had two things left to do. First, to bunch up the long dangling ends of the primers so that they were easier to work with, and second, setting the detonation cord to set off the round. We'd already, of course, timed the round by putting numbered Nonels in the holes. The holes were certain to go off in their proper order.

Jeff and his guys had been using the Nonel primers long before I came onto the scene, but they'd been rolling up their dangling ends and faithfully taping them neatly together with black electrical tape, as they'd been told. That was a waste of time.

I reached out, grabbed six or eight of the tubes, and bunched them together like I was rolling up a rope. I watched Jeff's reaction out of the corner of my eye as I did this. He looked amazed, but remained calm. The last part of timing Nonels requires the attachment of "det," or detonation, cord. The internally timed Nonels, of course, have no need of individual fuse primers to set each one of them off. Instead, their grips are snapped onto a continuous run of det cord. Then a single fuse primer is attached, using a special "folded back under" kind of a knot, to the end of the det cord.

It all took only a few minutes, looked like hell, but I knew it would work. I really think it took more time to convince Jeff of that than anything else. I looked at my pocket watch and saw that it was blasting time, so I lit the igniter end of the fuse primer and we walked on out toward the portal. As we left the tail drift and went into the main drift, we merged with the other miners who also were walking out of the mine.

We left the portal with the familiar dull thumps of dynamite exploding behind us. The other miners knew that I'd been cleaning up their round and they were really curious about how it was going to turn out. I think I heard, "How'd it go?" at least ten times that night. It was grand to be back mining again; I loved it.

The next day as Jeff, Zack, and I walked back into the drift to look at the results of our round, I felt confident that all had gone well. "After all," I thought, "I've been doing the exact same thing for a lot of years now." When we got back into the heading and shined our cap lights onto the face you couldn't even see any buttons (drill-bit markings) on the rock at all. The refurbished round broke the sandstone out like someone had cut it with a butter knife, leaving the face nearly as smooth as a baby's butt.

My credibility had been established. The drift crew was happy because they didn't have to shut down their operation to deal with their mess. They could keep right on running their loud, ear-splitting orange monster.

For the next few days, Zack put Jeff and me back to bolting up the walls again. Clayton was happy too. He had been working outside in the desert heat putting up a metal building, while loving every minute of it. I personally wouldn't have liked the heat and stuff like he did, but hey… whatever a guy likes, right?

A few days later, Zack told me about a really difficult round that had to be shot. As we walked into the mine together, I asked, "What kind of round is it?"

He elaborated, "Well, about 75 feet in from the portal we need to blast a round that will give us a 10-feet-long and 4-feet-wide notch in the right wall. It will be full height from the floor up to the back. It's for an air door." As we walked along, he pointed up to the left side of the drift near the back, "These power lines and pipes have to be protected somehow from flying rock when the dynamite explodes, so the blast's fly rock won't damage or destroy them. Phil is having the mechanics cut a couple of 10-inch diameter pipes in half, endo [meaning from end to end]. He wants us to hang the halves over the mine's 2,300 volt power line and the pipes, to protect them. And that's not to say what would happen to that 3-feet-wide ventilation line either if it gets hit. It's just a real dangerous deal."

By then we'd walked into the drift far enough that we'd come to the spot he was talking about. I could see that a side drift took off at about a 45 degree angle from the main drift. It looked like it went back in about 30 feet, or so, turned, and then ran parallel to the main drift. We walked back into it.

Then as we stood there looking around, Zack pointed back into the darkness and said, "It follows along back in there for about another 90 feet, turns to the left, and comes right back out into the main drift again down there. We are going to install a big ventilation fan in here for the mine."

Zack continued, "We had another man in here the other day and he assured us that he could drill it out, so we let him try."

Zack pointed out new drill holes that I hadn't noticed until then; they were back on the "tit" where the main drift connected with the side drift taking off to the right.

Zack continued, "This is where we want to put the air door. It goes across the main drift right here…" He held his arms outstretched and walked sideways following an imaginary line from one side of the drift to the other. He wound up standing beneath all of the lines and pipes and the jumbo's 4-inch-thick power line. He stopped, dropped his arms down to his side, and then pointing his right forefinger up, said, "See what I mean?"

I stood there for a second, grasping the situation and finally retorted, "Zack, if you shoot these holes the way they've been drilled you're gunna lose everything. They're paralleling the drift and when they go off they'll blast all the pipes and stuff to smithereens." I went on, "It looks like a good drilled round, but the holes should

"Silver Peak's version of an oil cartel." Sunshine's hiring-out office can be seen at far right.
Jerry Dolph

have been going the other way… away from the pipes and stuff, and straight into the wall and a bit further down the drift. That way when the powder goes off it'll blast the rock out toward the portal instead."

Zack looked at me again just like he had before the drift round and said, "Do you think you could drill it out?"

I sort of laughed and said, "Man you're looking at a bad-assed gypo from North Idaho. Hell, I eat crap like this for breakfast." Of course, I knew that I'd probably be working in the mine just a little while longer anyway because it was only a matter of time before the Lucky Friday and Sunshine bosses got their heads together and found out about my little fib. Besides, I'd learned from the short telephone calls I'd been making to Jo Ann every other day that our union negotiations were beginning to sound promising too.

I continued, "I'll tell you what pard. If I was in your shoes, I sure wouldn't shoot this round we have here on my shift. But you know what"… I was trying to make a joke, and a point… "why don't you just wait and let someone else blast it when you're not here? That way you'll have more seniority when the mine hires another shifter to replace the man they fired, because he's gunna be out walking down the road kicking tin cans wondering what went wrong."

I read the emotion in his worried face and knew that I'd really hit home. He said, "Well you did a good job on the drift round," and hesitantly continued, "Go ahead and do this too then, but be sure to hang the half-pipes over the power cords and pipes when the mechanics bring them in to you. Oh, I forgot to mention… Phil says that if we blast the power cord in two, it's going to cost the mine a couple of thousand dollars to repair it."

He turned quickly away and hurried off down the drift as if he were trying to distance himself from the problem.

Jeff had followed us into the mine, and silently stood by listening, though he'd caught only about half of the conversation. As Zack walked off, Jeff turned toward the left wall and looked up at the maze of power cords and pipes. With a doubting squint, he said, "We're not really going to shoot this today, are we?"

I exclaimed, "You bet, we'll shoot it at lunch. Let's get set up."

We got busy hauling in the jack-leg, hoses, and other miner's stuff. The round that had been drilled was just fine, and probably would have blasted the ground out just as good as anybody's. But, like I'd told Zack, "It was just going in the wrong direction."

I spent the rest of the morning drilling my holes 90 degrees straight into the wall opposite from the pipes and electrical wires. Finally, all was ready to blast by lunch. The holes had been drilled and loaded, and our tools were out of the way. The mechanics had brought in the cut pipes and even installed them for us by standing on the hood of one of the huge, swivel-in-the-middle muckers. The guys normally walked out of the mine for the short lunch break, since the air was a lot better outside. Since Jeff and I were working in the main drift, we were the object of many curious stares as the men passed by with their lunch boxes in hand. They knew how concerned the bosses were about blowing things up and they just shook their heads. Then I struck a match, lit our fuse primer, and Jeff and I followed them out of the mine.

It was a short walk to the structure serving as the dry and mine office, and by the time we'd all gotten settled in I was getting some weird looks from the crew. The round hadn't gone off yet.

Someone said, "That's all right Dolph, I hear they're hiring over in Arizona," and the crew erupted in laughter.

I felt pressure building up in my mind too as we all sat there waiting. Suddenly their laughter faded when the roar of high-explosive blasts rolled out of the mine. The crew fell into silence and listened. It's sort of a mystery, I guess, but when a miner hears exploding dynamite it's almost like a religious experience.

After we'd finished our lunches and waited long enough for most of the smoke to clear, we got up and started back into the mine. I was asked a number of times, "How do you think it went?" When we entered the portal there was a heavy blue acrid-smelling haze still hanging in the top of the drift. I thought, "Man… someone ought to make an after-shave out of the gas fumes and sell it to miners. They'd make a million."

As we approached the spot where my round had gone off, Zack walked by my side. Out of the corner of my eye I caught him glancing nervously over at me, every few feet. I didn't look back.

It had been a great round: the rock was blasted into fines leaving a smooth 10-feet-long, 4-feet-deep notch in the wall, just like what Phil had wanted. The neat pile of muck was just far enough out of the main drift too so as not to be in the way and cause anyone any inconvenience. I couldn't believe it; there was no fly rock at all. At least I didn't see any damage anywhere. I'd sort of expected for there to be some. You couldn't have stacked that muck up any better if you'd dumped it out of the back of a dump truck. But to tell you the truth, I'd been getting sort of worried about the round too, since I'd been the focus of every eyeball in sight during the whole episode.

Zack was elated, to say the least. Jeff and I spent the rest of the day cutting out old rock bolts and bent iron mats with a cutting torch. The torch looked a lot like the one I'd been using up in Idaho; I thought a lot about the dear old Lucky Friday Mine that day. A few minutes before quitting time, Zack came walking into the mine again and down the drift toward us. Jeff and I had quit for the day and were only waiting to walk outside with the rest of the crew.

When Zack approached, he had a stern look on his face and said, "Jerry, I've got some bad news for you. Phil found out that you and Clayton are both working up in Idaho for Hecla Mining Company's Lucky Friday Mine and that you're out on strike. He told me that you're either going to have to quit up there or down here, but you can't work in both places at once."

I just laughed because I'd expected that sooner or later we'd be found out. Jeff and I didn't wait for the rest of the crew, but instead walked out of the mine with Zack to the dry. I told him why we'd fibbed to Phil and that we were just plain damned tired of getting the runaround when trying to hire out.

Actually I was sort of excited about the news because I'd already decided that once this job was over we'd head back up north again. Clayton and I'd been bum-

16 to 1 Mine.
Sunshine Precious Metals Inc.

ming around down here in tarantula land for about six weeks now and that was plenty.

Word spread quickly among the crew as they came into the dry. Their initial surprise at the news was followed by delighted approval that someone had gotten away with something and bested the bosses. It was almost a carnival-like atmosphere as we loaded into the van. To top it all off, Phil came driving up in a company pickup after we'd all settled in our seats. He stopped next to the van and motioned for me to open my window. I did and we began to talk.

Phil said calmly, "I suppose Zack told you?"

I responded with a grin, "Yeah, he just couldn't keep a secret."

Then Phil sorta laughed and repeated the information Zack had told me. I assured Phil that I felt badly about fibbing to him, but needed the work, and, too, that I couldn't get the old lady to move down even though I'd already tried. He restarted the engine of his truck and was just about to drive off when I noted that the other guys in the van were intently listening to every word spoken. For their sake I yelled out to Phil, "The next time we go on strike, though, I'll come back down and look you up again."

The van instantly erupted with laughter. From Phil's half-smiling face and gleam in his eye as he drove away, I got the impression that I probably wouldn't be so warmly welcomed the next time around.

I really liked Phil; he acted more like a friend than a boss. I was deeply saddened when I heard a few years later that, in whatever hole he was working at the time, a giant slab of rock fell out of the back and crushed him to death.

When we finally emptied out the van near the mine's office in downtown Silver Peak (if there were such a thing), I saw Clayton and noticed that he had two paychecks in hand. I assumed that one of them was mine, and was right. Our past differences immediately were forgotten because we both sensed excitement at our pending return home.

We walked back down to the truck, which wasn't that far away, and soon we were driving out of town headed north. One good thing about living out of a camper, I was like a turtle. Whereas others had to take the time to pack their skivvies, all we did was get in and turn the key. I stopped near the post office and called my little lady up in "potato land" to tell her the good news. She was ecstatic and could hardly wait for me to get home.

I only assume that Clayton called his folks, too. I don't know; he could have been talking to his favorite bartender, I guess. I think I might have if I'd been his age and single. It had all happened so quickly that it took me another hour to realize that I was going home. We both settled in for the long drive north. ❀

CHAPTER 13

Home Again to the Hung Chute

Back in the Lucky Friday

The trip back home went smoothly. I watched Nevada's desert scenery slip by for many hours and then finally we entered Idaho. We drove all that night, and by early the next morning pulled the old truck, which by then was heaving and puffing and nearly used up, in front of my rented Pinehurst home. Boy did it look good too.

Jo Ann must have been expecting us about then because the front door opened, and she came out. Clayton disappeared down the street in a cloud of dust. Jo Ann and I began a full day of getting reacquainted.

One of the first things she said, though, was, "There is going to be a union meeting up in Mullan tomorrow to decide on a new contract offer from the Lucky Friday. It was on the news last night."

Bright and early the next day, I drove to Mullan, parked near an old three-story brick building, and climbed its concrete stairwell up to the union hall, which incidentally was just above an old four-lane bowling alley. Here, I mingled with many other "tired of the tramp" Lucky Friday miners. The company urged our negotiators to consider their contract proposal and they wanted us to vote by secret ballot. I suppose they figured we'd give into their offer in the privacy of the voting booth, rather than being swayed against the contract by the "We'll die together" mentality of mob rule.

It didn't matter though… we all knew it was time to go back to work. Even their usual threat of bringing in new employees to replace us—a standard ploy that most mines threatened to use—didn't affect our decision. We

had a show of hands and the die was cast. We were going back to work in the morning.

The next day I rose early as usual and readied myself to fight Mr. Air Blast, the "demon of the deep." I knew he was still down there someplace looking for me. As Jo Ann prepared my lunch, I said, "It was really neat that Clayton and I came back up from the desert country when we did. It seems like just one of those things that was supposed to happen, I guess."

As I drove the 25 some miles to the mine that morning, I really "checked out" the scenery. I was in awe of the thick forests that blanketed the mountainsides. Then, I remembered how parched and just "out and out dead-looking" the desert was, but then I also thought about how beautiful the sunset was over the red buttes and plateaus in Arizona. Of course, only a few weeks earlier when I was down there eating one soda cracker every four hours—which I had to hide from my voracious partner—I didn't really appreciate the landscape's beauty very much.

I even remembered driving out across the terrible, furnace-like dry lake bed of Casa Grande, and seeing my vulture friend flying along overhead. I had had a full tank of water in the camper and had decided to dump it all out so we could save gas by not having to carry around the extra weight. I had stopped the truck, walked back, undone the tap, and driven on down the road, letting the water dribble out of the camper's drain faucet. I hadn't thought at the time that the piddling little trickle of water was even getting a chance to spread out over the super heated pavement before it evaporated. Could have been too that the vulture following along had looked down thinking, "I wonder who

---

Drilling a round in the raise.
ASARCO Inc.

the idiot is who's dumping out that 'river' of water? I've never even seen that much water before."

My deep recollections faded as I passed by Mullan on Interstate 90 and took Exit 69. As I drove on the overpass above the freeway, I scanned the Lucky Friday's buildings, and remembered saying to Zack, who I'd left only three days before in Silver Peak, "Come on up if things don't work out for you here, and I'll try to get you on somewhere." I parked in the lot at the base of the hill just below the mine, and began the long climb up the 72-step metal staircase. It was great to be back.

I went into the dry with my official-looking flowered pillowcase full of diggers, and changed. After I'd finished dressing, I stepped out into the hallway ready for a new day, and a contract. Everything looked pretty much the same. That's when I saw big Betty. She worked as a motorman... or should I say, motorlady? Either way, she was a really good worker. I'd known her for a long time. Suddenly I remembered a story she'd told me years before about when she was a part-time driver for one of the madams there in Wallace. The madam had called Betty from Spokane, Washington, on the phone, and asked that Betty drive her car, a big black Lincoln, over to Spokane and pick her up. It's about a 1 and 1/2 hour drive.

Betty said, "I did like she asked and we were on our way back toward Wallace again. I guess I must have cut a trucker off on 4th of July Pass pass between Coeur d'Alene and Kellogg or something because all of a sudden a state patrolman pulled up alongside of us. I had the stereo turned up real loud and was sipping a glass of champagne that the madam had handed to me from over the backseat. I didn't notice him right away, but when I did, I rolled down my window like he was motioning me to do. Then he leaned over and yelled out through his open window, 'You've got one mad trucker behind you.' And I just said, 'To hell with the trucker,' and rolled my window back up. The officer grinned, threw up his hands, shrugged his shoulders, and dropped back. He had a smile on his face and was laughing hard the last time I saw him too."

I wandered a bit further on through the hallway and noticed the mine's seniority sheet still hanging on the wall. I stopped to check my status, and saw it was just as it had been before the strike. My seniority still didn't really amount to much, since most of the other miners had been working there much longer and had me beat by a mile. But I pushed my finger on up the sheet looking for my partner Bobby Burton's seniority number.

View from the lamp room into the Lucky Friday Mine at the beginning of another dark day.
Hecla Mining Company

Then I found it. There it was... right in between "Moses and Adam," a really important little item when it came to "bidding" on any new work places. I was checking the board just in case we were going to have to "bid out" of our place.

I was still looking at the board when I heard someone calling out to me, "Jerry... would you come in here for a minute?" I looked around and saw that it was George Lander, the mine's "silver-tongued" superintendent.

Right off, as I walked toward his office, I had a bad feeling about what he was probably going to say. I guessed that the ore chute in our stope probably was still hung up, and I had bitter memories of how I was screwed by George and the payroll office just before the strike began. My partner Bobby had just finished changing clothes and came out of the dry then too. I motioned for him to join me in George's office and he did. I don't know if George really expected both of us to walk through the door, but there we were anyway.

Just as I'd feared, he said, "Your chute is still hung up and we're going to have to pick up right where we left off. So go back down in there and see what you can do."

I instantly had a flashback to him sitting in that very same chair six weeks ago, telling me that I was about to face the cruel world of the unemployed again without the benefit of the contract check that he'd promised us. Now, I felt anger too, as I looked him squarely in the eyes and recalled my conviction at the time, "He'll never screw me like that again." It turned out, however, that none of the other Lucky Friday miners wanted to be toilet plungers in the hung-up chute, so it was an opportunity for payback time for Bobby and me.

Thus, much to George's chagrin probably, I replied with a smile, "I'm not going back in there without something written down this time. We went through all this before, George. You flatly refused to pay us the contract that we earned just before the strike because, as you said, 'We didn't have anything down in writing.' "

I knew full well that according to the union agreement the mine couldn't force Bobby and me, as a condition of further employment, to do something that we felt was unsafe. After all, just a small "thump" by Mr. Air blast in the right place could pinch off the chute and seal either Bobby or me in place forever.

George smiled back, like the seasoned professional he was, and said, "Give me a few days to think it over, but go on down into the stope anyhow. There must be some catching up to do down in there by now."

I figured he'd had his salaried shifters constantly appraising conditions in the workplaces during the strike, which was standard procedure at times like that. Bobby and I both agreed to go on down into the stope for the day and await his decision.

We left George's office and walked directly underground through the narrow drift that connected the mine's dry and office buildings with Number 2 Shaft. Many years before, when the mine's outbuildings were constructed, some engineer conveniently butted them snugly up against the base of the mountain and adjacent to the mine's portal. It wasn't necessary to walk outside to be able to go underground, which was an important feature for us during North Idaho's sometimes bitter winters—especially at the end of shift when we were soaked to the bone. Many other mines were laid out the same way too.

At the top station, Bobby and I began to talk as we stood there in the scattered crowd of miners waiting our turn to ride down. I found out that during the strike he hadn't left the planet to look for work like Clayton and I had. Of course, I couldn't have blamed him for not doing that either—what with his one glass eye and not being able to see very well out of the other one either. He said his family was doing well. Then somehow the conversation got around to hunting and he began telling another one of his stories.

He said, "Once, many years ago, I decided to buy a machine gun and use it for hunting. I thought it might work out since I sure can't see very much anymore with just this one eye. I figured that what with all those bul-

A miner descending a chute in a boatswain chair on the end of a tugger cable (three views).
Bruce Baraby, Wallace ID

Miner taking a break in his stope.
Bruce Baraby, Wallace ID

lets, a fella just had to hit something. Then one morning, as I was getting a glass of water at the kitchen sink, I looked up through the kitchen window at the side of the hill above the house and saw a herd of elk. I stepped out the back door with this thing, pulled back the hammer, closed my eyes, and just gave her hell. Man, you talk about bullets—it scared the hell right out of me, and probably the elk too because when the smoke cleared I'll bet there wasn't one within 200 miles of that hill."

He ended by saying, "Then I just got rid of the damned thing."

About then we boarded the skip's tiny six-man deck and soon were plummeting down the shaft toward the 3,850 level. As we zipped down, I could see the rotten old shaft timbers that constantly needed repairing, and, at 200 foot intervals, we flashed past the old abandoned stations of mined-out levels. It was good to be back.

It didn't take long to finish the "drop" to the 3,850 station. We exited the skip, and then Bobby and I walked on back toward our stope. Most everything looked the same—there stood the lunch table at the station, the same pipes and vent line were hanging in the drift, and we could see the familiar checkerboard pattern of rock bolts scattered across the rock walls and back.

"Oh, there's something new," I thought. Part of the wall on the left side of the drift had collapsed, just short of our stope, and the back had sagged down about a foot or so too. Mr. Air Blast was still alive and well. I sort of chuckled to myself and greeted Mr. Air Blast (I said this inwardly because I didn't want Bobby to think I'd gone nuts during the strike).

We spent the next two days cleaning up the mess—rebolting the back and then the walls, barring down the loose rock, and mucking up some. Then at the end of the second shift, after we'd left for the day, Mr. Air Blast hammered us again. When we came in the next morning and saw the new mess, I couldn't restrain myself. I walked right over to the top of our raise and yelled, "Now, cut that out." Bobby must have thought I was nuts, shouting at Mr. Air Blast like that.

I stood there for a while at the end of the tracks, looking down into the dark stope, while thinking, "Man that ore down in there in the chute really must be worth a bundle if the company's willing to spend all this money trying to save it."

We were both sort of afraid to climb down the 10 foot ladder into the stope, however, because of what we might see. By now we affectionately called it our "garbage pit." I remembered the gigantic 30-feet-wide slab that had fallen out of the back and crushed all of our stope timber. We both worried about what it was probably going to look like now, but we decided to wait and climb down the ladder the next day. "Besides," I reasoned with Bobby, "there's plenty of work for us to do right where we are."

This particular section of the mine was really ancient, dating back to the 1950s, I think. Carl Curl, a Lucky Friday miner approaching retirement, had finished mining out the stope directly above ours many years before, and there were other old dead places back behind us too.

Carl once told me that he'd left many tons of high-grade ore up there, "because we just couldn't get it all. And, it was anywhere from 40 to 50 feet thick in places. The ore up in there was just so rich that it makes a lot of the stuff that the mine's calling ore these days look like waste rock."

I could believe it too, considering that Bobby and I were starting to hit some of the richest ore that I'd ever seen as we came up underneath the bottom of Carl's old stope. I also think a reason we had so much ground movement in our place was because we were right underneath that air slacked, worked out, old stope with its rotted timbers.

We left the mine at the end of the third day knowing that we had job security for sure. This was especially so considering that we probably would be cleaning out the hung chute after we got the stope looking pretty again. We hadn't heard anything from George yet, but we decided this time we wouldn't be willing to do it as a "freebie," like before.

I came to work the next morning thinking hard about how Bobby and I were going to have to go down into the garbage pit. All of a sudden, as I was deep in my thoughts, I heard George's voice, "Jerry, will you come in here for a minute?"

I thought, "Uh, oh… here it comes," as I walked into his office.

George then said, "I've decided to go ahead and pay you the $200 a day for working down in the chute, but you'll have to get it done quickly so we can get back to mining again. The stope is taking a lot of weight now and we just can't afford to be down in there very long. Tell Bob will you?"

I replied, "We won't need any kind of a signed paper will we?"

Then George said, "No, I'll guarantee it this time."

I was filled by a sense of excitement and a new-found interest in our "wonderful" stope. I saw Bobby near the shaft and told him about our new-found wealth and

A rock burst blew the back down making this ground unsafe.
Bruce Baraby, Wallace ID

George's guarantee. We both decided it was time to go and look down into the hole.

Shortly, we were again standing at the top of our man-way, happy that Mr. Air Blast hadn't made another visit during the night. The air blasts we were taking usually occurred between shifts, largely because of the impact of exploding dynamite from other stopes and the shifting of blasted rock that occurred afterward. I suddenly had the curious thought that Mr. Air Blast was Mother Earth's way of complaining about the bellyache we were giving her.

I climbed down the ladder first and into the stope. I was really kind of surprised as I found myself standing in the slusher path near the very same spot where I'd nearly electrocuted myself. I looked in both directions, seeing only three caps that were partially broken. Bobby came down then and we walked hesitantly on back into the stope toward the hung chute, looking things over pretty good on the way. Man, talk about timber taking weight… the further back we got, the worse it was. The tree-thick overhead caps that we'd put in to replace the ones crushed by Mr. Air Blast had sunk nearly all the way through their headings, which were 18 to 24-inch thick stacks of headboards set between the ends of the caps and the rock walls. The ground had squeezed in so much that the big caps had taken all of the side squeeze that they were going to, and some were actually bowed down in the middle. The floor had heaved up so much too that the posts' ends also had sunk several inches deep up into the caps.

As I stood there staring in disbelief, I couldn't imagine how much end pressure it would take to cause a 24- to 30-inch thick "tree" to bend like that in the middle.

It just didn't look natural for some reason. A few of them were split down their sides too; I thought that I could almost see the wood quivering because of the pressure. I understood what George meant when he'd said, "Let's hurry along with it now."

We circumspectly walked the 110 feet back to the hung chute and the timber-slide. The last day we'd worked here, just before the strike, Bobby and I had covered the timber-slide with lagging boards so nothing would fall down into it. The lagging was still in place, and, surprisingly, the timber immediately around the chute didn't look bad at all. Unlike most of the rest of the stope, it looked pretty much like it did the day we left a couple of months before.

I looked over at Bobby, exclaiming, "This damned stope has just about had it. Now I see what George means about not being able to afford to be down in here for very long."

Bobby replied, "He's right. As soon as we get the chute cleared out, and the crib raised up, we can build a wall and sand all of this crap in. Then we'll be mining over the top of it."

We began checking our hose fittings and made sure we still had air pressure. I pulled on the tugger handle a few times, first one way, then the other. The little air motor sprang to life and blew so much condensation out of its exhaust ports that it looked like it had been nearly full of water.

I said, "Looks like everything is all right, doesn't it?"

About then, Bobby, who was checking the half-inch-thick safety rope, pulled it in two with his fingers. It had rotted through.

Seeing this, I said, "I'm sorta glad you did that, pardner. It would have been a bitch to get down in the tube, have the cable break, and then have to rely on that there 'rotten safety rope' to keep from free falling 100 feet down to the next level."

Our nipper walked up about then and we sent him back out to the shaft for some new rope, while Bobby and I checked out the rest of our gear. He returned about 20 minutes later dragging a new yellow 200-feet-long rope behind him. We untied the old rope from its moorings and replaced it with the new one. The nipper also had brought tanks of gas for the cutting torch—oxygen and acetylene—and we hooked them up.

I'd already decided to be the first to go down, "After all," I thought "might just as well get 'er going, right?"

I asked Bobby to help me into the boatswain's chair and get all my other stuff prepared. Now, we were ready to attack the hung chute again. Bobby took his place beside the tugger.

I said, "Take 'er up."

The little tugger reeled up the slack in the 3/8 inch cable, and my feet slowly came off the floor. Then my body swung out over the empty black hole. I felt hot air rushing up out of the darkness beneath me.

I looked up into Bobby's glass eye, and said, "Well pard, lower away… here we go again." ❀

Silver Valley Extracts

Earl H. Bennett

THE FABULOUS COEUR D'ALENE MINING DISTRICT

Sometime in February 1985, only a few months after the Coeur d'Alene district's 100th birthday, miners wrested the billionth ounce of silver from the district's mines. No sirens sounded that day. No Bands played. The achievement was just another digit in the production figures for the district. Nevertheless, upon that historic moment the Coeur d'Alene laid claim to being the largest silver mining district in the world. The other major silver districts, including Pachuca and Guanajuato, Mexico, and Potosi, Bolivia, have all mined since the 1500s and each has produced about a billion ounces of silver.

The Coeur d'Alene district is located in northern Idaho, with the town of Wallace at its bustling center. The district also claims records for silver mines in the United States: the deepest—the Star-Morning mine (7,900 [8,100] feet deep); the richest—the Sunshine mine (over 300 million ounces of silver); and the biggest—the Bunker Hill (over 180 miles of underground workings). The Sunshine is also the deepest mine below sea level (3,300 feet)...

In addition to silver, over 40 major mines in the district have yielded substantial amounts of zinc, lead, copper, antimony, and cadmium. Prior to closure in 1981, the Bunker Hill refining complex alone produced 20 percent of the nation's zinc and lead and 25 percent of its refined silver. By 1984, the district had produced over 8 million tons of lead and 3 million tons of zinc. Total metal production has a historic value of $4.6 billion...

—Earl H. Bennett, "The Fabulous Coeur d'Alene Mining District," *GeoNote 07*, Idaho Geological Survey, University of Idaho, Moscow, Idaho [1986].

∼

—Earl H. Bennett is the Idaho State Geologist, and the Associate Director of the Idaho Geological Survey, Moscow ID.

TOP PRODUCING SILVER MINES IN THE UNITED STATES, 1984-85

(production figures in millions of ounces)

Mines (United States)	1984	1985
1. Lucky Friday (ID) Hecla	4.8	4.7
2. Sunshine (ID) Sunshine	4.8	4.7
3. Galena (ID) Asarco, Callahan	4.2	4.1
4. Troy (MT), Asarco	4.3	3.6
5. Coeur (ID), Asarco, CDA Mines	2.5	2.6
6. Candelaria (NV), Nerco	2.7	2.5
7. Escalante (UT), Hecla	2.2	2.4
8. Delamar (ID), Nerco	1.7	1.5
9. Bingham (UT), Kennecott	n.a.	n.a.
10. Black Pine (MT), Inspiration	1.4	closed
11. Bulldog (CO), Homestake	1.3	closed
12. Taylor (NV), Silver King, Nerco	closed	closed

—"Selected Statistics for Silver Production—1986," *GeoNote 11*, Idaho Geological Survey: University of Idaho, Moscow; Boise State University, Boise; and Idaho State University, Pocatello.

∼

1993 UPDATE

Hard times have come to the Coeur d'Alene mining district... Silver that sold [in 1986] at $5.00 to $6.00 an ounce (a price range regarded low at the time) had dropped further by 1993 to under $4.00 an ounce. The present price is below the production costs of the district's mines. Consequently, recent mining activity has been mostly layoffs, closures, and bankruptcies...

The Bunker Ltd. Partnership formed the Bunker Hill Mining Company and reopened the giant Bunker Hill lead-zinc mine in 1988, only to go bankrupt in 1990. The mine may never reopen in its present configuration, although high-grade zinc ore is still underground. Also in 1988, Bunker Ltd. closed the Crescent mine, the first mine in the Silver Belt.

The Star Mine (a zinc mine) near Burke was opened in 1990 by the Star Phoenix Mining Company. Unfortunately, the company met the same fate as Bunker ...

Other mine closures in the district included the Coeur in 1991 and the Galena in 1992. Both mines were operated by Asarco...

The Sunshine mine, the most productive silver mine in the world with a historic total of over 325 million ounces, laid off two-thirds of its miners in 1991. The mine operated under Chapter 11 reorganization in 1992, despite discovering new high-grade ore and reducing mining costs to about $5.00 an ounce.

Hecla Mining Company continues working the Lucky Friday mine. The company has cut costs through a new mining method called the Lucky Friday Underhand Longwall system. The Friday has also benefitted from fair metal prices for the lead and zinc that are in the ore. The mine is operating at a loss but making

enough to insure that it is cheaper to take the loss than to close the mine and reopen it later . . .

The district will probably survive this protracted adverse market, but may not return to its heyday. Prices must greatly improve before the mines are even profitable again. One hopeful sign for the industry, as noted by the Silver Institute, is that world consumption has exceeded the supply of newly mined silver for the past three years. Still, a market surplus of over 280 million ounces remains stockpiled in COMEX warehouses. This excess continues to dampen investor enthusiasm for the metal.

Over 500 mining jobs were lost in the Silver Valley in 1992 alone. The towns of Kellogg, Wallace, and Osburn have tried to diversify their local economies into other enterprises besides mining. Tourism may be the most promising prospect for the immediate future. The area took a big step in this direction in 1990, when the longest gondola lift in the world was completed from Kellogg to the Silver Mountain ski resort at a cost of $18 million. The scenic ride provides an impressive year-round attraction.

Today, several mines outside the district, including the Greens Creek in Alaska and the Rochester in Nevada, vie for top silver producer in the United States. As recently as 1990, however, the district's Sunshine mine had ranked first, with an annual yield of over 5.2 million ounces of silver.

—Earl H. Bennett, "The Fabulous Coeur d'Alene Mining District—1993 Update," *GeoNote 24*, Idaho Geological Survey: University of Idaho, Moscow; Boise State University, Boise; and Idaho State University, Pocatello [March 1993].

Heroism at the Sunshine Mine, May 2, 1972

Gene Hyde

This synopsis of the Sunshine Mine tragedy is based on official reports and an account prepared by Gene Hyde, retired geological engineer, Post Falls ID.

On the fateful day of Tuesday, May 2, 1972, 173 men were working underground in the mine. The exact cause of the fire that proved fatal to over half of them has never been determined, but all possible origins have been eliminated except two—it appears to have been either "man" caused, or the result of spontaneous combustion. In order for the carbon monoxide gases to have built up to such deadly levels, it is thought by some that the fire had been smoldering for up to two weeks or more among rotted timbers and other combustible materials in old sealed off workings in the vicinity of the 910 raise on the mine's 3,400 foot level. The fire eventually burned through the surrounding old workings and entered into the mine's main ventilation system, where increased oxygen further enhanced the burning and the build up of deadly smoke and fumes.

11:40 A.M.

The fire was first detected at 11:40 A.M. when Roger Findley and Randy Peterson, cagers on the No. Ten Shaft chippy hoist, were leaving the 3,700 foot level with mechanics Dusty Rhoads, Richard Breazeal, and Wilbur Harris. The five men were on their way down Ten Shaft to the mine's 4,400 foot level. Upon arriving there, they smelled smoke and reported it to the hoistman.

At approximately the same time, on the 3,700 level Ten Shaft station, electricians Norman Ulrich and Arnold Anderson came out of the electrical shop; Anderson shouted "smoke!" to foremen Harvey Dionne

—Gene Hyde has been a frequent visitor to the Sunshine Mine, having been a monitor for the Hecla Mining Company, which owned 33.25 percent of the Sunshine Mine at the time of the tragedy. His last visit before the fire broke out was five days earlier, on April 27. His friend, Sunshine foreman Bob Bush, whom Hyde had known since 1937 when they were boys in Osburn, died in the mine. For 83 hours, Hyde participated in the rescue effort at the Silver Summit portal. In preparing his account, Hyde conducted an extensive investigation of government documents and reports.

and Gene Johnson, who were in a nearby fenced-off lunch area known as the "blue room." The two foremen immediately left the blue room and proceeded on foot out toward the Jewell Shaft, seeking the source of the smoke. (Beginning at Ten Shaft, prominent features along 3,700 level include the Strand substation, 910 raise, old No. 5 and No. 4 shafts, and finally the Jewell Shaft station.)

12:00 NOON

They discovered that the smoke was coming down and out of the bottom of 910 raise, which is about 850 feet from Ten Shaft, but they could not see any flames. Two other foremen, brothers Bob and Jim Bush, then joined them in the search and in initiating evacuation procedures.

At about 12 Noon, shift boss Gene Johnson, while at 3,700 level Ten Shaft station, telephoned maintenance foreman Tom Harrah at his office in the machine shop on the surface. Johnson requested that the stench warning system be activated and that oxygen breathing apparatus be sent down into the mine.

Harrah, in turn, contacted the company safety engineer, Robert Launhardt, at the mine safety office and relayed the request. The stench warning system, which is used to alert men to evacuate to the surface, was activated at 12:05 P.M. Foremen gave orders to close fire doors and for the men to evacuate via the Jewell Shaft.

At this time, shift boss Gene Johnson ordered Ira Sliger, hoistman on the main Ten Shaft hoist, to begin evacuating the mine by bringing men up to the 3,100 level where the hoist room is located, so the men could make their way from there over to the Jewell Shaft, about a mile away. Byron Schulz, the cager for No. Ten Shaft hoist, was down on the 5,600 level pulling muck at the time when he was signalled by hoistman Sliger to begin assisting in bringing men up to the 3,100 level.

12:13 P.M.
The first skip full of men was hoisted at 12:13 P.M., and for the next 48 minutes, or until 1:01 P.M., more men came up Ten Shaft (by 1:01 P.M., the evacuation effort would cease because men had collapsed from the increasingly deadly fumes in the Ten Shaft station vicinity). As the evacuation was continuing, hoistman Sliger began having respiratory problems in the increasingly smokey conditions. At 12:35 P.M., Sliger was told to evacuate to the Jewell Shaft; he was replaced by relief hoistman Robert Scanlan. Scanlan would bravely remain at his post, rescuing men, until his last breath at 1:01:30 P.M. He died shortly after he brought a last cage of men up from the 5,400 foot level to the 3,100 level.

Meanwhile, supervisors Gene Johnson, Virgil Bebb, and Charlie Casteel had remained on 3,100 station, aiding in the evacuation. Eventually all three succumbed to the deadly carbon monoxide, probably because of the numerous times they had to remove their self-rescuers from their mouths to give directions to fellow workers. Arnold Anderson and Roger Findley had volunteered to help Johnson count the men as they arrived on 3,100. Anderson went with Dusty Rhoads to the 3,400 level to await orders to shut off fans; both died there, still awaiting orders.

Greg Dionne, who volunteered to help hoist men up to 3,100 level, was overcome at the 5,000 level. Cager Schulz brought Dionne up to the 3,100 level in a col-

lapsed state. Before Schulz escaped, the last person he saw alive on the 3,100 level was Doug Wiederrick, who had been helping Schulz cage. Wiederrick slumped down after making a phone call in a desperate effort to find out where the nearest fresh air was located.

Schulz then headed for the Jewell Shaft, using his third self-rescuer, and passing by bodies everywhere along the way. (A "self-rescuer" is a filter-type respirator that is inserted into the mouth and over the nose to provide protection against carbon monoxide gas in underground fires. The protection lasts for an hour or so, depending on the severity of the conditions, and miners are required to immediately evacuate a mine after donning the devices. When a self-rescuer's chemical reaction causes a miner's lips to become hot or blistered, this is an indication to the miner that the carbon monoxide build-up is severe. Normally, a self-rescuer is carried in a small container hanging on a miner's belt.)

The men on 5,400 level did not have self-rescuers, as none were available on the lower levels of the mine. It appears that the 5,400 crews, already weakened by fumes, were hoisted into the deadly atmosphere of 3,100 station and did not get far in their mile-long trek toward the Jewell Shaft. Hoistman Scanlan had succumbed to the smoke before he could hoist any men from the 4,800 and 5,200 levels—at this time, some men were still alive on those two levels. A few of them in a tail drift on 5,200 level just off the station attempted to build a barricade, but died from carbon monoxide exposure before they could complete the job.

1:00 P.M.
At about 1 P.M., and within an hour after the stench warning system had been activated, the first rescue group to attempt to locate and save survivors went underground. This group consisted of four men. It was formed as safety engineer Bob Launhardt was bringing 10 McCaa two-hour self-contained breathing devices to the 3,100 level; Jim Zingler, Don Beehner, and Larry Hawkins volunteered to go with him. (Hawkins had come out of the portal just before smoke was detected, and Beehner had been one of the first men who had evacuated the mine after the alarm.)

At the Jewell Shaft station on the 3,100 level, the four men met motorman Alfred Smith, and each donned one of the "back-pack" type breathing devices.

They loaded the remaining units onto Smith's train and headed toward Ten Shaft, a mile away. After proceeding 1,500 feet or so, Smith was told to walk back to the Jewell Shaft because he was not trained in the proper operation of the McCaa breathing apparatus. The four remaining men then continued on with the train past No. 5 Shaft, and were over halfway to their destination when they met Roger Findley, who was having difficulty breathing. Zingler turned back with Findley to assist him in reaching the fresh air of the Jewell Shaft, while the other three men continued on.

In the next 500 feet or so, they met cager Schulz, who, as it already has been related, was the last man alive to leave Ten Shaft station. Despite wearing a self-rescuer, Schulz was in a state of near collapse and was pleading for oxygen. He told them that everyone was dead back near No. Ten Shaft. Beehner took off his own face mask to give oxygen to Schulz, but then collapsed as he attempted to put his face mask back on. Launhardt went to Schulz's assistance, and Hawkins took off his face mask and placed it over Beehner's face. Hawkins held his breath as long as possible before taking another breath from the mask. When Hawkins tried again to place his mask on Beehner's face he noticed blood gushing from Beehner's mouth and nose; Beehner also lost consciousness. Hawkins was unable to revive him. They tried unsuccessfully to lift Beehner into an ore cart.

A short time later, Hawkins had to retreat because his breathing apparatus was not working properly due to a tear in his hose. Launhardt, becoming concerned with Hawkins' safety, then left Beehner, and, with the train pulling a timber-truck with Schulz on it, headed for fresh air. As the train went by Hawkins, who had fallen twice, he jumped on the back of an ore car attached to the train and all three made it to safety. (It should be noted that on 3,700 level, motorman Robert Diaz and shift boss Paul Johnson lost their lives in an unsuccessful effort to save Bob Bush, Wayne Blalack, and Patrick Hobson. Launhardt and Hawkins likewise might have met the same fate had they tried to stay longer and lift collapsed men onto the train.)

1:10 P.M.
The last survivors to reach the surface on this day arrived there about 1:10 P.M.

2:00 P.M.
By 2 P.M., trained rescue recovery crews were being assembled from a number of locations, mainly neighboring mines. All rescue efforts for the remainder of that day, and for the following six days, were unsuccessful.

MAY 9, 5:43 P.M.
Seven days later (May 9), two miners—Ron Flory and Tim Wilkinson—were found alive at 5:43 P.M. on the 4,800 level by rescuers Wayne Kanack and Don Morris of the Bureau of Mines. Flory and Wilkinson had been working in a new bore hole when the fire broke out; foreman Harvey Dionne may have been responsible for their lives because he had the covering over the bore hole removed at the onset of the disaster. This provided fresh air to the 4,800 level. The two survivors wisely stayed in this flow of air rather than moving over into the deadly atmosphere at the No. Ten Shaft station.

Rescue teams from every mine in the district, plus teams from Canada, Montana, and Utah, participated in the rescue effort at the Sunshine and Silver Summit portals. Television and newspaper media from all over the nation came to cover the story, as the people of the Silver Valley grieved over their loss.

MAY 10-13
By early morning, May 10, 36 bodies had been recovered, 11 located, and 44 were still unaccounted for. By late afternoon, May 11, all of the bodies had been located and the last were removed from the mine on May 13.

JUNE 19
By June 19, the fire was brought under sufficient control to permit the Bureau of Mines to begin a full scale investigation into the cause of the fire.

In all, 173 men were underground on day shift, Tuesday, May 2, 1972—82 survived, while 91 died of suffocation from carbon monoxide.

In Memory

May 2, 1972

Robert H. Alexander, 50, stope miner
Billy W. Allen, 24, raise miner
Wayne L. Allen, 39, drift miner
Richard M. Allison, 37, drift miner
Arnold F. Anderson, 48, electrician
Robert L. Anderson, 37, boss
Joe E. Armijo, 38, stope miner
Benjamin S. Barber, 31, repairman
Barker, Robert E., 42, shaft repairman
Virgil F. Bebb, 53, shift boss
Donald G. Beehner, 38, nipper
Richard D. Bewley, 40, motorman
George W. Birchett, 40, stope miner
Wayne Blalack, 35, electrician
Robert A. Bush, 47, foreman
Floyd L. Byington, 35, stope miner
Clarence L. Case, 55, shift boss
Charles L. Casteel, 30, shift boss
Kevin A. Croker, 29, repairman
Duwain D. Crow, 39, drift miner
Roderick Davenport, 35, stope miner
John W. Davis, 28, diamond driller
Richard L. Delbridge, 24, stope miner
William R. Delbridge, 55, stope miner
Roberto Diaz, 55, motorman
Gregory G. Dionne, 23, pipeman
Carter M. Don Carlos, 47, repairman
Norman S. Fee, 27, motor helper
Lyle M. Findley, 30, repairman
Donald K. Firkins, 37, drift miner
Howard L. Fleshman, 38, stope miner
William L. Follette, 23, raise miner
Richard Garcia, 56, stope miner
Richard G. George, 20, motor helper
Robert W. Goff, 35, stope miner
Louis W. Goos, 51, raise miner
John P. Guertner, 54, repairman
William F. Hanna, 47, pumpman
Howard Harrison, 34, drift miner
Patrick M. Hobson, 57, repairman
Melvin L. House, 41, repairman
Merle E. Hudson, 47, stope miner
Jack B. Ivers, 44, stope miner
Fred E. "Gene" Johnson, 45, foreman
Paul E. Johnson, 47, shift boss
Wayne L. Johnson, 43, repairman

James M. Johnston, 20, motor helper
Custer L. Keough, 59, repairman
Sherman C. Kester, 60, trackman
Dewellyn E. Kitchen, 31, stope miner
Elmer E. Kitchen, 54, shaft miner
Kenneth C. La Voie, 29, repairman
Richard M. Lynch, 24, motorman
Donald J. McLachlan, 23, motorman
Delbert J. McNutt, 48, motorman
James C. Moore, 29, repairman
David J. Mullin, 34, stope miner
Joe R. Naccarato, 40, raise miner
Orlin W. Nelson, 32, stope miner
Richard D. Norris, 24, raise miner
Donald R. Orr, 50, stope miner
Hubert B. Patrick, 45, drift miner
Casey Pena, 52, shaft miner
John W. Peterson, 57, motorman
Francis W. Phillips, 42, repairman
Irvan L. Puckett, 51, shaft repairman
Floyd A. Rais, 61, pumpman
Leonard D. Rathbun, 29, stope miner
John R. Rawson, 27, drift miner
Jack L. Reichert, 45, hoistman
Delbert C. "Dusty" Rhoads, 57, lead mechanic
Glen R. Rossiter, 37, motorman
Paul M. Russell, 30, stope miner
Gene F. Salyer, 54, repairman
James P. Salyer, 51, foreman
Allen L. Sargent, 38, drift miner
Robert B. Scanlan, 38, hoistman
John Serano, 37, stope miner
Nick D. Sharette, 48, shaft miner
Frank R. Sisk, 31, stope miner
Darrell E. Stephens, 20, motor helper
Gustav G. Thor, 38, stope miner
Grady D. Truelock, 40, raise miner
Robert E. Waldvogel, 50, stope miner
William R. Walty, 29, repairman
Gordon Whatcott, 37, stope miner
Douglas L. Wiederrick, 37, shaft miner
Ronald L. Wilson, 41, drift miner
Willam E. Wilson, 28, hoistman
John D. Wolff, 49, stope miner
Don B. Wood, 53, hoistman